A BLUEPRINT *for* PROGRESS
• 2011 •

THE BCA's COMMITMENT TO ETHICS, JOB CREATION AND EDUCATION REFORM

BUSINESS COUNCIL
OF ALABAMA

Contributors: Anita L. Archie, William J. Canary, Mark Colson, Claire Haynes, Nancy Wall Hewston, Nathan Lindsay, Victor Vernon, Lenore Reese Vickrey, Pam Ware

Published for the Business Council of Alabama by:

Beers and Associates, LLC
Montgomery, AL

Publisher: Ronald P. Beers

Production Staff for *A Blueprint for Progress* • *2011*
Editor: Jennifer S. Kornegay
Managing Editor: Erin Mohajerin
Designer: Scott Fuller
Printer: Wells Printing Co.
Photography: Lenore Reese Vickrey, Bob Farley, Wynter Byrd

Published 2011
Printed in U.S.A.
First Edition
ISBN Number: 978-0-9796601-5-3

Dedication

This book is dedicated to the volunteer leaders who have led the Business Council of Alabama for the past quarter-century, with gratefulness for their vision, courage, integrity and commitment.

BCA Chairmen

2011 William W. Brooke
Venture Capital – Harbert
   Management Corporation

2010 Sandy Stimpson
Scotch Gulf Lumber Company, LLC

2009 Phil Dotts
Public FA Inc.

2008 David Muhlendorf
Paper and Chemical Supply Company

2007 Carol Gordy
Natural Decorations, Inc.

2006 Tom Hamby
Bellsouth – Alabama

2005 Johnny Johns
Protective Life Corporation

2004 C. Charles Nailen, Jr.
BBG Specialty Foods, Inc./Taco Bell

2003 Mike Thompson
Thompson Tractor Company, Inc.

2002 Mike Warren
Energen Corporation

2001 T. Keith King
Volkert & Associates, Inc.

2000 Roland Vaughan
Sherlock, Smith & Adams, Inc.

1999 J. Ab Conner
Conner Brothers Construction
   Company, Inc.

1998 D. Paul Jones
Compass Banchares Inc.

1997 Van L. Richey
American Cast Iron Pipe Company

1996 Robert "Bubba" Lee
Vulcan, Inc.

1995 Rex J. Lysinger
Energen Corporation

1994 Frank McRight
McRight, Jackson, Dorman, Myrick
   & Moore

1993 Elmer B. Harris
Alabama Power Company

1992 Robert W. Hager
The Boeing Company

1991 Dr. Peter Mannsfeld
Degussa Corporation

1990 Harry B. Brock, Jr.
Central Bank of the South

1989 Winton M. Blount III
Blount Strange Holdings, LLC

1988 James Miller
MacMillian Bloedel, Inc.

1987 Frank Mason
Mason Corporation

1986 Dick Dickson
Russell Corporation

Table of Contents

APPENDIX

Chapter 1
A Blueprint for Progress • 2011

The opening day of the Alabama Legislature often has been compared to the first day of a new school year after a long summer break. The same faces return year after year. The same cliques seem to naturally form. The same lessons are taught as everyone counts the days until the next vacation.

But the first day of the recently concluded 2011 legislative session was noticeably different. Many veteran lawmakers, including some who had served for decades and held high-ranking leadership positions, were gone. In their place were fresh-faced rookies eager for the challenge that the session would bring. A new attitude prevailed and, for the first time in several years, the body as a whole seemed to recognize that business interests, rather than being an enemy of the state, are the engine that drives Alabama's economy. While business for years has had a general floor plan for moving the state forward, it was now the time to draw a detailed blueprint.

Current BCA Chairman Will Brooke, then chairman of BCA's political action committee, ProgressPAC, sensed the difference. Shortly after the 2010 general election, he said, "Now that the legislature has been liberated, the Business Council of Alabama looks forward to working with a pro-business legislature that is committed to addressing the concerns of business, including job creation, establishing incentives for economic development, addressing ethics reform and addressing the changes needed in our public education system."

The lawmakers' priorities for the session were quickly apparent. To spur job creation and kick start Alabama's economy, the legislature approved a series of tax credits and incentives for businesses of all sizes. One bill provided state tax credits that offset federal tariffs to encourage corporations to invest in Alabama and build new factories and manufacturing facilities here. Another measure provided a $1,000 tax credit to small businesses and

1

companies for each employee they hire off the unemployment rolls. The Small Business Health Care Tax Deduction, which allows both employers and workers to deduct up to 20 percent of their medical coverage premium costs, also was expanded.

At a time when state finances were at their lowest and most unhealthy since the Great Depression, members of both parties joined to make the tough decisions needed to pass sensible budgets that require government to spend within its means. To ensure that public employees and teachers may one day collect the long-term pension benefits they earned, legislators began the process of shoring up finances in the state retirement system and, for the first time since 1974, made critical adjustments to the amount that workers contribute toward their future pension benefits.

Lawmakers also made the overdue decision to discontinue the state's fiscally irresponsible Deferred Retirement Option Program, which allowed a handful of upper-level government workers and union leaders to work past retirement age while banking their taxpayer-subsidized retirement in a lucrative, high-yield account and collecting a taxpayer-funded paycheck at the same time. This one act alone is estimated to save more than $58 million annually.

Because mid-year cuts in the education budget hurt our children's ability to learn and prevent needed resources from reaching the classroom, the legislature passed the innovative Responsible Budgeting and Spending Act. Under this measure, lawmakers will use a rolling 15-year average of revenues to appropriate money in the Education Trust Fund budget rather than rely upon undependable, finger-in-the-wind revenue estimates.

The Students First Act, passed in the second half of the session, streamlined and reformed the process for dismissing teachers who commit crimes, abuse our students and perform other acts worthy of termination. Instead of allowing teachers to continue accruing long-term pay and benefits during a lengthy and unwieldy termination and appeals process, the new law shortens the window for appeal while placing decisions in the hands of school boards and administrative law and circuit court judges.

In a December 2010 Special Session, the newly elected legislature approved a series of tough ethics laws. Public officials, candidates and the spouses of each now will be required to disclose any jobs or contracts they hold with government entities in the state. And the Alabama Ethics Commission, our state watchdog agency against corruption, is now shielded statutorily from retaliation by any public officials it investigates.

A new and unprecedented layer of transparency was added to Alabama's campaign finance system by blocking the ability to make anonymous and shadowy last-minute contributions to candidates. A new statutorily mandated electronic filing system will allow real-time reporting of contributions while providing the public the ability to conduct instant, in-depth searches of who donates and who receives specific campaign dollars.

A package of business-backed tort reform measures dealing with issues from post judgment interest and product liability immunity to venue selection and others successfully made its way through the legislative process. Voters soon will be given the opportunity to ratify a constitutional amendment guaranteeing the right to a secret ballot in all elections.

If many of the bills and initiatives detailed above sound familiar to you, they should. Many were priorities in the *2011 BCA State Legislative Agenda* while others have been on our list of priorities for nearly two decades. If any one of the bills detailed above had become law, it would have been occasion for much celebration, but to see so many fundamental reforms and changes take place at one time is, in a word, *unprecedented.*

The BCA has long worked toward accomplishing one stated goal — to provide Alabama's business community an equal opportunity to make a case and seek support for bills we back and programs we believe are important. Quite frankly, in the past, it was often frustrating, and, at times, infuriating to see worthy initiatives pushed to the side because competing interest groups found them threatening or simply did not support those who favored them.

The vision of the business community has now been sharpened into a blueprint for genuine progress. But make no mistake; there is still work to be done.

Alabama's schoolchildren still need and deserve quality schools that use innovative, outside-the-box ideas to achieve educational success. Our taxpayers still deserve an updated Bill of Rights guaranteeing a fair process when they appeal tax levies.

2010 BCA Chairman Sandy Stimpson aptly summed up the 2010 election results and laid the foundation for the rest of the quadrennium: "BCA has worked diligently for many years to see the creation of a pro-business legislature, and that dream is now reality. Now it is time for us to go forward boldly, but humbly, to see Alabama reach its full potential."

In the pages that follow, you will read how a bi-partisan group of lawmakers joined together to pass the pro-business legislation we have promoted for several years; these lawmakers took the blueprint and started building a foundation for progress for future generations. You will come to appreciate the determined legislative leaders who tirelessly pushed those bills through the process and changed the mindsets that had both chambers mired in the muck for far too long.

And you will learn the story of how Alabama was, once and for all, put firmly on the road to real reform.

2010 ELECTION RESULTS

FEDERAL OFFICIALS

U.S. Sen. Richard Shelby
Sen. Jeff Sessions, who won reelection in 2008, was not on the ballot in
    November 2010.

U.S. Rep. Robert Aderholt
U.S. Rep. Spencer Bachus
U.S. Rep. Jo Bonner
U.S. Rep. Mo Brooks
U.S. Rep. Martha Roby
U.S. Rep. Mike Rogers
U.S. Rep. Terri Sewell

STATEWIDE OFFICIALS

Gov. Robert Bentley
Lt. Gov. Kay Ivey
Attorney General Luther Strange
Secretary of State Beth Chapman
State Treasurer Young Boozer
Commissioner of Agriculture and Industries John McMillan
State Auditor Samantha Shaw
Public Service Commissioner Twinkle Andress Cavanaugh
Public Service Commissioner Terry Dunn
Supreme Court Justice Kelli Wise
Supreme Court Justice Mike Bolin
Supreme Court Justice Tom Parker

STATE SENATE

District 1: Sen. Tammy Irons
District 2: Sen. Bill Holtzclaw
District 3: Sen. Arthur Orr
District 4: Sen. Paul Bussman
District 5: Sen. Greg Reed
District 6: Sen. Roger Bedford
District 7: Sen. Paul Sanford
District 8: Sen. Shadrack McGill
District 9: Sen. Clay Scofield
District 10: Sen. Phil Williams
District 11: Sen. Jerry Fielding
District 12: Sen. Del Marsh
District 13: Sen. Gerald Dial
District 14: Sen. Cam Ward
District 15: Sen. Slade Blackwell
District 16: Sen. Jabo Waggoner
District 17: Sen. Scott Beason
District 18: Sen. Rodger Smitherman
District 19: Sen. Priscilla Dunn
District 20: Sen. Linda Coleman
District 21: Sen. Gerald Allen
District 22: Sen. Marc Keahey
District 23: Sen. Hank Sanders
District 24: Sen. Bobby Singleton
District 25: Sen. Dick Brewbaker
District 26: Sen. Quinton Ross
District 27: Sen. Tom Whatley
District 28: Sen. Billy Beasley
District 29: Sen. Harri Anne Smith
District 30: Sen. Bryan Taylor
District 31: Sen. Jimmy Holley
District 32: Sen. Trip Pittman
District 33: Sen. Vivian Davis Figures
District 34: Sen. Rusty Glover
District 35: Sen. Ben Brooks

STATE HOUSE

District 1: Rep. Greg Burdine
District 2: Rep. Lynn Greer
District 3: Rep. Marcel Black
District 4: Rep. Micky Hammon
District 5: Rep. Dan Williams
District 6: Rep. Phil Williams
District 7: Rep. Ken Johnson
District 8: Rep. Terri Collins
District 9: Rep. Ed Henry
District 10: Rep. Mike Ball
District 11: Rep. Jeremy Oden
District 12: Rep. Mac Buttram
District 13: Rep. Bill Roberts
District 14: Rep. Richard Baughn
District 15: Rep. Allen Farley
District 16: Rep. Daniel Boman
District 17: Rep. Mike Millican
District 18: Rep. Jonny Mack Morrow
District 19: Rep. Laura Hall
District 20: Rep. Howard Sanderford
District 21: Rep. Jim Patterson
District 22: Rep. Wayne Johnson
District 23: Rep. John Robinson
District 24: Rep. Todd Greeson
District 25: Rep. Mac McCutcheon
District 26: Rep. Kerry Rich
District 27: Rep. Wes Long
District 28: Rep. Craig Ford
District 29: Rep. Becky Nordgren
District 30: Rep. Blaine Galliher
District 31: Rep. Barry Mask
District 32: Rep. Barbara Boyd
District 33: Rep. Ron Johnson
District 34: Rep. Elwyn Thomas
District 35: Rep. Steve Hurst
District 36: Rep. Randy Wood
District 37: Rep. Richard Laird

District 38: Rep. Duwayne Bridges
District 39: Rep. Richard Lindsey
District 40: Rep. Koven "K. L." Brown
District 41: Rep. Mike Hill
District 42: Rep. Kurt Wallace
District 43: Rep. Mary Sue McClurkin
District 44: Rep. Arthur Payne
District 45: Rep. Owen Drake
District 46: Rep. Paul DeMarco
District 47: Rep. Jack Williams
District 48: Rep. Greg Canfield
District 49: Rep. April Weaver
District 50: Rep. Jim McClendon
District 51: Rep. Allen Treadaway
District 52: Rep. John Rogers
District 53: Rep. Demetrius Newton
District 54: Rep. Patricia Todd
District 55: Rep. Rod Scott
District 56: Rep. Lawrence McAdory
District 57: Rep. Merika Coleman
District 58: Rep. Oliver Robinson
District 59: Rep. Mary Moore
District 60: Rep. Juandalynn Givan
District 61: Rep. Alan Harper
District 62: Rep. John Merrill
District 63: Rep. Bill Poole
District 64: Rep. Harry Shiver
District 65: Rep. Elaine Beech
District 66: Rep. Alan Baker
District 67: Rep. Darrio Melton
District 68: Rep. Thomas Jackson
District 69: Rep. David Colston
District 70: Rep. Chris England
District 71: Rep. Artis "A. J." McCampbell
District 72: Rep. Ralph Howard
District 73: Rep. Joe Hubbard
District 74: Rep. Jay Love
District 75: Rep. Greg Wren

District 76: Rep. Thad McClammy
District 77: Rep. John Knight
District 78: Rep. Alvin Holmes
District 79: Rep. Mike Hubbard
District 80: Rep. Lesley Vance
District 81: Rep. Mark Tuggle
District 82: Rep. Pebblin Warren
District 83: Rep. George Bandy
District 84: Rep. Berry Forte
District 85: Rep. Dexter Grimsley
District 86: Rep. Paul Lee
District 87: Rep. Donnie Chesteen
District 88: Rep. Paul Beckman
District 89: Rep. Alan Boothe
District 90: Rep. Charles Newton
District 91: Rep. Barry Moore
District 92: Rep. Mike Jones
District 93: Rep. Steve Clouse
District 94: Rep. Joe Faust
District 95: Rep. Steve McMillan
District 96: Rep. Randy Davis
District 97: Rep. Yvonne Kennedy
District 98: Rep. Napoleon Bracy
District 99: Rep. James Buskey
District 100: Rep. Victor Gaston
District 101: Rep. Jamie Ison
District 102: Rep. Chad Fincher
District 103: Rep. Joseph Mitchell
District 104: Rep. Jim Barton
District 105: Rep. David Sessions*

* David Sessions was elected in a May 9, 2011, special election after Rep. Spencer Collier was appointed director of the state Department of Homeland Security.

RILEY CHALLENGES LAWMAKERS TO CHANGE HISTORY IN SPECIAL SESSION

Challenging the Alabama Legislature to "literally change the course of history" for the state, Gov. Bob Riley on Wednesday night kicked off the 2010 Special Session, which will take up the governor's seven tough ethics reform bills that, if passed, would give Alabama the toughest ethics laws in the United States.

"You will either be remembered as the leaders who finally changed the system or the ones who squandered a once-in-a-lifetime opportunity and became just like legislators of the past," Riley said. "If we are not successful in this mission, then we are not different from any of those who served before."

Riley's remarks preceded a public hearing in which lawmakers sponsoring ethics bills introduced each one, and proponents and opponents voiced their opinions. Sen. Bryan Taylor, R-Prattville, sponsor of SB 14, which would set up the new Code of Public Ethics and Accountability, said, "There is no better time than right now to improve accountability and transparency in state government."

"There is no greater disinfectant than sunlight," Taylor said.

Support for the ethics bill package came from state officials, including School Superintendent Dr. Joe Morton, newly elected Attorney General Luther Strange and Dr. Freida Hill, chancellor of the two-year community college system. Calling the ethics package "long overdue," Strange urged lawmakers to pass legislation that would be effective, easily understood and enforceable.

Danny Cooper, executive vice president of the Alabama Association of Realtors, said his thousands of members supported the legislation. "I want to lobby you to pass these bills. I also want you to restrict and limit what I can do to convince you to pass legislation in the future."

AEA Executive Secretary Paul Hubbert opposes the legislation that would ban payroll deductions for state employees who pay dues to AEA and the Alabama State Employees Association, saying it was more political than about ethics reform.

"It is clear that the results and outcome of this historic special session of the Alabama Legislature will change the ethical governmental 'family tree' for generations to come," said BCA President and CEO William Canary.

Riley pressed the lawmakers to stay true to the voters who elected them on November 2 to make a difference. "This is something you ran on," he said. "Don't let the people who voted for you down. The true difference and the true test will be in your leadership, your determination and steadfastness in the face of what is going to be powerful opposition to the reforms we want to make. Make no mistake. The people who sent you here will be watching. They will remember the outcome.

"If 49 other states can do it, Alabama can absolutely (do it)," he said. "I hope that this new legislature will be remembered as the greatest, most ethical, most honest, most reform-minded legislature in the history of Alabama."

BCA is monitoring all the bills in the governor's ethics reform package.

Senate Passes Bill to Ban Governmental Agencies from Collecting Membership Dues or Contributions for Political Purposes

The first bill to reach the floor and pass the newly elected Alabama Senate in the current special session on ethics and campaign reform was SB 2, by Sen. Del Marsh, R-Anniston. The bill passed by a vote of 22-12 and drew the vehement opposition of the Alabama Education Association (AEA), whose members filled the gallery in a show of force as senators who support AEA's position engaged in an afternoon-long filibuster. Opponents charged that the bill is politically motivated to target the AEA and diminish the voice of its membership, while proponents of the bill assert that it is unethical for public resources to be used for political purposes. A cloture vote by the Senate was needed to end debate and bring the bill to a vote.

Marsh's bill clarifies current state law to prohibit public property, public resources or the time of an employee, while employed by any governmental agency, from being utilized for political purposes. However, the bill specifically prohibits payroll deductions from public employees and educators for membership dues or contributions that would ultimately be expended for political purposes.

Senate Passes Bill Prohibiting Lobbyists from Spending on Legislators

The Alabama Senate rejected the committee-approved SB 14, by Sen. Bryan Taylor, R-Prattville, that would impose a $25 limit on gifts from lobbyists and instead approved a bill prohibiting any spending by lobbyists.

The Senate voted 33-2 to substitute Taylor's bill for a version by Sen. Scott Beason, R-Gardendale, which prohibits any spending by lobbyists. The substitute was approved by a vote of 35-0.

One apparent loophole of the substitute bill is that it does not bar the companies and people who employ lobbyists from spending money on legislators.

'Double Dip No More' Almost a Reality

The Senate, by a vote of 29-3 with one abstention, approved SB 3, by Sen. Jabo Waggoner, R-Vestavia Hills. The bill, known as the Legislative Double Dipping Protection Act, continues the movement started by the State Board of Education to prohibit a legislator from being employed by any branch of government or department, agency, board or commission of the state as well as any public educational institution while serving in elected office. If a legislator is employed as a state or public employee, he would have until November 5, 2014, the next legislative election, to terminate that employment.

Any legislator violating the law would be personally liable to the state for the amount of any employment compensation received while the violation occurred.

Senate Passes Ethics Commission Subpoena Bill

The Senate, for the first time ever, passed a bill that would grant subpoena power to the Alabama State Ethics Commission. SB 1, by Sen. Cam Ward, R-Alabaster, under certain conditions, would grant the Alabama State Ethics Commission authority to subpoena witnesses and compel their attendance, as well as to subpoena documents, books and other evidence in the course of an investigation.

If a person fails to comply with the Ethic Commission's subpoena, which was lawfully issued, then the director of the commission can notify the court of jurisdiction through application.

Under this legislation, the Alabama State Ethics Commission will have 180 days to determine whether probable cause exists after receiving or initiating a complaint. At the end of the 180 days from the date of receipt or commencement of a complaint, if the commission does not find probable cause, the complaint would be dismissed.

SB 1 also addresses the confirmation process for individuals seeking to serve on the Alabama State Ethics Commission. If an appointee is presented for confirmation, and the Senate fails to confirm the appointee before adjourning sine die, then that appointee is deemed confirmed. No appointee whose confirmation is rejected by the Senate may be reappointed.

This bill would also require the director of the Alabama Ethics Commission to be subject to Senate confirmation. This is a new standard. In the past, the director has served at the pleasure of the Alabama State Ethics Commission.

SB 1 also requires the commission to have an Alabama state licensed attorney in good standing as one of its members. The bill now goes to the House for consideration.

PAC-to-PAC Ban Passes House

By a vote of 104–0, the Alabama House passed HB 9, by Rep. Mac McCutcheon, R-Capshaw, which would make it illegal in Alabama to transfer money from one political action committee to another.

The legislation seeks to prevent political action committees (PACs) from swapping campaign contribution funds with other PACs. This kind of exchange allows PACs to effectively launder campaign contributions, thereby obscuring the identity of the individual or group that contributed to the PAC. The legislation would also prohibit principal campaign committees, which are effectively candidates' campaign accounts, from giving to other principal campaign committees, thus making it illegal for candidates to give money they have raised to other candidates.

The PAC-to-PAC transfer ban legislation moved out of the House Ethics Committee on a unanimous affirmative vote on Thursday before passing in the Alabama House today. House Ethics Committee Chairman Rep. Jim McClendon, R-Springville, stated clearly the purpose of banning PAC-to-PAC transfers: "The legislation is intended to introduce transparency into the election process in Alabama by allowing the public to easily identify who contributes money to a candidate."

Rep. Wes Long, R-Guntersville, along with Rep. Merika Coleman, D-Birmingham, offered an amendment to name the bill after Congressman Mike Rogers and former Rep. Jeff McLaughlin, D-Guntersville, who worked for years to pass legislation banning PAC-to-PAC transfers. The amendment passed with unanimous consent. HB 9 goes now to the Senate for consideration. BCA is monitoring this legislation.

Bill to Ban 'Pass-Through' Pork Unanimously Approved by the House

HB 10, by Rep. Mike Ball, R-Huntsville, passed the House by a vote of 104-0. The bill would put an end to the long-standing practice of legislators adding some non-itemized amount of funding to an agency's appropriation and later compelling the agency to expend the funds as the legislator directs. Fiscal transparency is undermined when powerful legislators hide "pass-through" appropriations within the state budgets, as it leaves both fellow legislators and taxpayers in the dark on how state funds are to be utilized. Although Gov. Riley issued an executive order that banned state agencies from participating in such schemes, a more far-reaching act of the legislature would carry the weight of law and apply the ban to all of state government.

Ethics Training Bill Passes House

On 104-0 vote, the House passed HB 11, by Rep. Paul DeMarco, R-Homewood. The bill requires mandatory ethics training for members of the Alabama Legislature, state constitutional officers, cabinet members, executive staff, municipal mayors, city council members, commissioners, county commissioners and lobbyists.

Lobbyists who fail to attend the training programs will not be allowed to lobby the legislature, executive branch, judicial branch, public officials or public employees. HB 11 provides timelines for the training to take place. This bill also directs the Alabama Ethics Commission to create a searchable database of all gifts and meals that have been given to public officials. HB 11 now goes to the Senate for consideration. BCA will continue to monitor this legislation.

Hubbard Elected House Speaker, Marsh Elected Senate Pro Tem

With a new majority in place for the special session, the Alabama Legislature elected new leaders. Republican Mike Hubbard (R-Auburn) was elected by a vote of 100-0 as Alabama's first Republican speaker of the House in 136 years.

Alabama state senators voted 32-0 to elect Sen. Del Marsh (R-Anniston) to be the Senate president pro-tem, its top leadership post. In the absence of the lieutenant governor, the Senate pro-tem presides over the Senate.

Both leaders will face another vote for their leadership posts when legislators choose their leaders in the legislature's organizational session that begins on January 11.

Chapter 3
Week of December 17, 2010
Faster Than a Moving Train, SB 14 Sent to the Governor

In the pre-dawn hours of Thursday morning, after numerous substitutes, amendments and a conference committee report, SB 14, by Sen. Bryan Taylor, R-Prattville, was transmitted to Gov. Riley for his signature. This bill was by far one of the most controversial, complicated and complex bills of the Special Session that sought to limit the influence of lobbyists with public officials.

Earlier in the day, the House debated the House Ethics Committee substitute to SB 14, during which numerous amendments were offered, including one offered and supported by the BCA working committee that would clarify the definition of "lobbyist" so that sales activities by an individual in the ordinary course of business would not be considered lobbying. The amendment by Rep. Greg Canfield, R-Vestavia Hills, passed 98-0, and the bill was sent to the Senate for concurrence.

However, the Senate voted to non-concur with the House version and sent SB 14 to conference committee. The conferees were: Taylor; Sen. Del Marsh, R-Anniston; Sen. Roger Bedford, D-Russellville; Rep. Jim McClendon, R-Springville; Rep. Randy Davis, R-Daphne; and Rep. Craig Ford, D-Gadsden.

After numerous recesses by the Senate with the various conference committees, both Houses automatically went to the next legislative day at 12:01 a.m. During this time, BCA President and CEO William Canary learned that the BCA-supported House amendment to SB 14 had been deleted as a part of the soon-to-be-considered conference committee report. Your BCA then worked to ensure that the deleted language from the conference committee report did not jeopardize our clarification of

Gov. Bob Riley signed the ethics bill package into law as Cub Scouts, including his grandson Bobby, looked on.

ordinary course-of-business sales activities. Various conferees and Senate President Pro Tem Del Marsh assured BCA that, based on negotiations by the conferees, the BCA-supported amendment was not necessary. However, if the bill is enacted, and there appears to be a problem, Marsh committed to BCA that the issue would be solved as a top priority during the 2011 Regular Session.

Specifically, SB 14 prohibits lobbyists and principals from offering or providing "a thing of value" defined as any gift, benefit, favor, service, gratuity, tickets to an entertainment, social or sporting event, unsecured loans (other than forbearances made in the ordinary course of business), reward, promise of future employment, honoraria, or other item of monetary value.

However, there are several exceptions:

Lobbyists would be able to buy public officials and their spouses a meal costing no more than $25, with a total limit of $150 per year. Principals — persons or businesses that employ a lobbyist — would be able to buy public officials and their spouses a meal costing no more than $50, with a total limit of $250 per year. However, the money spent would not have to be reported.

The bill bans persons who are not lobbyists or principals from giving a public official or their spouse "anything for the purpose of influencing action, regardless of whether or not the thing solicited or received (by the public official) is a thing of value."

The bill does not limit spending for transportation and lodging expenses, hospitality, meals, registration fee waivers and other similar costs necessary to facilitate the attendance of public officials at economic development functions and "educational functions"— meetings or events organized around a formal program or agenda — where the public official is a speaker for the event. Receptions hosted by civic clubs, chambers of commerce, charitable and education organizations, and trade and professional associations would also be exempt from spending limitations.

There also would be no limit on what a lobbyist or principals could spend on a "widely attended event," a gathering, dinner, reception or other event at which more than 12 people "with a diversity of views or interests" were expected to attend.

The Alabama Legislature concurred with the conference committee report, and the governor is expected to sign the bill. SB 14 was the centerpiece of the governor's reform package and will become effective in mid-March.

Legislature Bans Governmental Agencies from Collecting Membership Dues or Contributions Via Payroll Deduction for Political Purposes

The Alabama Senate moved quickly with a cloture vote on Wednesday morning to accept the changes made by the House to SB 2, by Sen. Del Marsh, R-Anniston. Marsh's bill clarifies current state law to prohibit public property, public resources or the time of an employee, while employed by any governmental agency, from being utilized for political purposes. However, the bill specifically prohibits payroll deductions by governmental agencies from the pay of public employees and educators for membership dues or contributions that would ultimately be expended for political purposes.

Earlier, the House leadership narrowly had won passage of the bill on a close vote of 52-49, after a nearly 18-hour filibuster, led primarily by House Democrats, that finally gave way to the vote. A week ago, the Senate voted for the measure 22-12, along party lines.

SB 2 drew the full opposition of the Alabama Education Association (AEA), which had urged both representatives and senators to block votes on the bill with delaying tactics in both chambers. Opponents charged that the bill was politically motivated to target AEA and diminish the political voice of its membership. Proponents of the bill asserted that it is unethical for public resources to be used for political purposes. The bill defines most election-related activities as "political purposes," but it excludes "lobbying," which was considered too far-reaching.

The bill now goes to the governor for his signature.

BCA Heralds New Standards; Ethics Training to Be Offered

Business Council of Alabama leadership expressed satisfaction with the outcome of the recently concluded special session. "Just as the November 2 elections set the stage for the liberation of the legislature, this session finally gave the people of Alabama what they deserve: the beginnings of an accountable government," said BCA Chairman Sandy Stimpson of Mobile. "Not only did the sun rise on Thursday morning, but now the sun shines on accountability and transparency and new standards of ethical behavior in our state."

Stimpson, who personally observed some of the activity at the State House this week, commended BCA President and CEO William Canary and Senior Vice President for Governmental Relations Anita Archie for working many long hours, including two nights with only two hours of sleep, to ensure that BCA's voice was heard by the lawmakers. BCA Board of Directors member Chester Vrocher of Mobile also spent long hours at the State House monitoring the progress of bills and amendments.

Double Dipping Prohibition Act Passes with Exceptions

SB 3, by Sen. Jabo Waggoner, R-Vestavia Hills, the Legislative Double Dipping Protection Act, prohibits a member of the legislature from being an employee of any branch of state government, any department, agency, board or commission of the state, or any public educational institution including, but not limited to, a local board of education, a two-year institution of higher education or a four-year institution of higher education.

The bill also provides for several exceptions, including:

• A legislator who is employed or is a member of certain areas of the armed forces;

2010 BCA Chairman Sandy Stimpson and Governmental Affairs Committee Co-Chair Chester Vrocher of Boise watched debate from the House Gallery.

- A legislator who has a contract with Medicaid as part of the ordinary course of his or her profession;

- A legislator employed on a part-time basis; and

- A legislator who has a substantial financial interest by reason of ownership of, control of, or exercise of power over an interest greater than 5 percent of the value of any corporation, partnership, company, joint venture or other business entity that is providing goods or services under any contract paid for by a branch, department, agency, board, commission or educational institution, including the Department of Postsecondary Education or a two-year institution of higher education.

Any legislator currently employed under any administrative or teaching contract may continue employment until December 31, 2014. Any legislator who has a state/public contract in force on December 1, 2010 may not continue the contract after November 5, 2014.

Ethics Training Bill On Way to Governor

On a 34-0 vote, the Alabama Senate passed HB 11, by Rep. Paul DeMarco, R-Homewood. This bill requires mandatory ethics training for members of the Alabama Legislature, state constitutional officers, cabinet members, executive staff, municipal mayors, city council members, commissioners, county commissioners, local board of education members and lobbyists.

Lobbyists who fail to attend training programs will not be allowed to lobby the legislature, executive branch, judicial branch, public officials or public employees. HB 11 requires the Alabama Ethics Commission to offer this training in person or online and provides for timelines for the training sessions.

The bill also expands the definition of lobbying to prohibit a member of the legislature from representing any person, firm, corporation, or other business entity before an executive department or agency for a fee, reward or other compensation, in addition to that received in his or her official capacity.

The bill also requires the Ethics Commission to create a searchable database of all gifts and meals given to public officials.

There appears to be a possible conflict or inconsistent definition of lobbying with the language in another bill, SB 14, as passed. BCA will analyze the language to determine its impact on our members.

The legislation now goes to the governor for signing.

PAC-to-PAC Ban Passes Legislature; Goes to Governor for Signature

After the House passed legislation last week that bans transfers of money among Political Action Committees (PACs), the Senate passed a similar measure by a vote of 34-0 on Tuesday.

This kind of exchange allows PACs to effectively launder campaign contributions, thereby obscuring the identity of the individual or group that contributed to the PAC. The proposed legislation would also prohibit principal campaign committees, which are effectively candidates' campaign accounts, from giving to other principal campaign committees, thus making it illegal for candidates to give money they have raised to other candidates.

The legislation, named the Congressman Mike Rogers/Jeff McLaughlin Campaign Finance Transparency Act, passed out of the Senate Ethics Committee on Monday. The Senate version, sponsored by Sen. Arthur Orr, R-Decatur, closely mirrored HB 9 by Rep. Mac McCutcheon, R-Capshaw; however, it was amended to prohibit 527 organizations and private foundations from making or receiving PAC contributions. (A tax-exempt 527 group can raise and spend money for political activities, including ads that attack or praise a candidate's positions but do not explicitly ask people to vote for or against the candidate.)

The bill would allow a corporation with a federal PAC to transfer money to its state PAC as long as contributions to the federal PAC only come from the corporation's employees and directors. The legislation now goes to Gov. Riley to be signed.

Ethics Commission Given Subpoena Power

The Alabama Legislature passed SB 1, by Sen. Cam Ward, R-Alabaster, which grants subpoena power to the Alabama State Ethics Commission. Under this legislation, the commission will have authority to subpoena witnesses and compel their attendance, as well as to subpoena documents, books and other evidence in the course of an investigation.

The bill allows any person or entity served with a subpoena to object to the issuance of the subpoena within 10 days after being served on the grounds set forth under Rule 17.3(c) of the Alabama Rules of Criminal Procedure. If this objection occurs, the subpoena will not be issued until an order to dismiss, modify, or issue the subpoena is entered by a state court of proper jurisdiction. The order must be entered within 30 days after a person files an objection to a subpoena.

If a person fails to comply with the subpoena, the director of the commission can notify the court of jurisdiction, and the court can compel that person to comply or face contempt charges.

SB 1 also addresses the confirmation process for individuals seeking to serve on the Ethics Commission. If an appointee is presented for confirmation and the Senate fails to confirm the appointee before adjourning sine die, the appointee is deemed confirmed. No appointee whose confirmation is rejected by the Senate may be reappointed.

The bill also requires the director of the Ethics Commission to be subject to Senate confirmation. In the past, the director has served at the pleasure of the commission.

The commission would have 180 days to determine whether probable cause exists after receiving or initiating a complaint. At the end of 180 days from the date of receipt or commencement of a complaint, if the commission does not find probable cause, the complaint would be dismissed.

The bill also requires the commission to have an Alabama state licensed attorney in good standing as one of its members.

Legislature Unanimously Approves Bill to Ban 'Pass-Through' Pork

HB 10, by Rep. Mike Ball, R-Madison, passed both houses of the Alabama Legislature without a dissenting vote. The bill would put an end to the long-standing practice of legislators adding non-itemized amounts of funding to an agency's appropriation and later compelling the agency to expend the funds as the legislator directs.

Fiscal transparency is undermined when powerful legislators hide "pass-through" appropriations within the state budgets, as it leaves both fellow legislators and taxpayers in the dark on how state funds are to be utilized. Although Gov. Riley issued an executive order that banned most state agencies from participating in such schemes, a more far-reaching act of the legislature would carry the weight of law and apply the ban to all of state government.

CHAPTER 4

March 7, 2011

AND SO IT BEGINS...

Key BCA-Backed Bills Clear Committees; On Their Way for Vote by Full House

The first week of the 2011 Alabama legislative session proved to be a clear win for several of the Business Council of Alabama's legislative priorities, as a number of key bills cleared hurdles in House committees and are on their way to be voted on by the full House of Representatives.

Several BCA members and staff were among those attending and speaking at public hearings on Wednesday. The BCA, represented by President and CEO William Canary, was the only business group testifying in support of HB 64, by Rep. Kurt Wallace, R-Maplesville, which would guarantee individuals the right to a secret ballot.

Other BCA-supported bills that sailed out of committees were HB 61, by Rep. April Weaver, R-Brierfield, which would allow businesses to deduct 200 percent of the amount they pay in health insurance premiums from state income tax; HB 57, the Responsible Budgeting and Spending Act, by Rep. Greg Canfield, R-Vestavia Hills, which would allow lawmakers to pass "proration-proof" budgets; and HB 59, by Rep. Barry Mask, R-Wetumpka, which would eliminate the Deferred Retirement Option Plan (DROP) for state employees without affecting those already participating.

The first week of the session followed a somber State of the State address by Gov. Robert Bentley on Tuesday, during which he proposed cuts to most state agencies and called on state employees and teachers to pay more for their health care and retirement costs. Bentley told lawmakers the realistic budgets are necessary to lessen the chances of proration when revenues fall short of projections.

Even before Bentley's address, Alabama House Speaker Mike Hubbard, R-Auburn, warned the BCA's Governmental Affairs Committee that no one should be surprised that state finances are in a "dire condition." But he added that for the first time in several years, the legislature, the Governor's Office and the Finance Department are working cooperatively in a hand-in-hand fashion to create the best solutions.

"It is nice to have the legislative leadership and the governor on the same team," he said. "It is nice for Gov. Bentley to call (Senate President Pro Tempore) Del (Marsh, R-Anniston), the budget committee chairs and me over to seek our input. I can tell you the budget that Gov. Bentley will offer is a very well thought-out plan on both the education and general fund sides."

The General Fund Budget, which funds most non-education state services, is in much worse condition than its ETF counterpart, according to Hubbard, and will require an intense review of each specific line-item to weed out wasteful programs and appropriations.

"Once something gets in the budget, it usually stays there year after year, and it will be nice to look at everything and determine what is working and providing a good return on investment and what is not," he said.

Rising costs related to public employee health insurance and pension programs will likely demand that state employees shoulder a larger portion of these costs, but doing so, Hubbard said, will bring a measure of fiscal responsibility and limit lay-offs, which is the ultimate goal.

"Reducing the employer [state government] contribution to the retirement system is not going to be popular with those who are going to be paying more, but it is something that those of us in the private sector have been doing for a long time," Hubbard said. "The taxpayers simply cannot sustain the growth in the employer contribution for retirement and health insurance, and if a private business had run its benefit program like the state has been doing, it would have gone bankrupt a long time ago."

Unprecedented Cooperation

Predicting unprecedented cooperation between the two chambers, Hubbard said the Republican House Caucus agenda consists of several items that were included in the Handshake with Alabama, an omnibus platform of specific issue-oriented bills that GOP legislative candidates across the state campaigned upon in 2010 and promised to pass if elected to office.

"We made a handshake deal with the people of Alabama, and we intend to keep that promise," he said.

Hubbard, principal architect of the successful effort to elect Republican supermajorities in both legislative chambers, is the first Republican Speaker to preside in Alabama since Lewis E. Parsons of Talladega held the gavel 136 years ago.

"We appreciate and value the professional classroom teacher," Hubbard said. "And we also understand we have a responsibility to craft a budget that provides the necessary funding for children in the classroom so teachers have the tools they need to educate kids."

Hubbard said the legislature is also duty-bound to appropriate money in a way that is accountable to the taxpayers, who fund government programs.

"We also have to be fair to the taxpayer because, at the end of the day, that's whose money we are spending — not some money that just magically shows up here in Montgomery," he said. "It's those in the private sector who are out creating jobs, taking risks, running businesses and paying taxes, and we must balance their needs, too."

He said that, ultimately, the top priority of the session is to pass bills that stimulate the economy and help small businesses create jobs, and any bill that does not work toward that goal should be considered "second tier." To assist this effort, Hubbard created the Speaker's Commission on Job Creation, a blue-ribbon panel tasked with soliciting ideas from business owners across the state and submitting a report on needed economic incentives by April 15.

Several BCA board members are serving on the commission, whose findings will be reviewed by the newly formed House Committee on Economic Development and Tourism, chaired by Rep. Barry Mask, R-Wetumpka, and developed into legislation.

Small Business Health Care Premium Tax Deduction on Fast Track

HB 61, by Rep. April Weaver, R-Brierfield, would allow qualifying employers and employees to deduct an additional 50 percent of the amount expended for health insurance premiums. Qualifying employers are those with less than 25 employees, and the qualifying employees are those whose annual wages do not exceed $50,000. The bill would help the smallest,

BCA Tax Committee Co-Chair Ron Box testified before legislative committee.

most vulnerable, yet essential, employers provide health coverage to their employees. The measure is considered an incentive for job creation and a way to reduce the numbers of citizens who otherwise would be added to the state's Medicaid and CHIP (Children's Health Insurance Plan) rolls. This would increase the 150 percent deduction, achieved during the 2008 legislative session, to 200 percent if passed and signed by the governor.

This item is a top-tier item in BCA's *2011 Legislative Priorities.* Ron Box, co-chairman of BCA's Tax Committee, and Ron Perkins, co-chairman of the Small Business Committee, took time off from their businesses in Birmingham to come to Montgomery to testify in support of the bill at a public hear-

BCA Small Business Co-Chair Ron Perkins also spoke to the committee.

ing before the House Commerce and Small Business Committee. This bill moves to the full House for consideration, where broad support in the legislature and from Gov. Bentley bodes well for its fate.

House Committee Approves BCA-Backed Private Ballot Bill

The BCA stood front and center in support of HB 64, by Rep. Kurt Wallace, R-Maplesville, as the bill passed the Alabama House Constitution, Campaigns and Elections Committee on Wednesday. HB 64 would ensure, via constitutional amendment, that every individual in the state of Alabama is guaranteed the right to privately cast a ballot in all elections, including union elections.

In the 2009 and 2010 legislative sessions, the BCA was the leading advocate for the "pro-private ballot" bill championed by Rep. Greg Canfield, R-Vestavia Hills, only to see the bill fail each year due to anti-business forces.

Continuing BCA's longstanding support of the measure in 2011, BCA President and CEO William Canary testified at the public hearing on Wednesday: "When an individual's voting record becomes public knowledge, the very system of democracy crumbles and in its place arises an environment where coercion, intimidation or even force can easily take root. The BCA strongly supports each Alabamians' right to vote by private ballot in all elections." Canary was the only person to testify at the public hearing in favor of the bill, and the only organization testifying in opposition was the AFL-CIO.

Voting with BCA in support of the measure were Committee Chairman Randy Davis, R-Daphne; Rep. Randy Wood, R-Anniston; Rep. Paul Beckman, R-Prattville; Rep. Paul DeMarco, R-Homewood; Rep. Juandalynn Givan, D-Birmingham; Rep. John Merrill, R-Tuscaloosa; Rep. Barry Moore, R-Enterprise; and Rep. Demetrius Newton, D-Birmingham.

Rep. Richard Lindsay, D-Centre, cast the only opposing vote.

Weary of Prorated Budgets, Panel Finds Favor with 'Responsible Budgeting' Concept

Gov. Bentley's declaration this week of 3 percent proration in the current education budget only added to the mounting evidence that the process used for years to craft budgets is seriously flawed and must be changed. HB 57, by Rep. Greg Canfield, R-Vestavia Hills, would reform the budgeting process by statutorily tying the amount of recurring revenue to spend to the education trust fund's 15-year average growth rate. Dubbed "Responsible Budgeting," HB 57 would end the practice of building budgets on revenue estimates some 18 months out, and in its place, a fiscally conservative formula would be used to determine the total amount that can be appropriated in a given year. The bill also would ensure that non-recurring revenue will not be used to fund recurring expenditures.

At Wednesday's public hearing, supporters advocated that the bill should move to the House floor because of the reliability and stable funding growth it would provide in coming years. In his testimony, Canfield quoted Jim Williams, the executive director of the Public Affairs Research Council of Alabama. In a 2009 editorial, Williams said, "Roller coasters are fun to ride in a theme park, but riding the ups and downs of the state's roller coaster education budget is no laughing matter for the public schools, colleges and universities of Alabama... The question is why budget in a roller coaster way that leads to such dilemmas? Everyone knows that the state's economy is cyclical, so why not budget with that in mind?"

Sally Howell, executive director of the Alabama Association of School Boards, told the committee Canfield's bill "just makes sense" because it provides much-needed stability. "We haven't had it. We need it," she said. Other proponents from the education community told of the dire effects three years of proration have had on their schools. "We have pulled every trick in the book to keep our heads above water," said Greg Pouncey of the state Department of Education.

Seeing the strong committee support, the bill's lone opponent, the Alabama Education Association, was complimentary of the bill, calling it a "step in the right direction." The AEA, however, contended that the legislation put too much of a premium on repaying debt over funding textbooks and supplies for the classroom and suggested that repayments to the Rainy Day account be made in three years rather than two. Canfield countered that the lack of supplies and textbooks was not due to the legislation, but instead, was due to proration.

The *BCA 2011 Legislative Agenda* calls for adopting policies and processes that ensure sound, sustainable funding for public education. HB 57 now moves to the full House for consideration.

Committee Votes to Drop 'DROP'

A sluggish economy and extremely tight budgets have compelled the legislature to find ways to reduce the overall growth of public employee benefits. HB 59, by Rep. Barry Mask, R-Wetumpka, takes aim at the Deferred Retirement Option Plan (DROP). Enacted in 2002, the DROP program was promoted as a way to discourage long-term, valuable state and education employees from early retirement. Critics of DROP saw the act as a "solution" to no real problem and believed it posed the very real potential of becoming yet another "entitlement," a fear that has proven prophetic.

The House Ways & Means General Fund Committee approved the bill, sending it to the full House for consideration. The bill would halt new enrollments in DROP after June 1, 2011. The bill also would reduce the amount of interest earned on the accounts of participants who complete DROP but continue working. It is estimated that the state could have saved $12 million in interest savings if DROP was in effect in 2010. Additionally, beginning in FY 2012, the state could save an estimated $27 million in employer contributions to the Teachers' Retirement System as well as an estimated $9.9 million in contributions to the Employees' Retirement System without the DROP program.

The *BCA Legislative Agenda* pledges to actively work to enact legislation that reduces the growth in state funded benefits for public educators and employees.

BCA Addresses Panel on Immigration Bill

HB 56, by Rep. Micky Hammon, R-Decatur, seeks to curb illegal immigration in Alabama by requiring state and local government officials to enforce federal immigration laws and by cracking down on employers who hire illegal immigrants. Modeled after the Arizona law, the bill would create specific penalties for employers who "knowingly or intentionally" hire illegal immigrants. The House Public Safety and Homeland Security committee, chaired by the bill's sponsor, heard testimony on the bill but delayed voting until next week.

Under the bill, all Alabama businesses would be required to use the federal E-verify program by January 1, 2012, to ensure they are hiring legal citizens as well as maintaining a record of the verification for up to three years. Employers who apply for economic development incentives after September 30, 2011, must provide proof they use the E-verify program to receive any economic development incentives. The legislation provides for an investigation by the attorney general or district attorney from the county in which the employer is located upon notification of a filed complaint that the employer is allegedly hiring illegal workers.

BCA Senior Vice President of Intergovernmental Affairs, Advocacy and Communications Anita Archie told the committee that BCA supports the concept and many of the principles behind HB 56 but also wants to ensure that it doesn't penalize Alabama employers. BCA was the only business association to address the committee.

BCA staff worked with Rep. Hammon this week to find language to address issues of concern. We feel confident that many of the issues have been alleviated in a substitute version that Rep. Hammon plans to present next week.

Environmental Bills Update

Many environmental bills saw action the first week of the session. Below is a recap:

HB 50, by Rep. Greg Canfield, R-Vestavia Hills, amends the solid waste laws by removing an existing exemption from regulation for ash waste, bottom ash waste, boiler slag waste and flue gas emissions control wastes from the burning of coal or other fossil fuels at electric generating plants and authorizes the Alabama Department of Environmental Management (ADEM) to regulate these wastes, once the federal EPA promulgates federal policy on management of such waste. SB 80, by Sen. Del Marsh, R-Anniston, is the companion bill. HB 50 was referred to the House Commerce & Small Business Committee. A public hearing was held on Wednesday, and after hearing from ADEM and several citizens complaining about a landfill in Perry County, the bill was voted out unanimously.

HB 68, by Rep. Micky Hammon, R-Decatur, exempts products manufactured and retained within the state from regulation by any federal cap and trade regulations. There are no such federal regulations at this time.

HB 106, by Rep. Steve Clouse, R-Ozark, amends state laws pertaining to civil penalties for violations of state environmental protection laws and orders by removing minimum penalty amounts for certain violations and limiting the penalties for violations subject to monthly reporting based on average compliance to not more frequently than once a month.

HB 126, by Rep. Randy Davis, R-Daphne, reauthorizes the state Forever Wild program for another 20 years. SB 140, by Sen. Scott Beason, R-Gardendale, is the companion bill. This program receives trust income from the Alabama Trust Fund for the acquisition of lands for public use. The House Committee on Economic Development and Tourism will hold a public hearing Wednesday.

In Other News...

The Legislative Council rejected a proposed rule change by the Department of Revenue that would deny the deduction of debt on the balance sheets of subsidiaries doing business in Alabama and thereby increase the amount of net worth subject to the business privilege tax. That action must be sustained by a joint resolution of the legislature. On Thursday, the Senate passed SJR 4, by Sen. Roger Bedford, D-Russellville, to effectively kill the proposed change.

The House Constitution, Campaigns and Elections Committee passed HB 19, by Rep. Kerry Rich, R-Albertville, requiring voters to show photo identification at the polls. A valid ID is defined as one issued by the United States, any U.S. state or territory or the State of Alabama, or any other government-issued ID such as those issued by the military. Someone without a photo ID could still cast a provisional ballot or a regular ballot if two election officials signed an affidavit identifying the person as an eligible voter.

The newly formed House Ethics and Campaign Finance Committee unanimously passed HB 58, by Rep. Mike Ball, R-Madison. The bill would require any public official, candidate or spouse of any public official or candidate to notify the Alabama State Ethics Commission no later than 30 days after the beginning of their employment with the state or within 30 days of the beginning of a state contract.

Washington Briefing
NAM Recognizes Three Alabama Congressmen

In the past week, three members of Alabama's congressional delegation, U.S. Sen. Jeff Sessions and U.S. Reps. Robert Aderholt and Mike Rogers were awarded the National Association of Manufacturers Award for Manufacturing Legislative Excellence. As the exclusive partner of the NAM in Alabama, BCA was proud to be on hand as these members were recognized for their efforts in the 111th Congress to improve manufacturers' ability to create jobs and compete.

U.S. Sen. Richard Shelby and U.S. Reps. Spencer Bachus and Jo Bonner are also recipients of the NAM Award for Manufacturing Legislative Excellence for the 111th Congress.

Federal Shutdown Averted, For Now

The Senate on Wednesday, by a vote of 91-9, approved a stopgap measure, H.J. Res. 44, that would keep the government funded through March 18. The two-week extension, which the president signed into law on Wednesday, averts a shutdown of the federal government. The measure cleared the House on Tuesday with bipartisan support, 335-91.

The continuing resolution cuts $4 billion in spending by targeting programs already marked for elimination, including the termination of funding for eight ongoing federal programs, which together total $1.3 billion.

The Congress still must come up with a plan to fund the government for the remaining seven months of this fiscal year. The House last month passed H.R. 1, Fiscal Year Continuing Appropriations Act for FY 2011, which would reduce spending by $61 billion. While the House bill doesn't have the support to pass in the Senate, the Senate has yet to produce its own funding plan. The marathon debate on this measure culminated in a 4:40 a.m.-roll call vote that saw the measure pass 235-189.

The Chairman's Intergovernmental Council met in February to prepare for the upcoming legislative session.

Chapter 5

March 11, 2011

Making History: Governor Signs First Bill into Law; Future Education Budgets to be More Fiscally Sound

Gov. Robert Bentley signed into law today the Responsible Budgeting and Spending Act, a bold step by legislators designed to reduce the chances of proration and help bring financial stability to future state education budgets.

HB 57, by Rep. Greg Canfield, R-Vestavia Hills, ends the practice of relying on revenue estimates that extend some 18 months in advance to determine the total amount of money available to appropriate. Accurate revenue estimates from such volatile tax sources have proven to be elusive for far too many years. Coupled with pressure on legislators to spend all available funds each year, it is easy to understand why more than one-third of the last 33 budgets have been subject to mid-year education budget cuts, commonly referred to as proration.

Beginning with the 2012 session, the legislature will use a fiscally conservative formula to determine the total amount that can be appropriated in a given year. This amount will be based on the historical 15-year growth rate of recurring revenue. The bill also ensures that non-recurring revenue will not be used to fund recurring expenditures.

"In passing this bill, the legislature took a big step in working to make sure Alabama always budgets responsibly," Gov. Bentley said. "By using a more sustainable budgeting process, proration in our education budget will soon be a thing of the past. The bill that I signed into law today provides sustainable growth and spending for the Education Trust Fund."

Gov. Robert Bentley signs the first bill of the session. Joining the governor were, from left: Rep. Greg Canfield; Speaker of the House Mike Hubbard; Alison Wingate, Alabama Retail Association; BCA President and CEO William Canary; Sen. Bryan Taylor; Myla Choy, Birmingham Business Alliance; and BCA Senior Vice President Anita Archie.

This is the third year Canfield had introduced the bill, which has wide support in the education and business communities. The Alabama Association of School Boards, the School Superintendents of Alabama, the Higher Education Partnership and the state Department of Education are among its many supporters. Canfield singled out the BCA, the Birmingham Business Alliance, the Shoals Area Chamber of Commerce and the Mobile Area Chamber of Commerce for rallying the business community to support the bill.

Although the bill passed in the minimum time possible, a cloture vote was needed to end debate and bring the bill to a vote on the Senate floor, where the bill passed 23-10. Opponents attempted to delay the bill's implementation and extend the repayment of some $437 million to the state's Rainy Day Fund, supposedly to catch-up on funding for the classroom, but the bill remained intact.

"We are grateful to Rep. Canfield for his hard work and persistence in bringing forward this commonsense approach to budgeting," said BCA President and CEO William Canary. "This is the first step in our journey to create a true business-education alliance in Alabama."

The *BCA 2011 Legislative Agenda* calls for adopting policies and processes that ensure sound, sustainable funding for public education.

Fiscal Reform a Necessity, BCA Told

Three days before passage, House Rules Committee Chairman Rep. Blaine Galliher, R-Gadsden, told BCA's Governmental Affairs Committee Tuesday that Canfield's bill would help rein in spending and allow the state to more easily absorb changes in a cyclical economy. It is one of several reform measures he and other lawmakers want to see passed to help the state cope with the fiscal shortfalls in the FY 2012 General Fund and Education Trust Fund budgets.

State finances are currently in the worst condition of his entire 17-year legislative career, he said. "Every year I have been in the legislature, we have balanced the budgets with 'one-time money,' but this year we are out of one-time money. The Education Trust Fund is in an uncomfortable situation, but it is nowhere near the catastrophic condition of the General Fund." He noted that in the spending plan recommended by Gov. Robert Bentley and State Finance Director David Perry, numerous state agencies are totally eliminated and others could face budget cuts of up to 50 percent, especially if the court system, Medicaid and the Department of Corrections are allowed to remain whole. When coupled with the pro-rated budgets and spending reductions of the past several fiscal years, many agencies will have difficulty carrying out their assigned duties, according to Galliher.

Other bills that will receive priority during the session include a package of Bentley-backed tax incentives offered to small businesses in return for jobs they create; a bill to increase the tax deduction for small employers offering health insurance to workers; and a state constitutional amendment guaranteeing a right to secret ballot elections, which is being offered as a counter to "Card Check" legislation previously considered on the federal level.

Full Reform Will Take Several Years

Calling business the "engine that runs the state," Senate Rules Committee Chairman Scott Beason, R-Gardendale, said he would focus on bills that help create jobs and make Alabama a friendly state in which all industries may prosper. "We cannot take it upon ourselves to decide which industries will be winners and which will be losers," Beason said. "Instead, we have to create a greenhouse environment in which all businesses are given the ideal conditions they need to grow."

Immigration reform will also take center stage at some point during the session, Beason said, but he added that he has been working with various segments of the business community to devise a measure that secures Alabama's borders without imposing undue strain and responsibilities upon employers.

He ended his remarks with a warning that Alabama faces many ills and entrenched ways of conducting business in Montgomery and said that fully reforming the system will not take place quickly, but will, instead, require a multi-year process.

"Don't be disappointed if all the changes you want to see made in Montgomery are not completed in the first year," Beason said. "This year we will focus on stopping the bleeding — putting the parts back on the car, if you will — but you will soon see us begin a three-year process of restructuring state government that makes things more efficient and gets rid of those things that do not work."

It was noted that Beason, as Rules chair, is allowing his committee to meet and have collective, public input in the calendars that are being offered as opposed to the previous practice of the chairman devising the agenda in private and alone. The difficulty, Beason said, is providing adequate public notice because the Rules Committee, in the preceding quadrennium, was the one panel not given access to post its agenda on the Internet. In an effort to work toward "total transparency," Beason said he will have the ability to post the agenda on the legislative website before lawmakers return from next week's traditional spring break recess.

House Approves BCA-backed Bill to Protect Citizens' Right to Vote by Private Ballot

By a vote of 63-31, the House passed BCA-supported HB 64, which would ensure, via constitutional amendment, that every individual in the state is guaranteed the right to privately cast a ballot in all elections, including union elections.

Bill sponsor Rep. Kurt Wallace, R-Maplesville, told the House, "This is a common-sense bill that ensures the fundamental right of Alabama citizens to vote in private and to be protected from threats of coercion and intimidation."

Following passage, BCA President and CEO William Canary said he was encouraged about the opportunity for this bill to pass the full legislature: "Having witnessed this important bill fail in the last two sessions in committee, I applaud those supporters of HB 64 in the House who voted to protect the rights of Alabama citizens and workers. This pro-private ballot measure is on the 10-yard line as it moves to the end zone in the Senate, and we encourage the members of the Senate to similarly protect Alabama citizens' right to vote by private ballot in all elections." The bill will be assigned to a Senate committee following the legislative spring break.

Immigration Bill Ready for Debate

HB 56, by Rep. Micky Hammon, R-Decatur, that seeks to curb illegal immigration received a favorable report Tuesday from the House Public Safety and Homeland Security Committee. The bill requires state and local government officials to enforce federal immigration laws and cracks down on employers who hire illegal immigrants.

Modeled after the Arizona law, the bill creates specific penalties for employers who "knowingly or intentionally" hire illegal immigrants. The bill is likely to be debated after the scheduled spring break.

Also under the bill, all Alabama businesses would be required to use the federal E-verify program by January 1, 2012, to ensure they hire legal citizens as well as maintain a record of the verification for up to three years. Employers who apply for economic development incentives after September 30, 2011, must provide proof they use the E-verify program to receive any economic development incentives.

Bill to Drop 'DROP' on Verge of Passing: Education Jobs to be Preserved

Enrollments in Alabama's Deferred Retirement Option Program (DROP) will cease April 1, if, as expected, the Senate concurs with a minor change, and the governor signs the bill when the legislature returns from spring break. In addition to ending new enrollments in the DROP program, SB 72, by Sen. Del Marsh, R-Anniston, provides that interest earned on the accounts of participants who have completed DROP but continue working will earn the lesser of the previous year's investment performance, up to 4.0 percent.

It is estimated that eliminating DROP will save the Education Trust Fund some $32.5 million and the General Fund $4 million in FY 2012, in addition to the savings realized from reducing the interest paid on the accounts of DROP completers.

The Senate is expected to concur with a House amendment that calls for the creation of a legislative interim committee that will study alternative plans to retain Alabama's best classroom teachers.

Opponents attempted to delay the date that new enrollments would cease and alter the eligibility requirements for DROP to make the bill "revenue-neutral," but those attempts were defeated.

DROP was enacted in 2002, for the purported intent of retaining Alabama's school teachers and allows state and education employees who are 55 years old with 25 years of service to continue working while also drawing retirement pay. However, the most damaging information to DROP supporters came when Rep. Lynn Greer, R-Rogersville, revealed the fact that those financially benefiting most from DROP were not school teachers, but instead, college presidents and deans, prominent coaches, and officials from organizations that are not a part of state or local government. In fact, the *Birmingham News* reported Thursday that 49 people have accumulated more than $500,000 in their DROP accounts, with the highest salaried employees typically having the highest balances.

It was noted during Tuesday's BCA Governmental Affairs Committee meeting that the two biggest beneficiaries of DROP are Alabama Education Association Executive Secretary Paul Hubbert, who wrote himself into the original bill and will earn a $1.37 million payout upon retirement, and his AEA deputy, Joe Reed, who will claim a $1.47 million windfall benefit.

The *BCA Legislative Agenda* pledges to actively work to enact legislation that reduces the growth in state-funded benefits for public educators and employees.

House Committee OKs Extending Forever Wild Program for Another 20 Years

In front of a standing-room-only crowd, the House Economic Development and Tourism Committee passed HB 126, by Rep. Randy Davis, R-Daphne, which reauthorizes Forever Wild, the state's land preservation program.

Forever Wild was established in 1992 by constitutional amendment to provide for the purchase of public recreational lands. To support its mission, the program receives 10 percent of the annual earnings of the Alabama Trust Fund (interest from the state's oil and gas royalties) with a cap not exceeding $15 million in any year.

Since its inception, Forever Wild has preserved more than 200,000 acres of wilderness for hunting, fishing, bird-watching and other outdoor activities. This program will expire in 2012 unless it is extended.

Proponents greatly outnumbered opponents in the committee room and included representatives from the state Department of Conservation and Natural Resources, the National Wildlife Federation and other organizations.

The bill now moves to the full House for consideration.

HJR 89, by Rep. Mike Hill, R-Columbiana, would create the Forever Wild Program Temporary Joint Legislative Committee. The Committee will study and review the operations and effectiveness of the Forever Wild Land and Water Acquisition and Stewardship Program, report to the legislature during the 2011 Regular Session as needed, and file a final report no later than May 3, 2011. The resolution was referred to the House Rules Committee. SJR 42, a similar resolution, was offered by Sen. Paul Sanford, R-Huntsville.

Bill Seeks Campaign Finance Transparency by Requiring e-Filing, More Frequent Reporting

The Senate Constitution, Campaign, Finance, Ethics and Elections Committee approved a measure that would require more frequent filing of campaign finance reports by political action committees (PACs) and principal campaign committees via electronic filing with the Secretary of State.

SB 136, by Sen. Arthur Orr, R-Decatur, would require that PACs and principal campaign committees file a campaign finance report with the

Secretary of State at the end of each month for the 12 months before a primary, special, runoff or general election. Additionally, the electronic filing of a campaign finance report would be required on each of the eight days before the election if contributions or expenditures of $5,000 or greater are made during that time. Also subject to the filing requirements are Section 527 organizations. From the 2014 election cycle forward, electronic filing would be mandated, and the Secretary of State would provide for campaign finance reports to be filed electronically.

The BCA strongly supports giving persons the opportunity to participate fully and equally in the political process and the opportunity to ascertain easily and in a timely manner what persons or entities may be supporting or opposing candidates. Specifically, the BCA supports the right to exercise free speech in all aspects of the political process as well as the timely and easily accessible reporting of all political contributions, financial commitments or expenditures.

Tort Reform on the Horizon

In the last two weeks, several tort reform measures were introduced in the Alabama Senate. Proposed legislation addressing tort reform has been a part of the BCA's Legal and Judicial Reform Committee *Legislative Agenda* for the last several years. Below is the list:

SB 59, by Sen. Cam Ward, R-Alabaster, and HB 132, by Rep. Greg Canfield, R-Vestavia Hills, would decrease the statute of repose for commencing an action against an architect, engineer or builder to four years.

SB 184, by Sen. Ben Brooks, R-Mobile, and HB 227, by Rep. Ron Johnson, R-Sylacauga, prohibit a product liability action for relief against sellers that are not manufacturers.

SB 187, also by Sen. Brooks, and HB 239, by Rep. Steve McMillan, R-Bay Minette, applies the more recent standard enunciated in the U.S. Supreme Court's decision in the 1993 Daubert case for the admissibility of expert evidence and testimony in all civil and criminal court actions, except for actions arising under and governed by the Medical Liability Act of 1987 or any judicial interpretations thereof.

SB 207, by Sen. Ward, and HB 236, by Rep. Canfield, would provide that judgments, other than judgments based on a contract action, would bear interest from the date of entry of the judgment at a rate equal to the weekly average one-year constant maturity Treasury yield, as published by the Board of Governors of the Federal Reserve System, for the nearest calendar week preceding the date of judgment, and provides that post-judgment interest would be computed daily to the date of payment and compounded annually.

SB 212, by Sen. Clay Scofield, R-Guntersville, and HB 228, by Rep. Johnson, provides that a wrongful death action may only be filed in a county where the deceased could have filed a civil action, if living.

Lobbying Statute Revisited

Earlier this year, House Speaker Mike Hubbard and Senate President Pro Tem Del Marsh said their respective houses of the legislature would be open to considering revisions to the Ethics Code that would make the law easier to understand and enforce. They said they would welcome advice from the Ethics Commission and Attorney General Luther Strange on such revisions.

"If parts of the Code need to be clarified or reinforced through legislation, we will certainly consider it," Speaker Hubbard said in January. "But, we're not going to weaken the law. This legislature is going to be a productive, responsive body that is accountable to the people. We're committed to moving Alabama forward and never back."

On March 4, Jim Sumner, director of the Alabama Ethics Commission, wrote a letter in which he was joined by John Gibbs, chief of the Public Corruption and White Collar Crime Division of the Attorney General's Office, recommending that Marsh and Hubbard introduce a minor technical amendment that would strengthen the new Ethics Law.

In response, Hubbard and Marsh introduced HB 224 and SB 213. These bills address vagueness and enforceability of certain provisions of Act 2010-764, enacted during the 2010 Special Session. The bills also would clarify that the prohibited offer, gift, solicitation or receipt of anything, as contemplated in Section 36-25-7, Code of Alabama 1975, as amended in the 2010 First Special Session by Act No. 2010-764, must be for the purpose of corruptly influencing official action.

Democrats Outline Agenda

House and Senate Democrats outlined their legislative agenda this week in a press conference. The group described their agenda as a "handshake with working people," and it includes removing the state's portion of sales tax on groceries, online filing of campaign finance forms and creating a searchable database.

House Rejects Revenue Department Rule Change

Following the lead of the Senate, the Alabama House rejected a proposed rule change submitted by the Department of Revenue that would deny the deduction of debt on the balance sheets of subsidiaries doing business in Alabama and thereby increase the amount of net worth subject to the business privilege tax. That action on SJR 4, by Sen. Roger Bedford, D-Russellville, completes the steps needed to kill the proposed rule change.

Bill Would Decrease Value of Dental Benefits

SB 154, by Sen. Paul Bussman, R-Cullman, would prohibit health insurance policies and plans from setting fees for dental services not covered under the plan or policy. The Senate Banking and Insurance Committee plans to vote on the bill March 23. BCA President and CEO William Canary and Senior Vice President for Intergovernmental Affairs Anita Archie met with the sponsor earlier this week to discuss the potential impact of the bill on health plan costs. We are committed to working with Sen. Bussman to address this issue and appreciate his open-door policy with business.

BCA Members Recognized for Trade Excellence

Three Business Council of Alabama members were among eight Alabama companies recognized for excellence in exporting during a ceremony at the State Capitol Thursday.

The three recipients of the Governor's Trade Excellence Award were Baron Services, Inc., of Huntsville; Process Equipment, Inc., of Pelham; and Scott Machinery & Supply Inc., of Helena.

Exporting was a $15.5 billion industry for Alabama in 2010 and supported some 300,000 jobs in the state according to the Alabama Development Office. Alabama ranks 27th among U.S. states in the dollar value of its exports and saw a 25.5 percent increase from 2009. The national average for this period was 20 percent.

"International trade in Alabama continues to see tremendous growth, and showcasing eight of Alabama's companies for success in selling their products overseas is exciting," said Governor Bentley. "These companies have helped sustain and create jobs by taking advantage of markets outside the United States."

The awards were established in 2005 to recognize Alabama manufacturers and service companies for excelling in global competition. The awards program is coordinated by the Alabama Development Office and the Export Alabama Trade Alliance and includes large, medium and small businesses as well as new-to-export companies from different parts of the state.

Washington Briefing
Threat of Government Shutdown Still Looms

The Senate on Thursday in two votes rejected the Republican and Democratic spending-cut proposals. The Republican bill, H.R. 1, which passed the House and would cut $57 billion from current spending, failed by a vote of 44-56. The Democratic alternative, which would cut less than $5 billion, failed by a vote of 42-58. The current continuing resolution is set to expire Friday, March 18, and Congress must find a way to keep the government funded through September 30.

Both U.S. Sens. Richard Shelby and Jeff Sessions took to the Senate floor on Wednesday to support the House-passed plan. Sessions, the ranking member on the Senate Budget Committee told his colleagues, "It's time for them to work with us on a responsible, long-term solution that funds our government for the rest of the year, makes responsible cuts and safeguards our fragile economic environment."

Shelby, the top Republican on the Senate Appropriations Subcommittee on Labor, Health and Human Services, and Education, called for a change in entitlement funding. "The greatest obstacle to our nation's fiscal stability is ignoring our increasing entitlement obligations. There is no way to control our debt without getting serious about entitlement reform."

It appears with both parties still so far from an agreement that a three- to four-week extension may be needed in order to cut a final deal to fund the government through the end of the fiscal year.

BCA Chairman William Brooke of Birmingham, right, discussed pending legislation with House Speaker Mike Hubbard, R-Auburn, at Hubbard's State House office in Montgomery.

Commission members from left, Carl Jamison, BCA second vice chairman; Charles Nailen; Shannon Speir; Cheryl Smiley Williams; Rep. Phil Williams; and Ben McNeil listened to testimony at a meeting of the Speaker's Commission on Job Creation.

Chapter 6
March 25, 2011

House Increases Tax Deduction for Small Business

By a vote of 83-6, the House passed HB 61, by Rep. April Weaver, R-Brierfield, which allows qualifying employers and employees to deduct from their state income tax an additional 50 percent of the amount spent on health insurance premiums. Qualifying employers are those with less than 25 employees, and the qualifying employees are those whose annual wages do not exceed $50,000.

The bill would help the smallest and most vulnerable, yet essential employers provide health coverage to their employees. The measure is considered an incentive for job creation and a way to reduce the number of citizens who otherwise would be added to the State's Medicaid and CHIP (Children's Health Insurance Plan) rolls.

If enacted, this measure would increase the 150 percent deduction, achieved during the 2008 legislative session, up to a deduction of 200 percent of qualifying premium payments. HB 61 has been assigned to the Senate Job Creation and Economic Development Committee, while its companion bill, SB 159, by Sen. Greg Reed, R-Jasper, received a favorable report from the Senate Health Committee this week.

Rep. Weaver was commended for her first sponsored bill in the *Shelby County Reporter* this week: "Even though Weaver is new to politics, it's safe to say she gets it. In today's economy, small businesses are where the jobs are. If our government representatives can help small businesses stay viable, it's their responsibility to do so."

This bill is a top-tier item on BCA's *2011 Legislative Agenda*.

DROP Dropped: Governor Signs Bill After Adding Executive Amendment

SB 72, by Sen. Del Marsh, R-Anniston, has been signed it into law. An executive amendment offered by Gov. Bentley effectively extended the deadline for enrolling in the Deferred Retirement Option Program (DROP) without actually extending the date of the deadline. The bill allows members who would otherwise be eligible for DROP and who had submitted the necessary paperwork to enroll up to the effective date of the act.

Opponents had argued the bill possibly was unconstitutional and was unfair to the final wave of nearly 300 state employees and teachers who had planned to enter DROP and had their paperwork pending but could not enroll because they had to retroactively submit their applications 30 days prior to the April 1 deadline created by the bill. The governor's executive amendment was generally accepted by both chambers as being fairer to those whose applications were pending and made the bill more likely to withstand a legal challenge.

The *2011 BCA Legislative Agenda* states that the BCA will actively work to enact legislation that reduces the growth in state-funded benefits for public educators and employees.

BCA Endorses Full Employment Act

Carl Jamison of Tuscaloosa, second vice chairman of the Business Council of Alabama, and BCA board member Greg Powell of Fi-Plan Partners joined Gov. Robert Bentley on the steps of the State Capitol this week as the governor introduced his plan to help small businesses hire employees.

"Small businesses are Alabama's job creators and the backbone of our economy," said Jamison. "Providing an incentive for job creation will enable small businesses to have the ability to grow, invest and create new jobs throughout the state in these challenging economic times."

The Full Employment Act of 2011, sponsored by Rep. Blaine Galliher, R-Gadsden, and Sen. Arthur Orr, R-Decatur, will provide a one-time tax credit to small businesses who hire additional employees.

"The Full Employment Act of 2011 will help small businesses create jobs by offering a financial incentive that will grow and expand their business

BCA Second Vice Chairman Carl Jamison and board member Greg Powell, left, joined Gov. Bentley and bill sponsor Sen. Arthur Orr at a press conference to endorse the Full Employment Act.

and get people back to work," said Gov. Bentley. "I appreciate the support of both Representative Galliher and Senator Orr to get this important bill introduced and passed in the Alabama Legislature."

In the governor's 2011 State of the State address, Gov. Bentley called the Full Employment Act of 2011 an enhanced version of the Reemployment Act of 2010 and the centerpiece of his legislative agenda.

Under the Full Employment Act of 2011, businesses with 50 or fewer employees will receive an income tax credit equal to $1,000 per new job paying more than $10 per hour.

"I commend Governor Bentley for making job creation in Alabama his top priority," said BCA President and CEO William Canary. "This one-time tax credit will provide small businesses the confidence and certainty they need to grow and hire new employees. Alabama's economic recovery is dependent on the ability of small businesses to generate jobs, and this common sense bill will help small businesses do just that."

Once the law is passed, the tax credit will be available for the tax year during which the employee has completed 12 months of consecutive employment and can begin on or after January 1, 2011.

Senate President Pro Tem: Lawmakers are Committed to Pro-Business Legislation

The state Senate's highest-ranking Republican outlined on Tuesday the three goals the majority caucus hopes to accomplish during the 2011 legislative session. Those goals include:

- Passing each of the Handshake with Alabama agenda items upon which GOP legislative candidates campaigned during 2010.

- Implementing reforms that will begin to put Alabama on a sound financial footing and replace past fiscal practices.

- Approving responsible budgets for public education and state agency appropriations in an expeditious manner that could result in early adjournment.

Senate President Pro Tem Del Marsh, R-Anniston, told BCA's Governmental Affairs Committee that fulfillment of the Handshake agenda began in December when lawmakers approved seven ethics bills in seven days during a special session called by then-Gov. Bob Riley.

He noted that one of the ethics bills, which regulated the entertaining of public officials by registered lobbyists, will require a "technical change" being requested by the Alabama Ethics Commission and Attorney General Luther Strange's office. Speaker Mike Hubbard, R-Auburn, is joining Marsh as a sponsor.

Marsh also touted the recent passage of the Responsible Budgeting and Spending Act, by Rep. Greg Canfield, R-Vestavia Hills, which was signed into law by Gov. Robert Bentley. The measure requires state revenue estimates to be based on a 15-year rolling average of tax collections rather than unreliable, "finger-in-the-wind" predictions.

Though the rolling average will provide more stable, conservative and dependable numbers with which to budget, the lawmaker said proration always will remain a threat.

"Using a rolling average will not eliminate proration, but we do believe it will greatly reduce the possibility," Marsh said. "We have run models going back 15 years, and in that time, there would have been proration even with the Canfield bill, but not nearly as often."

Referencing the most controversial measure yet to be considered, Marsh proved correct when he predicted lawmakers would wrap up work on his bill that repeals the state's Deferred Retirement Option Plan, a program that allows veteran public employees eligible for retirement to bank pension proceeds in a lucrative, high-yield account while continuing to work and receive a paycheck.

Indeed, the House voted 58-33 on Tuesday night to end the program, following a 21-13 vote earlier in the evening in the Senate on SB 72. After his legal advisor raised concerns the bill could be found unconstitutional, Gov. Bentley on Thursday added an executive amendment that would allow eligible applicants to enroll in DROP up to the effective date of the act. Both houses later concurred, and the governor signed it into law.

Labor unions for state workers and public education employees have fought efforts to repeal the expensive fringe benefit that they say was passed to discourage experienced workers and classroom teachers from retiring. It was noted, however, that those poised to receive the highest payouts from DROP include the leaders of the teachers' union and other high-paid enrollees far above the classroom level.

"Today, the DROP program costs the state anywhere from $45 million to $70 million, and the very responsible budget submitted to us by Gov. Bentley is based upon the repeal of that particular benefit," Marsh said. "Some want us to reform DROP rather than repeal it, but, quite simply, it is too flawed to fix."

Business to Be at Table When Immigration Bills are Debated

Immigration is another hot-button issue that soon could claim much of the legislature's attention, and Marsh said he expects to see several competing immigration bills combined into one measure after full input and advice from segments of the business community.

"We will probably see a committee formed and tasked with combining all of the immigration bills," Marsh said. "I promise the business community and others will be at the table, and we will come out with one bill that satisfies as many groups as possible while maintaining the promise we made in our Republican Handshake with Alabama."

Two new tax credits are being proposed for businesses that meet targeted goals in capital investment and job creation. The program, which is designed to increase employment and provide incentives for expansion, will be available to both new and existing businesses and industries.

Work also began this week on the General Fund and Education Trust Fund budgets with special emphasis placed on provisions to help shore up fiscal challenges faced by the state pension and public employee health insurance plans.

Marsh said moving the minimum years of service for full retirement from 25 to 30 years, requiring employees to contribute more to pension coffers and adjusting membership on boards overseeing fringe benefits are all items for consideration.

"Any study you look at shows that the public sector in pay, benefits, insurance and days off is ahead of the private sector in every case," Marsh said. "We have to bring parity back to Alabama, and we can no longer ask the private sector and taxpayers to carry the burden for public employees."

The ETF, Marsh indicated, will originate in the House with state agency spending plans conversely flowing down from the upper chamber.

Early Adjournment Possible?

A new air of openness and fairness exists in the Senate, according to Marsh, who said Democrats have proportional membership on important committees and will soon see their bills appear on calendars.

Once budgets are approved, the Handshake is fulfilled and "pro-business legislation is passed," lawmakers will not loiter long in Montgomery and could adjourn sine die before the mandated 30-meeting-days-within-105-calendar-days limitation is reached, Marsh said.

"Once we finish our business and do what's right by the people, we will go home," Marsh said. "Our plan is to pass the budgets early, pass what needs to be passed and get out of here early in order to save taxpayer dollars."

Dental Provider Bill Remanded for Further Study

SB 154, by Sen. Paul Bussman, R-Cullman, would prohibit health insurance policies and plans from setting fees for dental services that are not covered under the plan or policy. Sen. Slade Blackwell, R-Mountain Brook, and Senate Banking and Insurance Committee members accepted testimony from both proponents and opponents of the legislation. After much debate, Sen. Blackwell appointed a subcommittee to study the issue further. Subcommittee members Sen. Jabo Waggoner, R-Vestavia Hills; Sen. Roger Bedford, D-Russellville; and Sen. Bussman are to report back in three weeks. BCA will continue to be actively involved in the outcome of this proposed legislation. BCA opposes SB 154 in its current form.

House Passes Voter ID Bill

After extended debate Tuesday night, the Alabama House passed HB 19, by Rep. Kerry Rich, R-Albertville, which would require voters to show photo identification at the polls.

For years the state has required voters to show identification at the polls; however, many forms of non-photo IDs have been allowed, such as a utility bill or birth certificate that show only a voter's name and address.

This bill defines a valid identification as any photo ID issued by the United States, any U.S. state or territory, or any other ID issued by a government entity or agency such as the military.

Under this bill, someone without a photo ID still could cast a provisional ballot, or could cast a regular ballot if two election officials signed an affidavit identifying the person as an eligible voter.

The bill now goes to the Alabama Senate.

E-Verify Bill Sails Through Committee

The Senate Commerce and Small Business committee favorably reported SB 163, by Sen. Rodger Smitherman, D-Birmingham. The bill requires all public and private employers in Alabama to use the federal E-Verify program to verify legal status when hiring new employees. Businesses also must retain all documentation relating to the verification of legal status for at least three years after termination of employment.

According to the bill, businesses that wish to do business with the state must be registered with and utilizing the E-Verify program. Businesses found to have hired an illegal immigrant and that have not utilized the E-verify program will be subject to a 30-day license suspension upon the first violation and a permanent license suspension for the second offense. SB 163 now awaits consideration from the full Senate.

BCA is monitoring this legislation.

'Where Were These Textbooks?'

The House Ways and Means Education committee on Wednesday approved HB 211, The Teacher and Education Employee Protection Act, sponsored by Rep. Jay Love, R-Montgomery.

The bill would require the State Department of Education and the Department of Finance to implement a program that provides teachers and school support personnel with liability insurance. The state currently does not provide teacher and school support personnel with liability insurance, although it is provided to all other state employees. Teachers and school support personnel currently receive liability insurance through membership in private organizations, such as the Alabama Education Association.

"The state has always offered liability protection to state employees, and it's time we extend the same protection to our teachers," Love said at Wednesday's hearing. "No teacher should be forced to join an organization and pay dues out of fear of being financially ruined by a lawsuit. This is a basic service of state government, and it's something our teachers absolutely deserve."

Opponents contended that the state extending liability insurance to teachers and support personnel not only would remove a financial incentive for teachers to join the organizations, such as AEA, but that it is also an unneeded expense, especially given the current economic climate.

AEA Executive Secretary Paul Hubbert argued the money spent to create the new liability insurance program should be spent on classroom textbooks instead, and he brought visual aids. After Hubbert distributed several very worn textbooks to the committee, Love asked Hubbert, "Where were these textbooks [when you came before this committee arguing the state could afford to keep the DROP program]?"

In his testimony before the committee, Hubbert claimed AEA provides 92 percent of Alabama's teachers with liability insurance. The NEA purchases the insurance, and the current carrier is not an Alabama-based company.

The Legislative Fiscal Office estimates the cost to the state would be as low as just $475,000. With a favorable report from the committee, the bill now goes to the House floor for consideration.

Tort/Legal Reform Bills Set for Public Hearings

As previously reported, several tort/legal reform measures were introduced in the legislature and are set for public hearings.

Proposed legislation addressing tort reform has been a part of the BCA's Legal and Judicial Reform Committee *Legislative Agenda* for the last several years. BCA supports these bills as introduced:

SB 59, by Sen. Cam Ward, R-Alabaster, and HB 132, by Rep. Greg Canfield, R-Vestavia Hills, would decrease the statute of repose for commencing an action against an architect, engineer or builder to four years.

SB 184, by Sen. Ben Brooks, R-Mobile, and HB 227, by Rep. Ron Johnson, R-Sylacauga, prohibit a product liability action for relief against sellers that are not manufacturers.

SB 187, also by Sen. Brooks, and HB 239, by Rep. Steve McMillan, R-Bay Minette, apply the more recent standard enunciated in the U.S. Supreme Court's decision in the 1993 Daubert case for the admissibility of expert evidence and testimony in all civil and criminal court actions, except for actions arising under and governed by the Medical Liability Act of 1987, or any judicial interpretations thereof.

SB 207, by Sen. Ward, and HB 236, by Rep. Canfield, would provide that judgments, other than judgments based on a contract action, would bear interest from the date of entry of the judgment at a rate equal to the weekly average one-year constant maturity Treasury yield, as published by the Board of Governors of the Federal Reserve System, for the nearest calendar week preceding the date of judgment, and provides that post-judgment interest would be computed daily to the date of payment, and compounded annually.

SB 212, by Sen. Clay Scofield, R-Guntersville, and HB 228, by Rep. Johnson, provide that a wrongful death action may only be filed in a county where the deceased could have filed a civil action, if living.

BCA's Legal and Judicial Reform Committee's 2011 Tort Reform Package has recommended SB 184 for approval and support. This bill, a part of the Alabama Civil Justice Reform Committee's 2011 Tort Reform Package, addresses product liability litigation against Alabama retailers, wholesalers and distributors who may be sued even though they did not participate in the manufacture or design of the product. The suits cost Alabama businesses time and money while the true target of the suit is the manufacturer or designer of the product.

Environmental Bills Update

SB 80, by Sen. Del Marsh, R-Anniston, moved out of the Senate Commerce, Transportation and Utilities Committee on Thursday by a unanimous vote. This is the companion bill to HB 50, by Rep. Greg Canfield,

R-Vestavia Hills, which amends the state solid waste laws by repealing an existing exemption from regulation for fly ash waste, bottom ash waste, boiler slag waste and flue gas emissions control wastes from the burning of coal or other fossil fuels at electric generating plants. The bill further authorizes the Alabama Department of Environmental Management (ADEM) to regulate these wastes. BCA supports this legislation.

SB 181, by Sen. Marsh, was voted out of the Senate Judiciary Committee on Wednesday. This is the companion to HB 106, by Rep. Steve Clouse, R-Ozark. The bills amend state laws pertaining to civil penalties for violations of state environmental protection laws and orders, by 1) removing minimum penalty amounts for certain violations and by 2) limiting the penalties for violations subject to monthly reporting based on average compliance, to not more frequently than once a month. BCA is monitoring this legislation.

HB 143, by Rep. Alan Baker, R-Brewton, was voted out of the House County & Municipal Government Committee on Wednesday. HB 143 would change the state solid waste law on local government approval of "new" landfill sites. Present law states that if a local governing body does not take action on a landfill site application within 90 days, it automatically becomes approved. HB 143 would change the law from automatic "approval" to automatic "denial" if the local government takes no action. BCA is monitoring this legislation.

In Other News

Panel OKs Prevention of Davis-Bacon Act in Contracts

The House Commerce and Small Business Committee favorably reported out HB 214, by Rep. Jack Williams, R-Birmingham. The bill prevents the state or any political subdivision of the state from using the federal Davis-Bacon Act's prevailing wage provision in contracts. The Davis-Bacon Act of 1931 requires prevailing wages be paid on public works projects. For federally funded contracts in excess of $2,000, contractors and subcontractors must pay their workers no less than the local prevailing wage and benefits for similar work on comparable projects.

Since its enactment, the Davis-Bacon Act has been suspended a number of times, normally during national emergencies. Most recently, the act was suspended by President George W. Bush for designated areas in the Gulf Coast states directly impacted by Hurricane Katrina in 2005. The latest effort to repeal the Davis-Bacon act was by U.S. House Republicans in January of this year. As part of their effort to cut $2.5 trillion from the budget over the next 10 years, the "Spending Reduction Act of 2011" includes repealing the act, which would save upwards of $1 billion annually in discretionary spending.

Statute of Repose Bill Receives Favorable Report

The House Commerce and Small Business Committee also gave a favorable report to HB 132, by Rep. Greg Canfield, R-Vestavia Hills. The bill decreases the statute of repose for commencing an action against an architect, engineer or builder from 13 years to seven years. The original bill reduced the years to four, but after negotiations among interested parties, the compromise reached was seven years.

House Passes Bill Making Annual Appropriations to State Ethics Commission

In light of the new ethics legislation that placed additional responsibilities on the State Ethics Commission, the Alabama House passed HB 62, by Rep. Mike Jones, R-Andalusia, by a vote of 91-1. This bill provides that beginning with Fiscal Year 2012, the commission will receive an appropriation from the State General Fund in an amount equal to not less than one-tenth of one percent of the total funds appropriated from the State General Fund. The Commission's annual appropriation would not be reduced from that amount, unless two-thirds of the membership of the House and Senate vote to reduce the appropriation.

HB 62 has been referred to the Senate Committee on Finance and Taxation-General Fund. BCA is monitoring this legislation.

Tuesday, March 22, 2011:
BCA's Day of Advocacy and Leadership

BCA, Gov. Bentley Welcome New Board Members

The Business Council of Alabama welcomed several of the newest members of its Board of Directors to an orientation luncheon Tuesday. The group learned about *BCA's Legislative Agenda*, board responsibilities and policies and upcoming BCA events. Gov. Robert Bentley even paid the group a surprise visit and wished them well in their endeavors.

Attending the orientation meeting, held at the State Department of Archives and History, were new BCA board members Mark Hope, Wells Fargo; Greg Powell Fi-Plan Partners; Steve Holt, Shoals Area Chamber of Commerce; LaShaunda Holley, Jackson Area Chamber of Commerce; Chester Vrocher, Boise; Jan Wood, Wetumpka Area Chamber of Commerce; Denson Henry, Henry Brick Co.; Ronnie Boles, General and Automotive Machine; Ray Perez, Honda Manufacturing of Alabama; Terrance Brown, HEALTHSOUTH; Carl Jamison, Jamison Money Farmer P.C.; Ron Box, Joe Money Machinery; Jim Fincher, 3M Corporation; Shane Clanton, BBVA Compass; and Ron Perkins, Doozer Software.

Remaining new members unable to attend the meeting were: Paul Cocker, GKN Westland Aerospace; Greg Leikvold, BF Goodrich; Debbie Long, Protective Life Corporation; Douglas Markam, Books-A-Million; Joseph Rella, Austal USA; Markus Schaefer, Mercedes-Benz U.S. International; Lolly Steiner, Auburn Area Chamber of Commerce; David Ward, Hager Companies; and Dontá Wilson, BB&T.

Later that day, several board members visited the State House to observe from the galleries the proceedings in the House and Senate, including the House vote on HB 61, the small business heath care tax deduction increase legislation by Rep. April Weaver, R-Brierfield.

Salute to State Leaders Draws Large Crowd

BCA's annual reception saluting leaders of state government drew more than 500 persons on Tuesday at the Alabama Activity Center, including Gov. Robert Bentley, lawmakers, cabinet members and members of the Alabama judicial system. The event was co-sponsored by the Chamber of Commerce of Huntsville-Madison County and the Alabama Truck-

Gov. Robert Bentley stopped by to visit with BCA Second Vice Chairman Carl Jamison, his Tuscaloosa neighbor, and other BCA board members at their first meeting of 2011 at the State Department of Archives and History.

ing Association. A delegation of IT company owners and representatives from Moldova in Eastern Europe enjoyed the event as well, as many were able to network with others in the technology industry.

BCA Committee Chairmen Honored for Service

Three of the Business Council of Alabama's long-standing committee chairmen were honored for their years of service at Tuesday's BCA Board of Directors meeting. BCA Chairman Will Brooke presented special plaques to Health Committee Chair Bruce Windham, Environmental Committee Chair David Roberson and Tax Committee Chair William Dow. The three have served many years as chairmen of their respective committees, which recommend legislative policy to the full BCA board for incorporation in the annual *BCA Legislative Agenda*.

Washington Briefing

Congress Passes Sixth Funding Bill to Keep Government Open Until April 8

Before adjourning for a weeklong constituent work period, both the U.S. House and Senate voted on a resolution to keep the government running through April 8.

On a 271-158 vote, the House approved a continuing resolution that cuts another $6 billion from federal programs. The Senate followed by passing the measure 87-13, and the president signed it into law on Friday, Mar. 18, the day the previous continuing resolution was set to expire.

This marked the sixth time since the fiscal year began on October 1 and the second this month that Congress passed a stop-gap spending bill to keep the government running. Congress must still come to an agreement on how to fund the government through the end of the fiscal year.

Chapter 7
April 1, 2011
Resolve by Statute, Not Rule Change

Revenue Department Rule Change Would Unfairly Close So-Called 'Loophole' the Business Community Tried in Vain to Correct Through Sound Tax Policy

A valid tax issue that the Alabama Department of Revenue (ADOR) has with Alabama-based S corporations, partnerships, LLCs and other "pass-through" entities that earn income within and outside of Alabama needs to be resolved by statute and not by administrative rule change.

From the ADOR point of view, the current "gross income regulation" allows resident shareholders/partners of these companies to report only their shares of the entity's income allocated to Alabama at the entity level, although they also earn income from other states and at times from foreign countries. The Alabama resident shareholders and partners then are allowed to deduct 100 percent of their federal income tax deduction, which may markedly reduce or eliminate their Alabama taxable income.

The situation grew worse from the ADOR perspective when its administrative law judge ruled that the "gross income regulation" was invalid and that the Alabama resident shareholders'/partners' shares of income from all sources should be reported for Alabama income tax purposes. That ruling further muddied the water, in that it allowed resident shareholders and partners to select between reporting their shares of income earned in Alabama or reporting worldwide operations when they were heavily weighted with operating losses, whichever resulted in the lower tax liability.

Tax professionals within and outside of these companies are very familiar with ADOR's problems on this issue. Beginning in 2007, the BCA, along with other members of the Gross Income Regulation Coalition, worked in good faith to devise a fair solution and even introduced legislation in the 2007 session to resolve the issue. However, the bill gained no support because the Alabama Education Association said that it did not go far enough and raised too little revenue, some $15 to $20 million annually. Presently, the proposed unfair rule change is pending and written comments are sought from those affected, but it would be far better to have the issue resolved legislatively, and ample time remains in the current session to do so.

The recent move by the ADOR to repeal the "gross income regulation" under the proposed rule change results in a serious problem of double taxation, which means that ADOR's problems still will not be resolved fully, but a heavy tax burden would be shifted to the resident partners and shareholders and would raise between $25 to $40 million annually. The problem is that the rule change would fail to provide tax credits for taxes paid by the entity to countries outside of the United States, much less provide tax credits for any entity-level income or franchise taxes paid to other states. The 2007 Coalition legislation would have provided such tax credits and is clearly based on a fairer, more business-friendly tax policy.

Business Council of Alabama President and CEO William Canary spoke out against the proposed Revenue Department rule change this week, saying, "While we understand Alabama's dire budget situation, we certainly don't believe anyone expects the state's budgets to be balanced on the backs of the private sector, which is still facing a nearly 10-percent unemployment rate in Alabama.

"We have begun assessing the impact of the regulatory actions being taken by the Alabama Department of Revenue and how its proposed regulations would affect both job creation and future economic development efforts of existing businesses in Alabama. We look forward to discussing our findings in short order with the leadership in both the executive and legislative branches."

BCA will be working diligently with the legislative leadership of the House and Senate as well as officials in Gov. Bentley's administration to ensure that a fair, prospective, pro-business solution is reached through legislation rather than by rule. As we move forward, BCA also will set the record straight and show that the companies affected by this issue have been proactive in their attempts to resolve this issue, have only followed the laws in place and should not be vilified by negative labels or negative implications.

Since 2008, the *BCA Legislative Agenda* has stated that the BCA will support efforts to resolve the Revenue Department's problems and litigation over its "gross income regulation" that affects partnerships, S-corps, LLCs and other "pass-through" entities that earn income both in and outside of Alabama.

BCA Opposes Tax Measures

BCA opposes several AEA-initiated legislative proposals that would raise or impose new taxes totaling nearly $228 million. The proposals are:

HB 241, by Rep. John Knight, D-Montgomery - "This bill will amend Section 40-18-14, Code of Alabama 1975, to clarify that gross income for Alabama resident individuals includes an owner's entire allocable share of income from a pass-through entity."

HB 242, by Rep. Knight - This bill proposes "… to limit the state income tax deduction for federal income taxes for individual taxpayers; to exempt sales of food and over-the-counter drugs from state sales tax; and to prohibit local governments from levying separate sales taxes only on the sale of food or over-the-counter drugs."

HB 299, by Rep. Richard Lindsey, D-Centre - "… Alabama corporate income tax law is linked to federal corporate income tax law, which allows a domestic production activities deduction that is equal to a percentage of income earned from domestic production or taxable income, whichever is less. This bill would limit the Alabama deduction to three percent of qualifying income."

HB 300, by Rep. Lindsey - "…Alabama levies an income tax on corporations. Alabama corporate income tax law is linked to federal corporate income tax law, which allows a temporary increase in the bonus depreciation deduction from fifty percent (50%) to one hundred percent (100%) of the adjusted basis of qualified property pursuant to The Tax Relief, Unemployment Insurance Reauthorization, and Job Creation Act of 2010 (Public Law 111-312). This bill would limit the Alabama deduction to fifty percent (50%) of the adjusted basis of qualified property."

HB 301, by Rep. Lindsey, - "This bill defines unitary business and requires taxpayers who are part of a unitary business to use a combined report to determine their Alabama taxable income."

HB 302, by Rep. Lindsey - "This bill would limit the state depletion allowance for oil and gas to the amount allowed by the federal depletion allowance."

HB 347, by Rep. A.J. McCampbell, D-Gallion - "...Alabama corporate income tax law is linked to federal corporate income tax law, which generally provides that an acquiring corporation succeeds to the net operating loss (NOL) carryover of a loss corporation when the assets of the loss corporation are acquired. This bill would provide that a net operating loss (NOL) may be carried forward and allowed as a deduction only by the corporation that sustained the loss."

HB 373, by Rep. Joe Hubbard, D-Montgomery, would establish, for purposes of income taxes, a presence nexus standard for business activity.

'Full Employment Act' Now Moves to House, Senate

HB 230, by Rep. Blaine Galliher, R-Gadsden, and its companion bill, SB 173, by Sen. Arthur Orr, R-Decatur, received favorable reports from their assigned committees this week. The broad support for both bills reflects the premium that the governor and legislative leaders are putting on job creation this session. The bill would provide to employers of 50 or fewer employees a one-time income tax credit, beginning in the current tax year, equal to $1,000 for each new job that is created that pays at least $10 per hour, after the employee has completed 12 consecutive months of employment. Each bill is now in position to be voted on by members of their respective house of origin.

BCA supports this legislation.

Crowd Gathers for Hearing on Forever Wild as Senate Panel OKs Extension

The Senate Energy and Natural Resources Committee voted 5-3 to extend for 20 years the state's Forever Wild program. Voting in favor of SB 140, which reauthorizes the program as is, were: Sen. Ben Brooks, R-Mobile; Sen. Cam Ward, R-Alabaster; Sen. Gerald Allen, R-Tuscaloosa; President Pro Tem Del Marsh, R-Anniston; Sen. Bobby Singleton, D-Greensboro.

Voting against reauthorization of the program as is were: Sen. Greg Reed, R-Jasper; Sen. Jimmy Holley, R-Elba; and Sen. Tom Whatley, R-Auburn.

BCA supports this legislation. Will McCartney, representing his father, Tim McCartney, vice-president of McCartney Construction Co. and co-chair of BCA's Environment and Energy Committee, was prepared to speak on behalf of the bill before time constraints prevented it. However, his statement was delivered to the committee. In it, he reminded the group that reauthorizing Forever Wild for an additional 20 years is a BCA legislative priority.

"As you know, Forever Wild was established by constitutional amendment in 1992 with 83 percent voter support — the highest level of public support ever recorded for any state legislation establishing a government land acquisition program.

"Over the last 19 years, some of Alabama's greatest outdoor landmarks have been supported through Forever Wild — the Mobile-Tensaw Delta, Walls of Jericho, Sipsey River Swamp, Freedom Hills, Lillian Swamp, the Red Hills, Weogufka Creek, Ruffner Mountain, Turkey Creek, Hurricane Creek, Grand Bay Savannah, Little River Canyon, Old Cahawba Prairie, Hatchet Creek, Coon Gulf, Paint Rock River, Coldwater Mountain, Perdido River, Weeks Bay ... and the list goes on. Because of Forever Wild, these landmarks of Alabama will be preserved for generations to come.

"I also point out that Alabama's largest economic business is tourism. Hunting, fishing and wildlife viewing in Alabama has a $2.2 billion annual economic impact that benefits both local communities and the state. Forever Wild, since its inception, has preserved more than 200,000 acres of wilderness for hunting, fishing, bird-watching and other outdoor activities.

"Senators, Alabama's economic recovery hinges on a successful tourism industry, and during these challenging economic times, why would we not want to continue such a successful program, a program that helps attract tens of thousands of visitors each year?

"There is more work to do, and just as the legislature did in 1992, I urge this committee to protect the Forever Wild Land Trust and continue this worthwhile funding for another 20 years."

Immigration Bill Sponsor Working to Resolve Issues of Concern for Business

On Tuesday, the Senate Job Creation and Economic Development Committee heard testimony from opponents of SB 256, by Sen. Scott Beason, R-Gardendale. The bill, which seeks to curb illegal immigration in Alabama, would crack down on employers who knowingly hire illegal immigrants.

At Tuesday's hearing, Sen. Beason said, "What it will do is make Alabama a state where illegal immigration is frowned upon. The federal government is not enforcing its own law. Our goal is to make sure that we are not a sanctuary state." Beason went on to say that his goal is to produce "streamlined legislation where everyone understands the rules, and it's easy to enforce."

Under the bill, the penalties are extremely severe and could put companies out of business after only one violation. For example, employers who are found by a court to have knowingly hired an illegal immigrant would have to surrender their business licenses for up to 14 days. Due to the nature of some businesses, this provision could prove detrimental to the business.

SB 256 does not mandate the use of the E-Verify program to verify the employment status of a worker. An employer may use the E-Verify system if he or she so chooses, but the bill also allows for other forms of identification, like an unexpired Alabama driver's license or any valid government issued identification document that proves lawful status, to document that a person is legally present.

The bill would require employers to verify the legal status of all of the employees of companies with which they contract, placing a tremendous burden on the employer. For example, if a business contracts out for IT services and janitorial services, the employer would be responsible for verifying the legal status of all of the employees working for the IT and janitorial service companies. Employers who fail to verify the workers of the companies with which they contract would be subject to a $500 fine, upon a first violation, for each person employed that the employer does not have a file containing proof that the employee is legally present; a $5,000 fine, on a second offense, for each person for whom the employer lacks a file; and the $5,000 fine plus one-year business license revocation for the third offense.

BCA staff met with Sen. Beason to express our concerns. As a result, Sen. Beason is working to resolve our issues in a substitute version of the bill he plans to offer to the committee members next week.

Tort Reform Bills on Fast Track, Judiciary Committee Chairs Tell BCA Committee

BCA's Governmental Affairs Committee heard from the chairmen of both the House and Senate Judiciary Committees this week, as the pair told the group about a package of bills addressing tort reform, sentencing reform and other issues that they said would likely move swiftly through the legislative process.

House Judiciary Committee Chair Rep. Paul DeMarco, R-Homewood, quoted a series of statements from several governors and other elected officials across the county, each touting low taxes and a business-friendly environment as reasons employers give for locating in their respective states.

"I think everybody is looking at Alabama and saying we are headed in the right direction, and we can now write letters to business leaders across the country and tell them this is a place they want to do business," DeMarco said. "Our economic development prospects are ripe, but part of that is providing a good court system in which each and every business is given due process and treated fairly by the judiciary."

Senate Judiciary Committee Chairman Cam Ward, R-Alabaster, said it was difficult to imagine, "two or three years ago that you would have House and Senate Judiciary Committees actually willing to consider and pass the tort reform bills that you put before them this session."

He predicted that "four or five bills" in a package put forth by the Alabama Civil Justice Reform Committee could easily receive legislative approval this year.

Among them are measures dealing with post-judgment interest, product liability issues, venue selection and application of the Daubert Standard in state court cases, which allows a trial judge to make a preliminary assessment of whether an expert's scientific testimony is based on reasoning or methodology that is scientifically valid and can be applied properly to the facts at issue.

"We know in the past that those interests working against the business community have said, 'We'll just go to the committee chairmen, and these bills will never come up for a vote,'" Ward said. "Now we have the best possible climate for these civil justice reforms to pass, and the question is no longer if they will pass, but when in this session, they will pass."

DeMarco said he believes several bills will not require a public hearing and many will be considered by his committee as early as next week. He also noted that workers' compensation laws are another area that could be examined and reformed at some point during the current quadrennium.

The committees soon will consider sentencing reform, though not directly related to the business community, according to Ward. The state's desperate prison overcrowding situation and the threat of punitive orders by a federal judge — should the situation be taken to court — demand quick action by the legislature, he said.

"We don't have any money to build any new prisons, our system is the second most overcrowded in the nation, and it is the most overcrowded in terms of incarceration," Ward said. "We are going to have to look at some meaningful, thoughtful sentencing reform, and business leaders should be at the table discussing the situation because you will bear the burden if a federal judge orders us to spend $300 million a year to fix the overcrowding situation.

"The old mindset of lock 'em up and throw away the key looks great on a bumper sticker, but it is bad public policy," he added.

DeMarco urged business leaders to monitor the ongoing trial of *Lynch v. Alabama,* a case brought by parents in poor Black Belt counties who allege that the state's property tax system is historically rooted in racism and underfunds public education. He cited similar cases in Kansas and New York in which government entities were ordered by federal judges to raise taxes.

"If there is a ruling for the plantiffs, there could be some major tax consequences," DeMarco said. "We could have a federal judge setting tax policy in Alabama, and that is a scary thought, to say the least."

Committees OK Bills Amending Ethics Act

HB 253, by Rep. Mike Hubbard, R-Auburn, received a favorable report from the House Ethics & Campaign Finance Committee, while its companion, SB 222, by Sen. Del Marsh, R-Anniston, received a favorable report from the Senate Constitution, Campaign Finance, Ethics and Elections Committee. These bills amend the recent ethics legislation that prohibits a person from offering or giving anything to a public official or public employee, as well as members of their households or family to influence official action. Also, under this bill, a public official may not solicit or receive anything for the purpose of influencing official action.

To make this bill more effective and enforceable, an amendment was adopted to change the term "corruptly" to "corruptly influencing" to alleviate any questions relating to vagueness and enforceability. To clarify the meaning of the term "corruptly," it was defined to mean to "act voluntarily, deliberately and dishonestly to either accomplish an unlawful end or result or to use an unlawful method or means to accomplish an otherwise lawful end or result."

Each bill now goes to their respective chambers for consideration. BCA supports this legislation.

Environmental Bills Update

HB 50, by Rep. Greg Canfield, R-Vestavia Hills, passed the House Thursday and was transmitted to the Senate. HB 50 amends the solid waste laws by removing an existing exemption from regulation fly ash waste, bottom ash waste, boiler slag waste and flue gas emissions control wastes from the burning of coal or other fossil fuels at electric generating plants. It also authorizes the Alabama Department of Environmental Management (ADEM) to regulate these wastes, once the EPA promulgates federal policy on management of the waste. SB 80 by Sen. Del Marsh, R-Anniston, is the companion bill and is awaiting action in the Senate. BCA supports this legislation.

HJR 197, by Rep. Paul DeMarco, R-Homewood, urges the U.S. Congress to adopt legislation prohibiting the EPA from regulating greenhouse gas emissions without congressional approval. This was a model resolution pushed by the American Legislative Exchange Council (ALEC). The resolution passed the House on a voice vote on Tuesday and is now in the Senate Rules Committee. BCA supports this resolution.

Senate Committee Passes Health Care 'Opt Out' Bill

The Senate Health Committee approved SB 215, by Sen. Scott Beason, R-Gardendale, with only one dissenting vote. The proposed constitutional amendment would prohibit any person, employer or health care provider from being compelled to participate in any health care system if approved by the voters in the next statewide election. HB 60, by Rep. Blaine Galliher, R-Gadsden, received a favorable report from the House Health Committee on a party line vote earlier this month.

Both bills now await consideration by their respective houses.

BCA Joins in Support of Students First Act

In a demonstration of its commitment to a true business-education alliance, the Business Council of Alabama has joined the Alabama Association of School Boards, the State Department of Education and the Alabama Community College System to support the introduction of the Students First Act by Rep. Chad Fincher, R-Semmes. The proposed legislation substantially revises the current Tenure and Fair Dismissal Act by putting students first. The bill ensures fundamental fairness and due process for tenured employees, would ensure a high-quality, accountable and effective workforce for students, and would stop the incentive to file costly legal challenges of routine personnel decisions. Sen. Trip Pittman, R-Daphne, is expected to introduce the bill in the Senate.

Texting Bill on Way to Senate

HB 102, by Rep. Jim McClendon, R-Springville, received final passage by the House on Thursday. The bill prohibits a person from using text-based communications on a wireless communication device or manually operating a global positioning system (GPS) device or similar navigating device while operating a motor vehicle on a public road, street or highway.

Washington Briefing
Budget Deal Inching Closer

In February, the House approved a budget for the remainder of fiscal year 2011 cutting appropriations to $1.026 trillion, about $102 billion less than the president's initial request for 2011 and $61.3 billion less than the spending level under a continuing resolution that expired March 4. Congress has since passed two additional CRs, the second of which expires April 8.

The Senate has yet to counter with a proposal of its own after voting down the House bill. However, on Wednesday, negotiations began on a possible agreement that would cut federal spending through the end of September by $33 billion by cutting appropriations to $1.055 trillion, $73 billion less than the president's request for 2011.

Leaders on both sides of the Capitol have made it clear that no final deal has been reached and negotiations could break down over disagreement about how much to cut and from where. House Speaker John Boehner (R-OH) said this week, "Nothing will be agreed to until everything is agreed to."

Spending cuts are not the only sticking point in the negotiations. In their initial budget package, House Republicans included unrelated amendments, known as "riders," that would impose restrictions on federal agencies, including prohibiting federal funding to Planned Parenthood and weakening the ability of the Environmental Protection Agency to regulate carbon emissions.

These riders are expected to play a central role in the negotiations going forward. It has been suggested that in exchange for giving up some of the spending cuts, there will be pressure to accept some of the riders.

NAM Launches 'Affordable Energy' Campaign

Earlier this week, the National Association of Manufacturers (NAM) launched a multi-state, multi-million dollar initiative to oppose the Environmental Protection Agency's aggressive regulatory agenda. The campaign calls on Congress and the Administration to carefully consider the severe economic impact of the EPA's job-killing regulations on energy prices and on businesses and families across the country.

The unprecedented expansion of proposed regulations by the EPA — such as greenhouse gas regulations for stationary sources, more stringent ozone air quality standards, unachievable emissions limits on industrial and commercial boilers and several others — will cost manufacturers billions of dollars, lead to higher electricity prices and increase the cost of goods and services for consumers.

NAM's web page, www.NoNewRegs.org, contains a call to action so manufacturers, your employees and the general public can contact their member of Congress.

The BCA is the exclusive affiliate of the NAM in the state of Alabama.

CHAPTER 8

April 8, 2011

ALABAMA'S GROSS INCOME REGULATION: PROBLEMS ... AND A FAIR SOLUTION

This week, BCA President and CEO William Canary, Senior Vice President and Legal Advisor Anita Archie, BCA Tax and Fiscal Policy Committee Chairman Marty Abroms and immediate past Committee Chairman William Dow along with Rick Brown, chairman of the Business Associations' Tax Coalition (BATC) and president of the Alabama Retail Association, met with several state officials on the proposed change to the "gross income regulation." Included in the meetings were state Finance Director David Perry, Speaker of the House Mike Hubbard, Senate President Pro Tem Del Marsh and Alabama Commissioner of Revenue Julie Magee, along with key members of her staff.

These meetings represented a good-faith intent to assist state officials in crafting a legislative, pro-business remedy to long-standing problems with the Alabama income tax law, which is explained below.

The Alabama Department of Revenue's (ADOR) proposed rule change to the "gross income regulation" will require an Alabama S corporation shareholder or partner/LLC member to include income in his or her Alabama tax return from all sources, both foreign and domestic. However, if the resident owners are not allowed tax credits for entity-level taxes paid to other states and foreign countries, the proposed rule change will result in double taxation on the same income.

Presently, the regulation provides that only income that is allocated to Alabama at the entity level is required to be reported for Alabama income tax purposes. Income earned by the entity in another state is taxed by that state, assuming the other state levies an income tax. The Alabama resident is also allowed by the Alabama Constitution to deduct 100 percent of his/her federal income tax liability against the owner's Alabama source income, which could greatly reduce or even eliminate the resident owner's Alabama income tax liability.

Also presently in effect is a ruling by the ADOR's administrative law judge that requires Alabama resident shareholders/partners to report their shares of income from all sources, which directly conflicts with the provision in the above paragraph. Owners/partners who have heavy losses from their operations outside of Alabama will likely elect to report income (and losses) from all sources to reduce their Alabama income tax liabilities.

The two conflicting methods for reporting income, coupled with the ability to apply 100 percent of the federal income tax deduction drain the state's tax revenue and are unfair to other Alabama taxpayers who cannot select the more advantageous method for reporting income.

The solution to this dilemma is not to adopt the rule change as proposed by the ADOR and usher in double taxation because that will only open up new problems and possible litigation. In the prior term, the Legislative Council rejected the proposed rule change, wisely avoiding the substitution of new problems for old problems, which would impose an unfair tax burden on the resident owners.

Instead, this is a matter that should be resolved by the Alabama Legislature, and ample time remains to accomplish it. The legislation should be fair, prospective and based on sound tax policy that is pro-jobs and pro-business. To do that, every effort must be made to ensure that the Alabama resident owners/partners of such business entities are not subjected to double taxation.

Fortunately, much effort already has been put forth to find a just resolution to this issue. HB 829 of the 2007 Regular Session was proactively developed by members of the Alabama business community under the Gross Income Regulation Coalition. Alabama employers who are currently struggling in this fragile recovery need sound, sensible tax policy from the Alabama Legislature, and using this bill as model legislation to resolve these issues is a logical first step.

BCA Opposes Tax Measures

BCA opposes several AEA-initiated legislative proposals that would raise or impose new taxes totaling nearly $228 million. The proposals are:

HB 241, by Rep. John Knight, D-Montgomery - "This bill will amend Section 40-18-14, Code of Alabama 1975, to clarify that gross income for Alabama resident individuals includes an owner's entire allocable share of income from a pass-through entity."

HB 242, by Rep. Knight - This bill proposes "... to limit the state income tax deduction for federal income taxes for individual taxpayers; to exempt sales of food and over-the-counter drugs from state sales tax; and to prohibit local governments from levying separate sales taxes only on the sale of food or over-the-counter drugs."

HB 299, by Rep. Richard Lindsey, D-Centre - "... Alabama corporate income tax law is linked to federal corporate income tax law, which allows a domestic production activities deduction that is equal to a percentage of income earned from domestic production or taxable income, whichever is less. This bill would limit the Alabama deduction to three percent of qualifying income."

HB 300, by Rep. Lindsey - "... Alabama levies an income tax on corporations. Alabama corporate income tax law is linked to federal corporate income tax law, which allows a temporary increase in the bonus depreciation deduction from fifty percent (50%) to one hundred percent (100%) of the adjusted basis of qualified property pursuant to The Tax Relief, Unemployment Insurance Reauthorization, and Job Creation Act of 2010 (Public Law 111-312). This bill would limit the Alabama deduction to fifty percent (50%) of the adjusted basis of qualified property."

HB 301, by Rep. Lindsey - "This bill defines unitary business and requires taxpayers who are part of a unitary business to use a combined report to determine their Alabama taxable income.

HB 302, by Rep. Lindsey - "This bill would limit the state depletion allowance for oil and gas to the amount allowed by the federal depletion allowance."

HB 347, by Rep. A.J. McCampbell, D-Gallion - "... Alabama corporate income tax law is linked to federal corporate income tax law, which generally provides that an acquiring corporation succeeds to the net operating loss (NOL) carryover of a loss corporation when the assets of the loss corporation are acquired. This bill would provide that a net operating loss (NOL) may be carried forward and allowed as a deduction only by the corporation that sustained the loss."

HB 373, by Rep. Joe Hubbard, D-Montgomery, would establish, for purposes of income taxes, a presence nexus standard for business activity.

Dueling Immigration Bills Clear Hurdles

Two very different immigration bills cleared legislative hurdles in the Alabama Legislature this past week. HB 56, by Rep. Micky Hammon, R-Decatur, which seeks to curb illegal immigration in Alabama by requiring state and local government officials to enforce federal immigration laws as well as by cracking down on employers who knowingly hire illegal immigrants, passed the House by a vote of 73-28. The legislation, modeled after the Arizona law, creates specific penalties for employers who "knowingly or intentionally" hire illegal immigrants.

Under Hammon's bill, all Alabama businesses would be required to utilize the federal E-Verify program by January 1, 2012, to ensure they are not hiring illegal immigrants. Alabama businesses also would be required to maintain the verification records for up to three years. Employers with 25 employees or less would be able to use a telephone system created and maintained by the Alabama Department of Industrial Relations in lieu of the E-Verify system to verify their workers. In addition, employers who apply for economic development incentives after September 30, 2011, must prove they use the E-Verify program to receive any grant, loan or performance-based incentive awarded by a governmental entity.

Upon the first violation of employing an illegal immigrant, the employer must terminate the employment of all illegal workers and sign a sworn affidavit stating all illegal workers have been terminated, and the employer will not knowingly or intentionally employ an illegal immigrant in the state. The employer also will be subject to a three-year statewide probationary period. Upon the second violation, all business licenses issued in the county where the illegal immigrant performed work would be revoked permanently. The licenses would be revoked permanently statewide upon the third violation. Employers who can prove they utilize the E-Verify system or the state telephone system to verify their workers would be immune from these penalties.

SB 256, by Sen. Scott Beason, R-Gardendale, cleared the Senate Job Creation and Economic Development Committee with only one dissenting vote. Like Hammon's bill, SB 256 seeks to deter illegal immigration in Alabama by cracking down on employers who knowingly or intentionally hire illegal immigrants; however, there are significant differences between the two bills.

Under SB 256, an employer is not required to utilize the E-Verify program to determine the legal status of workers. Other forms of identification, such as a valid Alabama driver's license or any valid U.S. government-issued identification, may be used.

Employers found by the courts to have knowingly hired an illegal immigrant would be subject to a 14-day maximum business license suspension upon a first violation, a one-year license suspension upon a second offense and permanent license revocation upon a third violation. Employers seeking state contracts, grants or incentives must submit a sworn affidavit affirming they are not employing illegal immigrants. Employers found in violation would be fined 10 percent of the total contract and subject to possible contract termination upon a first violation. On a second violation, the contract would be terminated, the employer would be barred from doing future business with the state and the employer would forfeit 25 percent of the total contract. SB 256 includes a "whistle blower" provision that would award 50 percent of the damages collected by the courts to the person who reported the violation.

At this point, it is unclear whether the legislature plans to move SB 256 or HB 56. BCA staff will continue to monitor both bills and work with the bills' sponsors to ensure employers are not unfairly burdened or penalized by this legislation.

Finance Director Details State's 'Incredibly Difficult' Budgetary Planning for BCA Group

With looming shortfalls in both state budgets and talk of controversial proposals for new corporate taxes swirling around Montgomery, State Finance Director David Perry on Tuesday appeared before the BCA Governmental Affairs Committee to discuss Alabama's fiscal health. Allison Bell, the governor's legislative director, accompanied Perry.

Perry quickly acknowledged that a plan to address what he termed "corporate loopholes" in the state tax system was under way but indicated that the business community would be given a seat at the table to engage in the discussion. In fact, he met privately with BCA officials and the chairman of BCA's Tax and Fiscal Policy Committee immediately following his presentation in order to gather their insight on the issue.

The former practicing attorney assured attendees that Unitary Combined Reporting "is not on the table," but said other adjustments, both statutory and regulatory, in the corporate tax structure were likely.

Perry acknowledged that crafting state spending plans in the current economic environment is "incredibly difficult" and added that the General Fund, which funds non-education state agencies and is plagued by largely stagnant, flat-lined taxes, has proven "particularly challenging."

"On the campaign trail, a lot of the legislators now serving said they were interested in reining in unnecessary spending and cutting back on unreasonable employee benefits," Perry said. "The Bentley administration has put forward several proposals to increase the employee contribution rates to retirement and making changes to the state health insurance programs, but many in the legislature have been influenced by the employee groups to not follow through on these proposals."

Eliminating longevity pay, which provides state employees with yearly bonuses between $500 and $1,000 for merely remaining on the job for more than five years, will cost state agencies $10 million alone, according to numbers quoted by the finance director.

"By not following through on these employee benefit reforms, the pain is going to be that much worse in terms of layoffs and reductions in services," he said.

Perry said that both the General Fund and Education Trust Fund budgets would "begin to move very quickly" within the next two weeks with committee substitutes being offered for both, and he noted that having a governor work so closely and cooperatively with legislative leaders and budget chairmen on state spending plans has proven to be a rarity in Alabama history.

He noted that several education-related programs supported by BCA, including pre-kindergarten funding, the Alabama Reading Initiative, AMSTI, workforce training and others, were preserved in the governor's budget.

Tasked for the past few years with overseeing the flow of federal "stimulus" funding in state coffers, Perry said the FY 2012 budget will see the loss of $300 million of direct federal funding in the ETF and another $200 million once gathered by local school systems.

The General Fund is witnessing the loss of approximately $400 million in one-time revenues in the FY 2012 budget, and though both budgets are experiencing growth in revenue, it is not enough to replace the missing federal crutch.

Before Gov. Bentley's recent declaration of 15 percent proration in the General Fund, Perry said, the legislature approved supplemental appropriations for the Department of Corrections, the Alabama Medicaid Agency and a handful of other entities to lessen the blow of the cuts.

But Perry, who highlighted that he has had experience "both raising revenue and cutting costs" during his previous tenure as a staffer in the Riley administration Finance Department, added that the dramatic cuts that citizens and public employees will soon witness in the FY 2012 budgets are largely unprecedented.

"The cuts that will be coming this year are not pleasant, and the proposals are not necessarily ones that any administration would want to make in better times," he said. "But the governor is doing what he thinks is responsible to manage the budgets in the current economic crisis."

2011 Tort Reform Bills Poised For Legislative Debate

The BCA-supported Alabama Civil Justice Reform Committee (ACJRC) 2011 tort reform bills were considered Wednesday by both the Senate Judiciary Committee and the House Judiciary Committee, which met at the same time.

Senate Judiciary Committee Action:

SB 184, by Sen. Ben Brooks, R-Mobile, would protect retailers, wholesalers and other distributors of products from being sued in product liability actions where the product comes in a "sealed container." The bill only would protect retailers from the "innocent conduit" situations. It received a favorable report.

SB 207, by Sen. Cam Ward, R-Alabaster, as agreed, would provide that judgments, other than judgments based on a contract action, would bear a flat rate of 7.5 percent. It received a favorable report.

SB 212, by Sen. Clay Scofield, R-Guntersville, as agreed, provides that a wrongful death action may only be filed in a county where the deceased could have filed a civil action, if living and added that Rule 82 of the Rules of Civil Procedure would continue to apply to wrongful death actions. It received a favorable report.

SB 187, by Sen. Brooks, known as the Daubert bill, was not agreed upon by representatives of ACJRC and the trial bar but did receive a favorable report.

House Judiciary Committee Action:

HB 251, by Rep. Wes Long, R-Guntersville, as agreed, protects retailers, wholesalers and other distributors of products from being sued in product liability where the product comes in a "sealed container." The bill only protects retailers from the "innocent conduit" situations. It received a favorable report.

HB 236, by Rep. Greg Canfield, R-Vestavia Hills, was carried over to the call of the chair after Rep. Paul Beckman, R-Prattville, raised questions. The bill is a companion to SB 207 and would provide that judgments, other than judgments based on a contract action, would bear a flat rate of 7.5 percent.

HB 228, by Rep. Ron Johnson, R-Sylacauga, as agreed, provides that a wrongful death action may only be filed in a county where the deceased could have filed a civil action, if living and added that Rule 82 of the Rules of Civil Procedure would continue to apply to wrongful death actions. It received a favorable report.

HB 239, by Rep. Steve McMillan, R-Bay Minette, companion bill to SB 187 known as the Daubert bill, was not considered.

BCA supports these bills.

House Republicans Keep Handshake Promise

The Alabama House of Representatives this week passed all of the bills included in the 2010 Republican Handshake with Alabama, an agenda of specific, issue-oriented bills that were considered legislative priorities if Republicans gained one or both houses of the Alabama Legislature. Republicans hold a majority in both houses of the Alabama Legislature, and the Senate Republicans are expected to push for final passage of the bills during this session.

"I commend my fellow House members for staying true to the commitments we made to the people of Alabama," Speaker Mike Hubbard said. "Passing the entire 'Handshake' agenda in just 10 legislative days is a remarkable accomplishment."

Several bills relating to ethics reform were enacted during the 2010 Special Session of the Alabama Legislature. The remaining bills were:

HB 56, by Rep. Micky Hammon, R-Decatur, gives local law enforcement the authority to verify the residency status of those detained; requires business owners to verify legal status of new workers with the E-verify system; and mandates that recipients of taxpayer-funded public services must be legal residents of the United States.

HB 57, by Rep. Greg Canfield, R-Vestavia Hills, the "Responsible Budgeting and Spending Act," bases state revenue estimates upon a 15-year rolling average, absorbing cyclical economic changes and enabling lawmakers to pass "proration-proof" budgets.

HB 58, by Rep. Mike Ball, R-Madison, requires public disclosure of the names of public officials or candidates or spouses of public officials or candidates.

HB 60, by Rep. Blaine Galliher, R-Gadsden, proposes an amendment to the Constitution of Alabama of 1901, which, if ratified, will prohibit any person, employer or health care provider from being compelled to participate in any health care system.

HB 61, by Rep. April Weaver, R-Brierfield, allows small business employers and employees to deduct 200 percent of the amount they pay in health insurance premiums from their state income tax.

HB 62, by Rep. Mike Jones, R-Andalusia, protects the Alabama Ethics Commission from political retaliation by ensuring that its annual appropriation in the State General Fund Appropriations Act is an amount equal to .1 percent of the total funds appropriated from the State General Fund in the State General Fund Appropriations Act.

HB 64, by Rep. Kurt Wallace, R-Maplesville, proposes an amendment to the Constitution of Alabama of 1901, which, if ratified, would classify as "fundamental" the right of individuals to vote for public office, public votes on referenda, or votes of employee representation by secret ballot.

Committee Approves Education Budget

House Ways and Means-Education Committee Chairman Rep. Jay Love, R-Montgomery, received favorable support, on a vote of 10-5, for his version of next year's spending plan for public schools and colleges. The committee substitute for HB 123 and the accompanying spending bills for FY 2012 appropriate some $92 million more than Gov. Robert

Bentley recommended. As with the governor's recommended budget, it reduces the FY 2011 rates paid by the state for teachers' retirement from 12.51 percent to 10 percent and for educators' health insurance from $752 to $714 per month.

The loss of 1,100 state-funded teacher units is mitigated by the fact that there are approximately 1,500 teacher retirements each year, according to State Superintendent of Education Joe Morton. The committee version of the budget adds more than $10 million to other current expenses, which schools use to pay utilities and other operational expenses; from that amount, an estimated 2,000 essential support worker jobs will be preserved. The statewide school transportation system is fully funded under Rep. Love's substitute with an increase of $25 million more than the governor's recommendation.

The substitute education budget also reflects the even more dire financial status of the state's General Fund budget, as $32.4 million in funding for the Department of Public Health's Children's Health Insurance Program was shifted from the General Fund over to the Education Trust Fund.

The following table lists other changes made in the House committee version compared to the governor's recommendation:

K-12:

- Teacher Liability Insurance $1.5 million
- At-Risk Schools, Systems $3.0 million
- Student Exit Exam Assistance $3.0 million

Two-Year College System:

- Operations & Maintenance $2.2 million
- AL Industrial Dev. Training — Workforce Development $2.5 million
- Colleges and Universities (collectively) $7.6 million

  BCA is monitoring this legislation.

Senate Passes Bill Amending Ethics Act

The full Senate passed SB 222, by Sen. Del Marsh, R-Anniston, by a vote of 28-0. Its companion, HB 253, by Rep. Mike Hubbard, R-Auburn, received a favorable report from the House Ethics & Campaign Finance

Committee last week. These bills change the term "corruptly" to "corruptly influencing," to alleviate any questions relating to vagueness and enforceability. The Alabama Ethics Commission and the Attorney General recommended the change.

SB 222 has been referred to House Ethics & Campaign Finance Committee.

BCA is monitoring this legislation.

Environmental Bills Update

HJR 197, by Rep. Paul DeMarco, R-Homewood, urges the U.S. Congress to adopt legislation prohibiting the EPA from regulating greenhouse gas emissions without congressional approval. This was a model resolution by the American Legislative Exchange Council (ALEC) and is referred to as the "EPA Trainwreck Resolution" because of the aggressive regulations the EPA is pushing to impose on business and industry. The resolution passed the Senate on a voice vote today. This was the result of an effort by BCA and supporting member companies and organizations with our Environment & Energy Committee Chair taking the lead with the legislature.

HB 406, by Rep. Alan Baker, R-Brewton, would create a 24-month moratorium on new commercial Subtitle D (household garbage) and C&D (construction and demolition) waste landfills. During this period, the Alabama Department of Environmental Management (ADEM) and the Alabama Department of Public Health (ADPH) will review their programs pertaining to this issue and advise the legislature of any needed new legislation to carry out their duties or to promulgate additional regulations to enhance their existing programs. The original legislation was much more comprehensive than just the moratorium, but BCA members and others talked to Rep. Baker, and he understood the need to narrow the scope to better serve his intended purpose. BCA will monitor the legislation.

SB 224, by Sen. Del Marsh, R-Anniston, with companion bill HB 285, by Rep. Randy Wood, R-Anniston, would provide a procedure where the owner of a motor vehicle could transfer to an automotive dismantler and parts recycler or a secondary metals recycler a motor vehicle without a title, if certain conditions are met, and the owner of the motor vehicle signs a statement regarding the ownership, value and identifying characteristics of the motor vehicle. Several members of BCA and other interested parties had discussions with the Department of Revenue on correct language before committee action. The BCA Environment & Energy Committee adopted this legislation as part of its *2011 Legislative Agenda*. The bill would help to eliminate problems associated with cars no longer in use that may allow fluids to leak into the environment. BCA supports this legislation.

In Other News

Senate Approves Lean General Fund Budget

The Alabama Senate passed the General Fund Budget that funds state government operations for the 2012 fiscal year that totals $1.76 billion, an increase of $210 million over this year's prorated level, but $56 million less than the total recommended by Gov. Robert Bentley. The budget protects funding for prisons and Medicaid while cutting funds for the legislature and most other agencies of state government.

Of note was a $35 million reduction in the general fund appropriation to the Court System, but that reduction was offset by a transfer of $35 million in funding from the Alabama Department of Transportation. Also noteworthy was the shift of $32.4 million in funding under the Department of Public Health for the Children's Health Insurance Program from the general fund to the Education Trust Fund. Both of these actions indicate the extent to which the budget is short of funding.

The bill now moves to the Alabama House for consideration.

Ignore the Myth, Know the Facts: Students First Act

SB 310, by Sen. Trip Pittman, R-Daphne, and HB 46, by Rep. Chad Fincher, R-Semmes, overhaul Alabama's 2004 tenure and dismissal laws for education personnel and shift the focus from adults to children. The Alabama Association of School Boards gives the facts on the Students First Act on its web site, www.alabamaschoolboards.org, as these bills ensure fundamental fairness and due process for tenured employees; would help maintain a high quality, accountable and effective workforce for students; and stop the incentive to file costly legal challenges of routine personnel decisions.

BCA supports the Students First Act, further demonstrating our commitment to a true business-education alliance.

PSC OKs Rate Measures to Help Local Economies

The Alabama Public Service Commission this week approved several rate measures aimed at helping to revitalize local economies. The PSC approved an Alabama Power Company proposal to broaden the terms of its small business rate (Rate LPS - Light and Power Service - Small), which would qualify some 8,000 more customers for benefits. Small churches, investment-type businesses, realty offices and small retail shops could now qualify for the small business rate.

For small and medium-sized businesses, the PSC also accepted a Power Company proposal to provide a one-year, 15 percent discount incentive for any new account established at a location that has been unoccupied for at least six months. The commission also approved a proposal to provide a two-year discount on the base bill of customers who meet Alabama Department of Revenue criteria for receiving Capital Investment Tax Credits. Qualifying customers will receive a 10 percent discount in year one and a 5 percent discount in year two. The discounts apply to additional electric usage and will be offered through December 31, 2013.

Former BCA Board Member Now on Attorney General's Staff

Jessica Medeiros Garrison, a former member of the board of directors of BCA and ProgressPAC, has joined the staff of Attorney General Luther Strange where she is serving as deputy attorney general and chief counsel.

A graduate of the University of Alabama and UA School of Law, she managed Strange's recent campaign. She earned a partnership in the Tuscaloosa law firm of Phelps, Jenkins, Gibson & Fowler, L.L.P.

Washington Briefing
Federal Budget Deal Elusive

At press time, a deal to keep the federal government from shutting down remained elusive. In fact, neither side could even agree on what the specific policy hang-up is that is preventing an agreement on just how far to cut the 2011 federal budget.

The current stopgap funding measure expires at midnight.

On Thursday, the House, by a vote of 247-181, passed H.R. 1363, a one-week extension for federal funding that cuts $12 billion while funding the Defense Department for the remainder of the fiscal year. The Senate has not considered the measure.

Senate and House Vote on EPA's Regulatory Agenda

On Wednesday, the Senate voted 50-50 against an amendment, sponsored by Republican Leader Mitch McConnell (R-KY), which would have blocked the Environmental Protection Agency's authority to regulate greenhouse gas emissions. The measure was proposed as an amendment to the Small Business Innovation Research and Small Business Technology Transfer Reauthorization Act of 2011 (S. 493).

The Senate also voted against three other amendments addressing greenhouse gas regulations sponsored by Sens. John Rockefeller (D-WV), Max Baucus (D-MT) and Debbie Stabenow (D-MI).

The Baucus amendment would have limited the application of greenhouse gas permitting requirements to sources that emit more than 75,000 tons of emissions and also exempted certain agricultural activities from regulation. It was defeated 7-93.

The Rockefeller amendment was rejected 12-88. It would have delayed the EPA regulation of stationary sources for two years from the date of enactment; however, the amendment only covered two greenhouse gases — carbon dioxide and methane.

Sen. Stabenow's amendment, which failed by a vote 7-93, was a combination of the Rockefeller and Baucus amendments. It would have delayed the EPA regulation of stationary sources for two years, exempted agricultural facilities from regulation, prevented any future California waivers for tailpipe greenhouse gas emissions and extended the 48C Advanced Energy Manufacturing Tax Credit. However, the EPA could still develop regulations and issue guidance during the two-year suspension of the regulations. These regulations would then become effective at the end of this two-year period.

On Thursday, the House voted 255-172 to pass the Energy Tax Prevention Act (H.R. 910), a bipartisan approach that protects jobs and restores the Clean Air Act to its original purpose by repealing the EPA's efforts at regulation. All seven members of the Alabama House delegation voted in support of this bill.

Repeal of 1099 Mandate Headed to President's Desk

On Tuesday, the Senate voted 87-12 to pass H.R. 4, the Small Business Paperwork Mandate Elimination Act of 2011, which would repeal the 1099 IRS requirement that was part of last year's health care law.

Under the Patient Protection and Affordable Care Act, businesses would have been forced to file form 1099 reports for all purchases and services in excess of $600 in a calendar year, beginning in 2012. This onerous mandate would have dramatically increased accounting costs and created time-consuming paperwork burdens for businesses of all sizes, particularly small businesses.

The House passed H.R. 4 last month by a vote of 314-112. The bill now goes to the president, who is expected to sign it into law.

Repealing the 1099 provision is a priority of the BCA's *2011 Federal Legislative Agenda.*

BCA Education Committee Chair Bob Powers endorsed Students First Act.

CHAPTER 9
April 15, 2011
STUDENTS FIRST ACT: A NEW LEVEL
OF ACCOUNTABILITY IN THE CLASSROOM

The House and Senate on Wednesday held a joint public hearing before a crowded room on SB 310, by Sen. Trip Pittman, R-Daphne, and HB 46, by Rep. Chad Fincher, R-Semmes, which is an overhaul of the state tenure law.

Under current law, a teacher who is fired by a local school board is provided an arbitration hearing, and the teacher remains on the payroll throughout the process. The Students First Act would make termination effective upon action by the school board, stop pay and benefits upon termination, provide a review process comparable to state merit employees and require full compensation and benefits if termination is reversed upon appeal.

More than a dozen supporters of the bill testified that the current tenure system's elaborate rules make it nearly impossible to fire a teacher. School superintendents gave numerous examples of employees collecting a paycheck as they appealed to an arbitrator, some remaining on the payroll for 200 days or more, despite offensive, even criminal behavior.

Emphasizing BCA's commitment to a true business-education alliance in Alabama, Bob Powers, chairman of BCA's Education & Workforce Preparedness Committee, testified in support of the bill at the public hearing. "After thorough research, discussion, input, feedback and prioritizing of education and workforce issues facing Alabama's business community, BCA's Education & Workforce Preparedness Committee, Governmental Affairs Committee, Chairman's Intergovernmental Council, Executive Committee and Board of Directors designated in *BCA's Legislative Agenda* to 'fundamentally reform teacher tenure and fair dismissal laws' as a critical and top priority.

"The BCA has long been an advocate for the professional teacher and has a record of support for quality classroom initiatives for our children," he said. "The business community is the number one consumer of the product called education, and our support for the Students First Act is an outgrowth of the concept we have been championing, a true business-education alliance in Alabama.

"The current tenure system and fair dismissal laws are counterproductive and a serious impediment to the education of our children and their preparation for higher education, training and the ability to compete in a global economy. The current system leaves less than competent teachers in positions that can be filled by willing, capable and competent teachers. Our students deserve to have high quality teachers in every classroom; both their education and our future depend on it."

Dr. Freida Hill, chancellor of the Alabama Community College System, said the current system is "broken," "expensive" and "cumbersome."

Sally Howell, executive director of the Alabama Association of School Boards, told the committee, "When we can't fire employees who show up to work drunk, we need to return accountability to the local level, and we need to put students first."

BCA supports this legislation.

House, Senate Education Committee Chairs Brief BCA on Spending Priorities

As state spending plans move through the legislature faster and sooner than any other time in recent history, the chairmen of the House and Senate education budget committees appeared at the weekly BCA Governmental Affairs Committee meeting Tuesday to brief members on items they considered spending priorities.

Prior to the House of Representatives passing the Education Budget Tuesday night, House Ways and Means Education Committee Chairman Jay Love, R-Montgomery, discussed the loss of approximately $600 million in federal "stimulus" dollars that will no longer be available in the FY 2012 budget cycle. The shortfall, he said, either will have to be replaced with new revenue or cut from the budget, along with the programs, benefits and other expenses it funds.

"We have made tremendous strides in education over the last few years by going from the bottom 40s to our most recent ranking of 25th in the nation," Love said. "We have seen areas where certain programs have made a vital impact in the performance of students, and those are the areas where we want to avoid cuts at all costs."

According to Love, the proven education initiatives producing results include BCA-supported programs such as the Alabama Math, Science and Technology Initiative (AMSTI), the Alabama Reading Initiative and the ACCESS Distance Learning Program, which allows every high school in the state to offer advanced placement classes to qualifying students through interactive videoconferencing and web-based courses.

Love complimented the proposed budget submitted to legislators by Gov. Robert Bentley, and he said the only potentially weak area was a lack of funding for operating expenses, such as school bus operations, utility costs and salaries for essential support personnel. He estimated the cost of funding for "Other Current Expenses," colloquially referred to as "OCE" in the Education Trust Fund budget, to be between $110 million and $120 million.

"Working with State School Superintendent Joe Morton and the school boards, we searched for the best way to fund these essential needs without harming other areas of the budget," Love said. "It makes no sense to pay teachers if we don't have the money to bus the kids to school or turn on the lights or provide an environment in which children can learn."

The best solution devised by the group was raising the classroom divisor by a half-unit, which translates to increasing the student-to-teacher ratio by a half-student in each classroom. Such a change, he said, would generate approximately $80 million that could be shifted to other areas.

And, while raising the divisor technically would require laying off about 1,100 public school teachers, Love said roughly 1,800 to 2,000 educators retire, quit or move to other employment each year, so any necessary job losses would simply be absorbed by natural attrition.

In addition to requiring new revenue to be raised through regulatory changes in the corporate tax structure, Love said Bentley's budget also called for an increase in the percentage of salary that teachers and other education workers contribute to the retirement plans.

"If the bill I am sponsoring passes, on May 1 of this year, employees will pay an additional 1 percent toward their retirement, on October 1 of this year, another percent will be added, and, finally, in October 2012, another half-percent will be required," Love said. "By asking employees to pay an additional 2.5 percent, we will bring them in line with what our other surrounding states require."

He added that the current 5 percent contribution required of employees has not been adjusted since 1975.

Love also is carrying the Bentley administration's "double-weighted sales tax" bill that would change tax allocations based upon the presence a corporation has in Alabama compared to other states. Using property taxes, payroll taxes and sales figures in a formula, the bill would have no effect on businesses operating solely in Alabama, he said, but multi-state corporations with large sales in Alabama and little property and payroll domestically would see their taxes increase.

Love said providing public school teachers with state-funded liability insurance would be a new line item in the budget if his Teacher Protection Act legislation is approved, but the budget approved by the House late Tuesday night did not include that item. The House-passed version is $5.587 billion, which is $93 million more than the total recommended by Gov. Bentley and $240 million more than the current year's total. However, the budget does not contain some $502 million in federal stimulus funds, which supplemented the total appropriated from the Education Trust Fund in each of Fiscal Years 2010 and 2011.

Democratic legislators continued to criticize the spending plan, objecting to it being predicated on higher employee contributions for retirement and the loss of some 1,125 teacher units, which enlarges class sizes. Supporters contend that the loss of units will not necessarily translate into lost teachers because about 1,500 teachers retire each year. The Democratic leaders also continued to hammer away at the need to close corporate "loopholes" in the state tax laws as a way to avoid budget cuts.

A looming challenge in the ETF is $437 million that must be repaid to the state's "Rainy Day" proration prevention account over the next four years, as required by constitutional mandate. No portion of the repayment has been set aside in the FY 2012 budget, so Love said funding could become even tighter in future cycles.

Turning his attention toward higher education, Love said public colleges and universities are slated to receive a 6 percent increase over last year's appropriation, and two-year colleges saw their request for workforce development dollars fully funded.

Senate Finance and Taxation Education Committee Chairman Trip Pittman, R-Daphne, opened his remarks by discussing the BCA-supported Students First Act, a bill he is sponsoring that reforms the dismissal process for disciplined teachers and support workers. (See previous story.)

Currently, under the Fair Dismissal Act, which was last revised by the legislature in 2004, terminated teachers are privy to a long review process involving mandatory arbitration and appeals to the Circuit Court system with the government paying the associated costs. Because they continue to receive a salary throughout the slow and lengthy process, even the most guilty and unsatisfactory teachers are provided a natural incentive to extend their appeal for as long as possible.

Pittman's bill, sponsored in the House by Rep. Chad Fincher, R–Semmes, saves considerable dollars by immediately ending an employee's salary upon termination with paychecks presented in arrears only if an appeal is later validated. Hearing officers and arbitrators also are removed from the process, among several other provisions.

"The Students First Act does not take away teacher tenure; instead, it returns accountability to the local school boards and the local superintendents," Pittman said. "I think it is fundamental to achieving the kind of success that we all want to achieve in our public school system."

He added that his bill would require a majority of local school board members to ratify a superintendent's decision to terminate an employee after depositions are taken and a judicial-like process takes place. Employees also would be given the decision of holding the hearing process in public or in closed-door session.

Appeals, he said, should take a maximum of 90 to 120 days, if his legislation is enacted.

Senate Passes BCA-backed Bill Providing Tax Deduction to Small Businesses; Heads to Governor for Signature

The Senate on Thursday passed HB 61, by Rep. April Weaver, R-Brierfield, by a vote of 29-1, which would allow qualifying employers and employees to deduct an additional 50 percent of the amount expended for health insurance premiums. Qualifying employers are those with less than 25 employees, and qualifying employees are those whose annual wages do not exceed $50,000. The bill passed the House of Representatives on March 22 by a vote of 83-12. Sen. Greg Reed, R-Jasper, who carried the bill for Rep. Weaver in the Senate, worked diligently to remove concerns raised by other senators.

"This bill allows my IT consulting firm to directly compete with well-established firms when trying to hire highly skilled employees," said Craig

Bacheler, owner of Bacheler Technologies in Montgomery and BCA member. "I am able to absorb the high cost of health coverage knowing that I will get some tax credit relief at the end of the year. Without this bill being passed I do not know if I would have been able to offer health insurance to my employees."

The measure now increases the 150 percent deduction, approved during the 2008 legislative session, to a deduction of 200 percent of qualifying premium payments.

"This is the perfect incentive for creating jobs," said BCA President and CEO William J. Canary. "At a time when business owners and state government are coping with tighter budgets, this will help reduce the number of citizens who otherwise would be added to the state's Medicaid and Children's Health Insurance Plan rolls. We applaud Rep. April Weaver and Sen. Greg Reed for their leadership in enacting this legislation."

HB 61 was a top-tier item in the BCA's *2011 Legislative Agenda* and now goes to the governor for his signature.

House Votes to Reauthorize Popular Forever Wild Program

The House on Thursday voted 69-24 to extend for 20 years the state's Forever Wild program. Rep. Randy Davis, R-Daphne, sponsored HB 126, and SB 140, by Sen. Scott Beason is the companion bill.

Forever Wild was established by constitutional amendment in 1992 with 83 percent voter support, the highest level of public support ever recorded for any state legislation establishing a government land acquisition program. This program receives payments into the Forever Wild Land Trust for acquisition of lands for public use. HB 126 has been referred to the House Committee on Economic Development and Tourism.

Voting YES to reauthorize the program for another 20 years were:

Rep. Mike Ball, R-Madison; Rep. Jim Barton, R-Mobile; Rep. Paul Beckman R-Prattville; Rep. Marcel Black, D-Tuscumbia; Rep. Napoleon Bracy, D-Prichard; Rep. K.L. Brown, R-Jacksonville; Rep. James Buskey, D-Mobile; Rep. Greg Canfield, R-Vestavia Hills; Rep. Terri Collins, R-Decatur; Rep. Randy Davis, R-Daphne; Rep. Chad Fincher, R-Semmes; Rep. Berry Forte, D-Eufaula; Rep. Victor Gaston, R-Mobile; Rep. Dexter Grimsley, D-Newville; Rep. Micky Hammon, R-Decatur; Rep. Steve Hurst, R-Munford; Rep. Ronald Johnson, R-Sylacauga; Rep. John Knight, D-Montgomery; Rep. Barry Mask, R-Wetumpka; Rep. Alan

Baker, R-Brewton; Rep. Richard Baughn, R-Lynn; Rep. Elaine Beech, D-Chatom; Rep. Barbara Boyd, D-Anniston; Rep. Greg Burdine, D-Florence; Rep. Mac Buttram, R-Cullman; Rep. Merika Coleman, D-Midfield; Rep. David Colston, D-Hayneville; Rep. Paul DeMarco, R-Homewood; Rep. Joe Faust, R-Fairhope; Rep. Craig Ford, D-Gadsden; Rep. Blaine Galliher, R-Gadsden; Rep. Todd Greeson, R-Ider; Rep. Laura Hall, D-Huntsville; Rep. Alan Harper, D-Aliceville; Rep Mike Hill, R-Columbiana; Rep. Mike Hubbard, R-Auburn; Rep. Jamie Ison, R-Mobile; Rep. Wayne Jonson, R-Huntsville; Rep. Yvonne Kennedy, D-Mobile; Rep. Jay Love, R-Montgomery; Rep. Lawrence McAdory, D-Bessemer; Rep. Jim McClendon, R-Springville; Rep. Mac McCutcheon, R-Capshaw; Rep. Darrio Melton, D-Selma; Rep. Mike Millican, R-Hamilton; Rep. Jeremy Oden, R-Vinemont; Rep. Arthur Payne, R-Trussville; Rep. Kerry Rich, R-Albertville; Rep. John Robinson, D-Scottsboro; Rep. John Rogers, D-Birmingham; Rep. Rod Scott, D-Fairfield; Rep Elwyn Thomas, R-Oneonta; Rep. Allen Treadaway, R-Morris; Rep. Pebblin Warren, D-Shorter; Rep. Greg Wren, R-Montgomery; Rep. Mary Sue McClurkin, R-Pelham; Rep. Steve McMillan, R-Bay Minette; Rep. John Merrill, R-Tuscaloosa; Rep. Mary Moore, D-Birmingham; Rep. Charles Newton, D-Greenville; Rep. Becky Nordgren, R-Gadsden; Rep. Jim Patterson, R-Meridianville; Rep. Bill Poole, R-Northport; Rep. Oliver Robinson, D-Birmingham; Rep. Howard Sanderford, R-Huntsville; Rep. Harry Shiver, R-Bay Minette; Rep. Patricia Todd, D-Birmingham; Rep. Mark Tuggle, R-Alexander City; and Rep. Kurt Wallace, R-Maplesville.

Voting NO, against reauthorization of Forever Wild, were:
Rep. Alan Boothe, R-Troy; Rep. Steve Clouse, R-Ozark; Rep. Allen Farley, R-McCalla; Rep. Lynn Greer, R-Rogersville; Rep. Ed Henry, R-Hartselle; Rep. Alvin Holmes, D-Montgomery; Rep. Mike Jones, R-Andalusia; Rep. Paul Lee, R-Dothan; Rep. Wes Long, R-Guntersville; Rep. DuWayne Bridges, R-Valley; Rep. Donnie Chesteen, R-Geneva; Rep. Juandalynn Givan, D-Birmingham; Rep. Ralph Howard, D-Greensboro; Rep. Ken Johnson, R-Moulton; Rep. Richard Laird, D-Roanoke; Rep. Richard Lindsey, D-Centre; Rep. Thad McClammy, D-Montgomery; Rep. Barry Moore, R-Enterprise; Rep. Johnny M. Morrow, D-Red Bay; Rep. Lesley Vance, R-Phenix City; Rep. Dan Williams, R-Athens, Rep. Phil Williams, R-Huntsville; Rep. Bill Roberts, R-Jasper; and Rep. Randy Wood, R-Anniston.

Voting present or not voting were:

Rep. George Bandy, D-Opelika; Rep. Daniel Boman, R-Sulligent*; Rep. Chris England, D-Tuscaloosa; Rep. Joe Hubbard, D-Montgomery; Rep. Thomas Jackson, D-Thomasville; Rep. A.J. McCampbell, D-Gallion; Rep. Joseph Mitchell, D-Mobile; Rep. Charles Newton, D-Greenville; Rep. April Weaver, R-Brierfield and Rep. Jack Williams, R-Birmingham.

Over the last 19 years, some of Alabama's greatest outdoor landmarks have been supported through Forever Wild, including the Mobile-Tensaw Delta, Walls of Jericho, Sipsey River Swamp, Freedom Hills, Lillian Swamp, the Red Hills, Weogufka Creek, Ruffner Mountain, Turkey Creek, Hurricane Creek, Grand Bay Savannah, Little River Canyon, Old Cahawba Prairie, Hatchet Creek, Coon Gulf, Paint Rock River, Coldwater Mountain, Perdido River, Weeks Bay and many more. Because of Forever Wild, these landmarks of Alabama will be preserved for generations to come.

Alabama's largest economic business is tourism. Hunting, fishing and wildlife viewing in Alabama has a $2.2 billion annual economic impact that benefits both local communities and the state. Forever Wild, since its inception, has preserved more than 200,000 acres of wilderness for hunting, fishing, bird-watching and other outdoor activities.

House Speaker Mike Hubbard, R-Auburn, supported the extension. "Forever Wild has been a great program for the state," Hubbard said. "It's not going to cause the government to own the majority of the land. But it does give to the average person who can't afford to belong to a hunting club. This land is for them."

Davis told his colleagues, "This is a real opportunity for the state of Alabama, an opportunity to leave a legacy. Each of you in your vote today will be able to leave a legacy to your children and grandchildren, to say that Alabama the beautiful shall remain."

During the debate, Rep. John Robinson, D-Scottsboro, focused on the original sponsors of Forever Wild when the program was created 19 years ago. Robinson called the original sponsors "the Teddy Roosevelts of Alabama," comparing their legacies to that of the 26th president, who worked to create national parks and proclaim historic landmarks throughout the United States.

BCA supports this legislation.

---

* Rep. Boman changed his party affiliation to Democrat after this vote.

BCA Opposes AEA Tax Measures

BCA opposes several AEA-initiated legislative proposals that would raise or impose new taxes totaling nearly $228 million. The proposals are:

HB 241, by Rep. John Knight, D-Montgomery - "This bill will amend Section 40-18-14, Code of Alabama 1975, to clarify that gross income for Alabama resident individuals includes an owner's entire allocable share of income from a pass-through entity."

HB 242, by Rep. Knight - This bill proposes "... to limit the state income tax deduction for federal income taxes for individual taxpayers; to exempt sales of food and over-the-counter drugs from state sales tax; and to prohibit local governments from levying separate sales taxes only on the sale of food or over-the-counter drugs."

HB 299, by Rep. Richard Lindsey, D-Centre - "... Alabama corporate income tax law is linked to federal corporate income tax law, which allows a domestic production activities deduction that is equal to a percentage of income earned from domestic production or taxable income, whichever is less. This bill would limit the Alabama deduction to three percent of qualifying income."

HB 300, by Rep. Lindsey - "...Alabama levies an income tax on corporations. Alabama corporate income tax law is linked to federal corporate income tax law, which allows a temporary increase in the bonus depreciation deduction from fifty percent (50%) to one hundred percent (100%) of the adjusted basis of qualified property pursuant to The Tax Relief, Unemployment Insurance Reauthorization, and Job Creation Act of 2010 (Public Law 111-312). This bill would limit the Alabama deduction to fifty percent (50%) of the adjusted basis of qualified property."

HB 301, by Rep. Lindsey - "This bill defines unitary business and requires taxpayers who are part of a unitary business to use a combined report to determine their Alabama taxable income.

HB 302, by Rep. Lindsey - "This bill would limit the state depletion allowance for oil and gas to the amount allowed by the federal depletion allowance."

HB 347, by Rep. A.J. McCampbell, D-Gallion - "...Alabama corporate income tax law is linked to federal corporate income tax law, which generally provides that an acquiring corporation succeeds to the net operating loss (NOL) carryover of a loss corporation when the assets of the loss corporation are acquired. This bill would provide that a net operating loss

(NOL) may be carried forward and allowed as a deduction only by the corporation that sustained the loss."

HB 373, by Rep. Joe Hubbard, D-Montgomery, would establish, for purposes of income taxes, a presence nexus standard for business activity.

Senate Committee Approves Bill Guaranteeing Private Ballot Voting

By a vote of 5-1, the Senate Constitution, Campaign Finance, Ethics and Elections Committee gave a favorable report to BCA-supported HB 64, by Rep. Kurt Wallace, R-Maplesville, which would ensure, via constitutional amendment, that every individual in the state of Alabama is guaranteed the right to privately cast a ballot in all elections, including union elections.

Before committee passage, a public hearing was held on HB 64. Testifying at the public hearing, BCA President and CEO William Canary reinforced BCA's longstanding support of the bill: "For over three years, the BCA has voiced its support to ensure the right of Alabama citizens to vote by private ballot in all elections, but until 2011, the legislature would not even consider this bill." Canary thanked the senators for considering this important constitutional amendment and applauded bill sponsor Rep. Wallace for his efforts in getting HB 64 passed in the House by a vote of 63-31. Also testifying in support of the bill were representatives from the NFIB and Associated Builders and Contractors.

Voicing opposition was a representative from the AFL-CIO who threatened that lawsuits would result if the legislature passed the bill because he believed that it would violate federal law. The threat of legal action results from four other states (South Dakota, South Carolina, Arizona and Utah) passing similar constitutional amendments to guarantee that citizens are able to vote by private ballot. Attorneys general from these states have been informed that the National Labor Relations Board (NLRB) is considering legal action to challenge the laws' constitutionality. Responding to a question from a committee member Canary said, "We strongly believe that an Alabama constitutional amendment guaranteeing a person's right to vote a private ballot does not violate federal law." HB 64 now heads to the full Senate for consideration.

Those voting in support of HB 64 and business were: Sen. Bryan Taylor, R-Prattville; Sen. Phil Williams, R-Rainbow City; Sen. Paul Bussman, R-Cullman; Sen. Shad McGill, R-Scottsboro; Sen. Trip Pittman, R-Daphne; and Sen. Arthur Orr, R-Decatur.

Those opposing HB 64 and supporting labor: Sen. Tammy Irons, D-Florence.

Sen. Billy Beasley, D-Clayton, was not present.

BCA supports this bill.

Committees Approve Job Creation Legislation Matching Industrial Incentives in Other States

In keeping with their pre-session promise to focus intently on job creation, Gov. Robert Bentley and a bipartisan group of legislators announced this week the introduction of the Jobs Creation and Retention Act that would provide the state with an additional tool to attract, retain and expand industry and jobs in Alabama.

HB 478, by Rep. Barry Mask, R-Wetumpka, and its companion SB 373, by Sen. Phil Williams, R-Rainbow City, allows new and expanding industry to retain as much as 90 percent of state income tax withholdings from employees associated with the project, which the company may use to offset the costs of constructing or equipping the new facility.

The legislation is similar to incentives currently offered by states such as Kentucky, Georgia and Mississippi, and proponents contend that it is needed to keep Alabama competitive with those states in attracting industry. The measure is also similar to incentives once offered by the State of Alabama to successfully lure Mercedes-Benz and other companies to the state in the early 1990s. That legislation was repealed shortly thereafter because education groups objected that the withheld taxes should flow to support public education.

The heads of the Alabama Development Office and the Department of Revenue would negotiate the extent of the incentive to be offered on an individual project basis. Up to 90 percent of the employees' withheld taxes may be retained by the company for new and expansion projects, while up to 75 percent of the withheld taxes may be retained for projects deemed to retain jobs. The employees will receive state income tax credits for the taxes withheld. Once the company recoups the costs of its capital investment, the employees' taxes will no longer be retained. Failure by a company to meet its agreed-upon jobs level and capital investment requirements could result in the state recapturing the withholding incentives or terminating the agreement.

2011 Tort Reform Bills to be Debated

The BCA-supported Alabama Civil Justice Reform Committee (ACJRC) 2011 tort reform bills are scheduled to be debated in the Alabama Senate as early as next week. The House Judiciary Committee gave a favorable report to HB 236, by Rep. Greg Canfield, R-Vestavia Hills, on Wednesday. The only remaining bill to be considered by the House Judiciary Committee is HB 239, by Rep. Steve McMillan, R-Bay Minette.

Senate Tort Package:

SB 184, by Sen. Ben Brooks, R-Mobile, protects retailers, wholesalers and other distributors of products from being sued in product liability actions where the product comes in a "sealed container." The bill only protects retailers from the "innocent conduit" situations.

SB 207, by Sen. Cam Ward, R-Alabaster, as agreed, would provide that judgments, other than judgments based on a contract action, would bear a flat rate of 7.5 percent.

SB 212, by Sen. Clay Scofield, R-Guntersville, as agreed, provides that a wrongful death action may only be filed in a county where the deceased could have filed a civil action, if living and added that Rule 82 of the Rules of Civil Procedure would continue to apply to wrongful death actions.

SB 187, by Sen. Brooks, known as the Daubert bill, has been agreed upon by representatives of ACJRC and the trial bar.

House Tort Package:

HB 251, by Rep. Wes Long, R-Guntersville, as agreed, protects retailers, wholesalers and other distributors of products from being sued in product liability where the product comes in a "sealed container." The bill only protects retailers from the "innocent conduit" situations.

HB 236, by Rep. Canfield, as agreed, would provide that judgments, other than judgments based on a contract action, would bear a flat rate of 7.5 percent.

HB 228, by Rep. Ron Johnson, R-Sylacauga, as agreed, provides that a wrongful death action may only be filed in a county where the deceased could have filed a civil action, if living and added that Rule 82 of the Rules of Civil Procedure would continue to apply to wrongful death actions.

HB 239, by Rep. Steve McMillan, R-Bay Minette, companion bill to SB 187 known as the Daubert bill, has not been considered.

BCA supports these bills.

Environmental Bills Update

SB 80, by Sen. Del Marsh, R-Anniston, came up for debate on Tuesday, but the sponsor asked that it be carried over to the call of the Chair. The companion bill, HB 50, by Rep. Greg Canfield, R-Vestavia Hills, moved out of the Senate Energy & Natural Resources Committee on Thursday and received a second reading. When SB 80 is recalled by the Senate Chair, HB 50 can be substituted for it, and the bill can receive final passage. The legislation amends state solid waste laws by repealing an existing exemption from regulation for fly ash waste, bottom ash waste, boiler slag waste, and flue gas emissions control wastes from the burning of coal or other fossil fuels at electric generating plants. The bill further authorizes the Alabama Department of Environmental Management (ADEM) to regulate these wastes. BCA supports the legislation.

SB 224, by Sen. Del Marsh, R-Anniston, as substituted, moved out of the Senate Commerce, Transportation & Utilities Committee on Thursday and received its second reading. SB 224 and companion bill, HB 285, by Rep. Randy Wood, R-Anniston, would provide a procedure where the owner of a motor vehicle could transfer to an automotive dismantler and parts recycler or a secondary metals recycler a motor vehicle without a title if certain conditions are met and the owner of the motor vehicle signs a statement regarding the ownership, value and identifying characteristics of the motor vehicle. This legislation is needed to correct legislation passed last year that prevents "any" vehicle from being sold for recycling or scrap without a title. For many older model vehicles that have not been in use for years, there is no existing title, and owners who want to sell the vehicles will not go through the Department of Revenue to buy a new title when they are selling the car for scrap.

BCA President and CEO William Canary and Senior Vice President of Intergovernmental Affairs and Legal Advisor Anita Archie have attended meetings on this legislation and were present at the Senate Committee meeting to show their support for BCA members caught in this dilemma. The BCA Environment & Energy Committee adopted this legislation as part of its *Legislative Agenda* during 2010 Committee Days. The bill would help to eliminate problems associated with cars no longer in use that may leak fluids into the environment or cause blight in communities. BCA supports this legislation.

In Other News

House Gives Unanimous Approval to Full Employment Act

The Alabama House passed the Full Employment Act, HB 230, by Rep. Blaine Galliher, R-Gadsden, by a vote of 96-0 on Thursday, and it awaits committee assignment in the Senate. The bill would provide to employers of 50 or fewer employees a one-time income tax credit, beginning in the current tax year, equal to $1,000 for each new job that is created that pays at least $10 per hour, after the employee has completed 12 consecutive months of employment.

BCA supports this legislation.

Internet Purchasers to be Advised on Use Tax Obligations

Many Alabamians routinely purchase products via the internet because they falsely assume that no sales tax applies to such purchases, but that may change very soon. The fact is that state and local sales or use taxes do apply to such transactions, and a new law will require internet sellers to advise purchasers that they may owe use tax on the transaction. HB 365, by Rep. Jamie Ison, R-Mobile, will require that before the sale is completed, the seller must give the purchaser notice of his use tax obligation, and the purchaser must acknowledge that he or she understands their tax responsibility.

The internet seller also is required to issue to the purchaser at year end an annual compilation of his or her purchases from the previous calendar year. The purchaser will use the compilation to calculate the amount of use tax that is due, which the purchaser may remit with his or her state income tax return.

The *2011 Legislative Agenda* states that the BCA will support efforts to streamline and simplify our sales/use tax system so that in-state and out-of-state retailers are on a level playing field. This bill is consistent with that agenda item.

House Members Take Pay cuts, Refuse COLA

Nearly 60 members of the House of Representatives have cut their pay or refused cost of living adjustments. Speaker of the House Mike Hubbard and 54 House Republicans voluntarily cut their pay 15 percent and refused the COLA. Twenty-eight senators refused the cost of living adjustment in the upper chamber. Both chambers continue to study ways to adequately compensate legislators.

Taxpayers' Bill of Rights II Favorably Reported by House Judiciary Committee

HB 427, by Rep. Paul DeMarco, R-Homewood, received a favorable report from the House Judiciary Committee, which puts the bill into position to be considered by the full House. The legislation has been listed on the *BCA Legislative Agenda* for several years. It combines provisions for updating the original Alabama Taxpayers' Bill of Rights act and provisions to create an independent tax appeals tribunal, often referred to as the Alabama Tax Appeals Commission (ATAC).

The bill separates the tax appeals function from the Alabama Department of Revenue and is intended to give taxpayers more confidence that their tax appeals will be adjudicated in a fair and impartial manner, by eliminating its connection to the department.

Among its many provisions, the bill will: 1) allow taxpayers to appeal final tax assessments from self-administered cities and counties (and their private auditing firms), unless the governing body of the locality opts out; 2) extend the period that a taxpayer can appeal a preliminary or final assessment from 30 to 60 days; 3) conform two sets of federal changes to the innocent spouse rule; 4) increase the penalties for negligence, fraud, frivolous returns and appeals to conform with federal law; and 5) correct the statute that imposes a minimum $50 penalty for late filing, even when the taxpayer owes no tax.

Senate Committee Passes General Funds Appropriation for Ethics Commission

The Senate Finance and Taxation General Fund Committee favorably approved HB 62, by Rep. Mike Jones, R-Andalusia. This bill provides that beginning with Fiscal Year 2012, the Alabama Ethics Commission will receive an appropriation from the State General Fund of not less than one-tenth of 1 percent of the total amount appropriated from the State General Fund. The amount appropriated would not be reduced from the approved amount unless two-thirds of the membership of the House and Senate specifically vote to reduce the appropriation. The funding floor provided by the bill assures that the Commission will have sufficient funding to fulfill all of its statutory responsibilities.

HB 62 now goes to the full Senate.

Washington Briefing
Congress Passes 2011 Funding Deal to Keep Government Running Through Late September

The House on Thursday passed H.R. 1473, the Fiscal Year 2011 Continuing Resolution that will keep the government running through the end of the fiscal year while cutting $38.5 billion in federal spending.

The CR passed the House on a bipartisan 260-167 vote. Just hours later, the Senate passed the funding deal by a vote of 81-19. President Obama must sign the measure into law by midnight tonight to avert a government shutdown.

Following passage of the CR, the House then moved to debate on two concurrent resolutions to the CR, which were considered separately from the underlying concurrent resolution. The first, H.Con.Res. 35, would have directed the clerk of the House to make a correction in enrolling H.R. 1473 after Senate passage. The resolution would have directed the clerk to add a section at the end of H.R. 1473 to provide that no funds should be made available to implement any aspect of the Affordable Care Act.

The second resolution, H.Con.Res. 36, would have directed the clerk to add a section at the end of H.R. 1473 — after Senate passage — to provide that no funds in the bill should go to Planned Parenthood. The Senate rejected both resolutions.

The House then moved to consideration of H.Con.Res. 34, the Republican budget resolution for fiscal year 2012 as introduced by U.S. Rep. Paul Ryan (R-WI), chairman of the House Budget Committee. The resolution would establish the federal budget for fiscal year 2012 and set budgetary levels for fiscal years 2013 through 2021 as well as fundamentally change federal entitlement programs. The Republican budget passed the House on Friday on a party-line vote of 235-193, with all but four Republicans in support and all Democrats opposed.

Small Business May be Required to Pay More Taxes

A corporate tax overhaul that eliminates business tax credits and deductions could mean that small business owners who pay taxes as individuals would pay an average of 8 percent more in income taxes, according to a report by Ernst & Young. Many businesses that pay taxes through the individual code use tax deductions, such as accelerated depreciation, which could be eliminated to pay for changes in the corporate code.

Joining Gov. Bentley for the bill-signing were BCA President and CEO William Canary; Ron Box of Joe Money Machinery Company and co-chairman of BCA's Tax and Fiscal Policy Committee; bill sponsors Sen. Greg Reed and Rep. April Weaver; Ron Perkins of Doozer Software and co-chair of the Small Business Committee; Rick Roden, president of the Greater Jackson County Chamber of Commerce and chairman of BCA's Small Business Committee; and BCA Senior Vice President and Legal Advisor Anita Archie.

C H A P T E R **10**

April 22, 2011

GOVERNOR SIGNS BCA-BACKED BILL GIVING TAX DEDUCTION TO SMALL BUSINESS OWNERS

On Thursday, Gov. Robert Bentley signed into law HB 61, by Rep. April Weaver, R-Brierfield, which is a tax deduction bill affecting small businesses that provide health insurance for their employees. On hand for the bill signing were BCA board members Greg Powell, president of Fi-plan Partners; Rick Roden, president of the Greater Jackson County Chamber of Commerce and chairman of BCA's Small Business Committee; Ron Perkins of Doozer Software and co-chair of the Small Business Committee; and Ron Box of Joe Money Machinery Company, co-chairman of BCA's Tax and Fiscal Policy Committee.

The new law allows employers and employees to deduct an additional 50 percent of the amount expended for health insurance premiums. Qualifying employers are those with less than 25 employees; qualifying employees are those whose annual wages do not exceed $50,000. Sen. Greg Reed, R-Jasper, sponsored the bill in the Senate.

The measure now increases the 150 percent deduction, approved during the 2008 legislative session, to a deduction of 200 percent of qualifying premium payments.

BCA board member Greg Powell told the Associated Press after the bill-signing ceremony that he has provided health insurance for his employees since 2005, and the money he will save under this new law will allow him to add two additional employees to his 10-employee firm.

BCA member Craig Bacheler, owner of Bacheler Technologies in Montgomery, was also supportive of the new law. "This bill allows my IT consulting firm to directly compete with well-established firms when trying to hire highly skilled employees," said Bacheler. "I am able to absorb the high cost of health coverage knowing that I will get some tax credit relief at the end of the year. Without this bill being passed I did not know if I would have been able to offer health insurance to my employees."

Also attending the bill signing on behalf of the BCA were President & CEO William Canary and Anita Archie, senior vice president for inter-governmental affairs, advocacy and communications and legal advisor.

HB 61 was a top-tier item in the BCA's *2011 Legislative Agenda.*

Senate Passes 2011 Tort Reform Bills

On Tuesday, the BCA-supported, Alabama Civil Justice Reform Committee (ACJRC) 2011 tort reform bills passed the Senate with over-whelming support. During the debate, Senate Judiciary Committee Co-Chairman Sen. Cam Ward, R-Alabaster, specifically thanked the business community for its work in helping to craft the package.

Senate Tort Package:

SB 59, by Sen. Ward, would decrease the statute of repose for commencing a civil action against an architect, engineer or builder from 13 years to seven years. SB 59 passed 29-1.

SB 184, by Sen. Ben Brooks, R-Mobile, would protect retailers, whole-salers and other distributors of products from being sued in product liability actions where the product comes in a "sealed container." The bill only protects retailers from the "innocent conduit" situations. During the debate on the Senate floor, Brooks stressed that the legislation would offer retailers "a layer of protection" and "save small businesses money." SB 184 passed 34-0.

SB 207, by Sen. Ward, as agreed, would provide that judgments, other than judgments based on a contract action, would bear a flat rate of 7 percent. Sen. Roger Bedford, D-Russellville, took "personal exception" to the bill and predicted the legislature will revisit this issue when interest rates go back up. The bill passed by a vote of 30-3, with one abstention.

SB 212, by Sen. Clay Scofield, R-Guntersville, as agreed, provides that a wrongful death action may only be filed in a county where the deceased could have filed a civil action, if living, and added that Rule 82 of the Rules of Civil Procedure would continue to apply to wrongful death actions. The bill passed 32-1.

SB 187, by Sen. Brooks, would require the federal expert witness rule, known as the "Daubert Standard," to be applied in Alabama and be limited to scientific evidence. The U.S. Supreme Court mandated the Daubert standard in all federal courts in 1993; however, Alabama remains one of the final states that has not adopted the rule. Brooks said the legislation will "improve the reliability of testimony a jury hears," and will promote a fairer, more just system. The bill passed 31-1.

House Tort Package:

HB 251, by Rep. Wes Long, R-Guntersville, as agreed, protects retailers, wholesalers and other distributors of products from being sued in product liability where the product comes in a "sealed container." The bill only protects retailers from the "innocent conduit" situations.

HB 236, by Rep. Greg Canfield, R-Vestavia Hills, as agreed, would provide that judgments, other than judgments based on a contract action, would bear a flat rate of 7.5 percent.

HB 228, by Rep. Ron Johnson, R-Sylacauga, as agreed, provides that a wrongful death action may only be filed in a county where the deceased could have filed a civil action, if living, and added that Rule 82 of the Rules of Civil Procedure would continue to apply to wrongful death actions.

HB 239, by Rep. Steve McMillan, R-Bay Minette, companion bill to SB 187 known as the Daubert bill, has not been considered.

BCA supports these bills.

Rep. Robinson Thanks BCA for Support of Partnering for Progress conference

Rep. Oliver Robinson, D-Birmingham, a longtime BCA ally and 2010 ProgressPAC-endorsed candidate, appeared before the Governmental Affairs Committee meeting this week to share his perspective as a legislator who spent his entire career in the House majority, but following the 2010 election cycle, now joins his fellow Democrats in the chamber's minority.

"I thought after November 2 that the world was coming to an end because for the first time in 12 years I would have no chairmanship, and I would not help determine the direction of the House," Robinson said. "But I must say that, under the leadership of Speaker Mike Hubbard, things have been fair, and in the end, all you really want is fairness."

Robinson did note that few bills sponsored by Democrats moved through the House before the session's halfway point, which was marked last week, but conceded that similar action occurred when his party held the gavel.

"During my 12 years in the legislature, the Republicans had the same problem (with moving bills through the House)," Robinson said. "It is nothing any different from quadrennium to quadrennium, no matter who is in charge."

Referring to the Republican Handshake with Alabama, an omnibus platform of bills and initiatives upon which GOP legislative candidates across the state campaigned during the 2010 elections, Robinson said he is glad that each measure in the agenda has finally cleared the lower chamber so lawmakers may turn their attention to other areas.

Unity among Republicans has been tested since House approval of the Handshake package, according to Robinson, and GOP lawmakers have been quarreling among themselves over some of the measures.

"Sometimes the Republicans start fighting with each other, and for me, that is a pretty good thing to see," Robinson told the group. "Anytime the Republicans start fighting over a piece of legislation, it starts to make the few Democrats left in the chamber more relevant in the process. With the Handshake bills, you always knew when you pressed the button to vote that it was going to be all of the Republicans for it and all of the Democrats against."

He thanked BCA for its support of the Partnering for Progress conference, held each fall at the Grand Hotel in Point Clear, and its efforts to build better relationships between the business community and African-American members of the legislature, among others.

Business, Caucus Benefit From Conversation

"You may not readily see it, but I see how it is beginning to influence the members of the black caucus and other elected officials around the state," Robinson said. "Having the opportunity to get to know members of the business community and better understanding business issues makes for better conversation between the groups."

Robinson said job creation is the top priority for every member of the legislature — whether Democrat or Republican — because more employment leads to additional tax revenue, which results in more funding for public education and state services.

Calling upon his experience in the banking industry, Robinson compared state government to corporations who must be accountable to shareholders, or, in his example, taxpayers.

"We have to create an environment in which the shareholders are happy with the leadership of our corporation, and the only way to do that is to produce profits and use good business practices," he said. "And, ultimately, that is the same thing that taxpayers expect from the leaders of our state — good leadership, good results and good business practices."

Asked about the fiscal health of his native Jefferson County, Robinson said a recent court ruling nullifying the occupational tax and continued difficulties with the financing of the local sewer system have created a tenuous situation.

Members of the county commission, according to Robinson, have asked lawmakers to approve a measure of home rule that will allow for more local tax increases without having to navigate bills through the State House. Un-earmarking currently earmarked dollars is among the other requests being made by the commission, but the lawmaker said he does not feel Republicans or Democrats in the legislature are prepared to grant any of the wishes.

"The Jefferson County Public Health Department does have $70 million in reserves, and I think we can look at taking that money and bridging the county's needs until we can hold another referendum on bringing the occupational tax back," he said.

Immigration Bill Passes Full Senate with Changes

SB 256, by Sen. Scott Beason, R-Gardendale, which seeks to curb illegal immigration in Alabama by cracking down on employers who knowingly or intentionally hire illegal immigrants, cleared the Senate Thursday by a vote of 26-6.

Under SB 256, an employer is not required to utilize the E-Verify program to determine the legal status of workers unless he or she is applying for a government contract. Other forms of identification, such as a valid Alabama driver's license or any valid U.S. government-issued identification document, may be used.

Employers seeking state contracts, grants or incentives must submit a sworn affidavit affirming that they are not knowingly employing illegal immigrants in addition to providing proof they are a registered participant with the federal E-Verify program. Employers found in violation would be fined 5 percent of the total contract and be subject to possible contract termination upon a first violation. On a second violation, the contract would be terminated, the employer would be barred from doing future business with the state, and would forfeit 25 percent of the total contract. SB 256 includes a "whistle blower" provision that would award 50 percent of the damages collected by the courts to the person who reported the violation.

An employer who uses E-Verify cannot be found liable of violating the law.

SB 256 does not require subcontractors to utilize the E-Verify program. Instead, subcontractors must submit an affidavit, like contractors, affirming they do not employ unauthorized aliens. Under the bill, contractors cannot be held liable for the practices of a subcontractor so long as the contract between the two entities includes a provision stating that the subcontractor is not knowingly employing illegal immigrants.

For private contracts, employers found by the courts to have knowingly hired an illegal immigrant would be subject to a 14-day maximum business license suspension upon a first violation, a one-year license suspension upon a second offense, and permanent license revocation upon a third violation.

SB 256 now goes to the House of Representatives. BCA staff will continue to monitor the bill and work with the sponsor to ensure that employers are not unfairly burdened or penalized by this legislation.

Students First Act Clears Senate Panel

The Senate Education Policy Committee this week debated and approved a substitute to SB 310, by Sen. Trip Pittman, R-Daphne, which is an overhaul of the state's tenure law. Rep. Chad Fincher, R-Semmes, is sponsoring the companion bill, HB 465, in the House. Before a packed room, the committee voted 6-2 to send the bill to the full Senate.

Under current law, a teacher who is fired by a local school board is provided an arbitration hearing and remains on the payroll throughout the process. Under the Students First Act, teachers would have 30 days to notify the State Department of Education that they are seeking to appeal the dismissal to an administrative law judge chosen by the State Department of Education who would have the option of overturning or affirming the board's decision within 45 days. If the administrative law judge affirms the board's decision, the teacher would have the option of appealing to the circuit court. Under the Students First Act, the teacher's pay would cease upon notification of termination. Should the administrative law judge or an appeals court reinstate the teacher at a later date, back pay and benefits would be restored.

Under the original bill, a teacher could be fired for continual poor student performance. That has since been removed; however, Rep. Fincher said at a press conference on Wednesday, "We listened to teachers, took concerns and made changes to the legislation to make it better. They'll have that fair, impartial decision made."

Voting YES for the Students First Act were:

Sen. Trip Pittman, R-Daphne; Sen. Dick Brewbaker, R-Pike Road; Sen. Gerald Allen, R-Tuscaloosa; Sen. Slade Blackwell, R-Mountain Brook; Sen. Bill Holtzclaw, R-Madison; and Sen. Del Marsh, R-Anniston.

Voting NO to the Students First Act were:

Sen. Quinton Ross, D-Montgomery, and Sen. Hank Sanders, D-Selma.

The bill now goes before the full Senate for debate.

BCA supports this legislation.

Charter School Legislation Gains Support

The House Committee on Education Policy held a public hearing on HB 459, by Rep. Phil Williams, R-Huntsville, which provides for charter schools in Alabama on a pilot basis as separate and distinct public schools under local boards.

The bill is expected to be substituted when it comes up for a committee vote and will specify that the pilots be located in Class 1 and Class 2 municipalities of the state. Birmingham is the state's only Class 1 municipality and Montgomery, Huntsville and Mobile are the state's Class 2 municipalities.

At the public hearing on Wednesday, there was more support for this year's version of the bill, compared to legislation proposed in 2010, due in large part to the bill limiting the number of charter schools that would be formed and placing more oversight under local boards of education.

BCA's Senior Vice President for Intergovernmental Affairs, Advocacy and Communications and Legal Advisor Anita Archie told the committee, "Those who argue against charter schools fight for the status quo while those who support them believe we can rise above mediocrity and provide Alabama's children the education they deserve."

Tracey Meyer with the Alabama Department of Education also testified in support of the bill, saying, "the innovations [charter schools] bring will do great things."

John Hill with the Alabama Policy Institute called charter schools "hubs of innovation and creation for students and teachers."

Some 39 states allow for charter schools in some form as an alternative to traditional public schools. Charter schools are required to provide instruction for the grade level, as are other public schools, but many other regulations and procedures that other public schools must follow are waived.

The *2011 Legislative Agenda* states that the BCA will support efforts to enact legislation allowing public charter schools in Alabama.

House Committee OKs Bill to 'Double-Weight' Sales Factor in Apportioning Income of Multi-State Corporations

Corporations subject to Alabama income tax that sell tangible property and operate in several states currently apportion their income equally among the three factors — sales, property and payroll. HB 434, by Rep. Jay Love, R-Montgomery, would change the apportionment method to double the weight of the sales factor. This change would reward companies that invest relatively more heavily in the state, in terms of company property and payrolls, compared to their sales in Alabama, by sourcing less income subject to Alabama's income tax. Conversely, the change would source more company income to Alabama taxation when the company sells more in Alabama relative to its investments in property and payrolls in Alabama.

Alabama is the only state in the Southeast that does not either double-weight the sales factor or employ a single sales factor.

HB 434 also provides that multi-state corporations that sell intangible property or services will be sourced where the intangible property is used or where the service is delivered. This change would again reduce the amount of company income that is sourced to Alabama to be taxed when the company has relatively greater sales of intangible property or services to non-Alabama purchasers.

The Alabama Department of Revenue estimates that double-weighting the sales factor will produce a net increase in tax revenue of $15 million annually, while the change to the sourcing rule for intangible property or services will yield a net increase in tax revenue of $5 million annually.

BCA is monitoring this legislation.

House Passes Alabama Tax Appeals Commission/Taxpayers' Bill of Rights II

HB 427, by Rep. Paul DeMarco, R-Homewood, passed the Alabama House on Thursday by a vote 88-0. The legislation has been listed on the *BCA Legislative Agenda* for several years and combines provisions for updating the original Alabama Taxpayers' Bill of Rights act and provisions to create an independent tax appeals tribunal, often referred to as the Alabama Tax Appeals Commission (ATAC).

The bill separates the tax appeals function from the Alabama Department of Revenue and is intended to give taxpayers more confidence that their tax appeals will be adjudicated in a fair and impartial manner, by eliminating its connection to the Department.

Among the many provisions included in the legislation, the bill will: 1) allow taxpayers to appeal final tax assessments from self-administered cities and counties (and their private auditing firms), unless the governing body of the locality opts out; 2) extend the period that a taxpayer can appeal a preliminary or final assessment from 30 to 60 days; 3) conform to two sets of federal changes to the innocent spouse rule; 4) increase the penalties for negligence, fraud, frivolous returns and appeals to conform with federal law; and 5) correct the statute that imposes a minimum $50 penalty for late filing, even when the taxpayer owes no tax.

BCA supports this legislation.

House Approves Streamlined Sales and Use Tax Commission

On a vote of 94-0, the Alabama House passed HB 355, by Rep. Mike Hill, R-Columbiana, which provides for the Alabama Streamlined Sales and Use Tax Commission to implement the procedures and identify the statutory changes necessary to bring Alabama into compliance with the Streamlined Sales and Use Tax Agreement. Several states have entered into the multi-state agreement in anticipation of the enactment of federal law that would simplify the collection of sales taxes nationwide.

The Commission will be comprised of eight members: 1) two representatives of municipal government appointed by the Alabama League of Municipalities; 2) two representatives of county government appointed by the Alabama Association of County Commissioners; 3) two employees of the Alabama Department of Revenue; 4) one representative of the retail community appointed by the Alabama Retail Association; and 5) one representative from the business community appointed by the Business Council of Alabama.

BCA supports this legislation.

State Budgets for 2012 May be Dire, But Bill Gives Hope for Job Creation

As reported in the *Birmingham News* on Wednesday, Rep. Jim Barton, R-Mobile, Chair of the House Ways and Means General Fund Committee, predicts hundreds of state layoffs due to shortage of funds for the 2012 budget. However, a bill making its way through both houses of the legislature may be an option to resolve some of the budget shortfalls.

The Alabama Jobs Creation and Retention Act, HB 478, by Rep. Barry Mask, R-Wetumpka, and its companion, SB 373, by Sen. Phil Williams, R-Rainbow City, allows Alabama companies which undertake new, expansion or retention projects to retain a percentage of state income taxes withheld from full-time employees at the project.

The program is discretionary, meaning companies must apply to the Alabama Development Office to participate, and any projects must create a positive return for the Alabama economy. Simply put, for companies looking to locate or expand in Alabama, the state will not give away what it does not have. It must be a positive return on the state's investment for a company to receive the incentive. For existing industries, the bill is designed to give the state the ability to preserve jobs in situations where jobs would otherwise be lost.

BCA supports this legislation.

Environmental Bills Update

HB 285, by Rep. Randy Wood, R-Anniston, was referred to the Environmental Subcommittee of the House Commerce & Small Business Committee following a public hearing. The subcommittee recommended the bill to the full committee without any changes, and Committee Chair Rep. Greg Canfield, R-Vestavia Hills, has added the bill to the committee agenda next Wednesday. The legislation would provide a procedure for the owner of a motor vehicle to transfer to an automotive dismantler, parts recycler or secondary metals recycler a motor vehicle without a title if certain conditions are met, including a signed statement by the motor vehicle owner regarding its ownership, value and identifying characteristics. This legislation is needed to correct legislation enacted last year that prevents "any" vehicle from being sold for recycling or scrap without a title. For many older model vehicles that have not been in use for years, there is no existing title, and owners who want to sell the vehicles will not go through the Department of Revenue to buy a new title when they are selling the car for scrap.

Senior Vice President of Intergovernmental Affairs and Legal Advisor Anita Archie spoke in support of the bill during the public hearing, pointing out to the committee that this bill is on the *BCA 2011 Legislative Agenda*. The legislation passed last year has caused operating problems for several BCA member companies. The bill would help to eliminate problems associated with cars no longer in use that may lose fluids into the environment or cause blight in communities. BCA supports this legislation.

HB 143, by Rep. Alan Baker, R-Brewton, passed the House on Tuesday. HB 143 would change the state solid waste law on local government approval of "new" landfill sites. Present law states that if a local governing body does not take action on a landfill site application within 90 days, it is automatically approved. HB 143 would reverse the law from automatic "approval" to automatic "denial" if the local government takes no action. BCA has been talking to the sponsor and will continue to work with him on the bill.

HB 406, also by Rep. Baker, would set a two-year moratorium on the permitting of "new" commercial Subtitle D or Construction & Demolition waste landfills. During the two-year period, ADEM and the Alabama Department of Public Health will review their programs and propose legislation or update regulations as needed. BCA is monitoring the legislation.

BCA Given Award for Support of Pre-K Education and Early Childhood Advocacy

On Wednesday, The Alabama Department of Children's Affairs presented the Business Council of Alabama with the First Class Friend for Alabama's Children Award for BCA's support of early childhood development.

The BCA and its leadership have identified Pre-K education and early childhood investment as a top priority and are partnering with a number of reform-minded education groups to see that Alabama's first class Pre-K program is expanded and adequately funded.

Accepting the award on behalf of BCA were BCA President and CEO William Canary and Senior Vice President for Intergovernmental Affairs and Legal Advisor Anita Archie. "The successes in Pre-K education and early childhood investment are great examples of how business and education, working together through a Business Education Alliance (BEA) can transform the future of Alabama," Canary said. "Investing in our children is the best investment we can make."

Canary made opening remarks at a special Pre-Kindergarten Forum and Reception Wednesday night, reaffirming BCA's commitment to early childhood education. The keynote speaker was Ronnie Herndon, director of the Albina Head Start Program in Portland, Oregon, and chairman of the National Head Start Foundation.

The Alabama Partnership for Children and the Alabama School Readiness Alliance, among others, also received recognition for their work in early childhood education.

Chambers Visit Montgomery, BCA Offices

Delegations from two local chambers of commerce brought delegations to Montgomery this week to meet with their local legislators and BCA staff. The Calhoun County Chamber of Commerce, led by President Sherri J. Sumners, CCE, and the Greater Jackson County Chamber of Commerce, led by President Rick Roden, brought groups to the capital city. Both chambers are members of the Chamber of Commerce Association of Alabama and The Partnership, BCA's formal relationship with the CCAA.

Senate Committee OKs Forever Wild

The Senate Energy and Natural Resources Committee voted 6-3 to approve HB 126, by Rep. Randy Davis, R-Daphne, which reauthorizes Forever Wild, a state program that has bought and preserved land for environmental and recreation reasons. The bill could be acted on by the full Senate next week. BCA supports this legislation.

Washington Briefing
President Targeting Political Contributions of Contractors

The White House is drafting new rules that would require companies seeking federal contracts to disclose their political contributions. The draft executive order includes stopping certain contributions during negotiation and performance of a government contract.

Although some spending already is disclosed to the Federal Election Commission, the order would require that entities seeking contracts compile and disclose information on contributions by their political action committees and executives as part of the contracting process. The draft order would also require the disclosure of contributions "made to third-party entities with the intention or reasonable expectation" that the money would be used to fund independent campaign expenditures or electioneering communications.

The White House says the draft executive order is an effort to improve transparency and accountability in the federal contracting system.

Senate Republican Leader Mitch McConnell (R-KY) said in a written statement, "No White House should be able to review your political party affiliation before deciding if you're worthy of a government contract."

As you may recall, early last year the Supreme Court ruled in *Citizens United v. FEC* that corporations and unions can pay for political ads anonymously. In the wake of that decision, Congress tried to pass the DISCLOSE Act, which would have placed onerous restrictions on corporate free speech. The bill passed the House but failed in the Senate.

Alabama to Receive $100 Million from BP Agreement

The Natural Resource Trustees for the Deepwater Horizon oil spill announced on Thursday that BP has agreed to provide $100 billion toward early restoration projects in the Gulf of Mexico to address injuries to natural resources caused by last year's spill.

Alabama as well as Florida, Mississippi, Louisiana and Texas will each receive $100 million in projects. In addition, the Federal Resource Trustees, the National Oceanic and Atmospheric Administration (NOAA) and the Department of the Interior will each select and implement $100 million in projects. The remaining $300 million will be used for projects selected by NOAA and DOI from proposals submitted by the state trustees.

"Alabama's natural resources are environmentally diverse and an economic engine for our state and nation. Ecosystem restoration is vital to the economic vitality of the Alabama Gulf Coast," said Gov. Robert Bentley. "Obtaining funding for these restoration projects is a major step forward in addressing the oil spill's damage to our precious natural resources. I have the utmost confidence that the Alabama trustees will consider and identify projects and use these funds toward restoring our natural resources."

Boeing Receives Contract for SM-3 IIB Concept Design

BCA member Boeing in Huntsville has been awarded a contract by the U.S. Missile Defense Agency (MDA) to develop the Standard Missile-3 Block IIB (SM-3 IIB) and continue work on the development of the Next Generation Aegis Missile (NGAM). This $41.2 million, 32-month contract is for the concept definition and planning phase of the project.

NGAM is a key component of the Department of Defense's Phased Adaptive Approach for missile defense in Europe. It will provide capability against emerging longer-range ballistic missile threats.

"We'll begin work immediately on the development of this advanced defensive capability," said Boeing's Ken Tucker. "The Boeing NGAM program office will be located in Huntsville. This effort will create approximately one dozen jobs initially, growing to more than 40 jobs by mid-2012."

Chapter 11

April 29, 2011

Committee Hears Testimony on Business-Backed 'Gross Income Regulation' Fix; Vote Expected Tuesday

The Alabama Department of Revenue's (ADOR) proposed rule change to the "gross income regulation" will require an Alabama resident shareholder of an S-corporation or a partner or member of an LLC to include income in his or her Alabama tax return from all sources, both foreign and domestic. However, if the resident owners are not allowed tax credits for entity-level taxes paid to other states and foreign countries, the proposed rule change will result in double taxation on the same income.

State Finance Director David Perry testified at the House Ways and Means Committee public hearing saying, "The Administration is supportive of the bill as a whole...and the Administration and the business community are on the same page."

Presently, the regulation provides that only income that is allocated to Alabama at the entity level be reported for Alabama income tax purposes. Income earned by the entity in another state is taxed by that state, assuming the other state levies an income tax. The Alabama owner is also allowed by the Alabama Constitution to deduct 100 percent of his/her federal income tax liability against the owner's Alabama source income, which could greatly reduce or even eliminate the resident owner's Alabama income tax liability.

Also presently in effect is a ruling by the ADOR's Administrative Law Judge that requires Alabama resident shareholders/partners to report their shares of income from all sources, which directly conflicts with the provision in the above paragraph. Owners/partners who have heavy losses from their operations outside of Alabama will likely elect to report income (and losses) from all sources to reduce their Alabama income tax liabilities.

The two conflicting methods for reporting income coupled with the ability to apply 100 percent of the federal income tax deduction drain the state's tax revenue and are unfair to other Alabama taxpayers who cannot select the more advantageous method for reporting income.

These issues pose serious tax consequences for many employers and must not be resolved by an administrative rule change, but rather, by legislation. Any legislation proposed to resolve this issue should be fair, prospective and based on sound tax policy that is pro-jobs, pro-business and avoids double taxation. However, Susan Kennedy with the Alabama Education Association stressed that the rule be changed through regulation, not legislation.

Alabama employers, who are struggling in this fragile recovery, need sound, sensible tax policy from the Alabama Legislature that will resolve the matter without inciting new rounds of litigation.

Following the introduction of HB 548, by Rep. Jay Love, R-Montgomery, officials of the ADOR offered three recommendations to the original bill: 1) that the credit for taxes paid to other states be limited to taxes based on income or gross receipts, not those based on net worth; 2) that the amount of the credit for taxes paid to other states be limited to the amount of tax that would have been paid if the income had been earned in Alabama; and 3) that the resident taxpayer receive a deduction rather than a credit for income or gross receipts-based taxes paid to foreign countries.

The business community agreed to conditions 1 and 2 above but is holding firm in rejecting condition 3, to be consistent with the tax treatment provided for in Act # 2007-366, which applies to only a very small number of companies. It is estimated that HB 548 will generate $25 million annually.

BCA Tax and Fiscal Policy Chairman Marty Abroms told the committee members, "he believes good tax policy is important, and the business community does not want a loophole." He also said that he recognizes that

BCA Tax Committee Chair Marty Abroms spoke at the public hearing on HB 548.

tax law is not perfect, and, "since 2007, the BCA has adopted as part of its *Legislative Agenda* to develop a pro-jobs and pro-growth fix to the gross income regulation."

House Judiciary Sends 2011 Tort Reform Bills to Full House

The BCA-supported, Alabama Civil Justice Reform Committee (ACJRC) 2011 tort reform bills received a favorable report from the House Judiciary Committee on Wednesday.

Senate Tort Package:

SB 59, by Sen. Cam Ward, R-Alabaster, would decrease the statute of repose for commencing a civil action against an architect, engineer or builder from 13 years to seven years.

SB 184, by Sen. Ben Brooks, R-Mobile, would protect retailers, wholesalers and other distributors of products from being sued in product liability actions where the product comes in a "sealed container." The bill only protects retailers from the "innocent conduit" situations.

SB 207, by Sen. Ward, as agreed, would provide that judgments, other than judgments based on a contract action, would bear a flat rate of 7 percent. Sen. Roger Bedford, D-Russellville, took "personal exception" to the bill and predicted the legislature will revisit this issue when interest rates go back up. The bill passed by a vote of 30-3, with one abstention.

SB 212, by Sen. Clay Scofield, R-Guntersville, as agreed, provides that a wrongful death action may only be filed in a county where the deceased could have filed a civil action, if living, and added that Rule 82 of the Rules of Civil Procedure would continue to apply to wrongful death actions.

SB 187, by Sen. Brooks, would require the federal expert witness rule, known as the "Daubert Standard," to be applied in Alabama and be limited to scientific evidence. The U.S. Supreme Court mandated the Daubert standard in all federal courts in 1993; however, Alabama remains one of the final states that has not adopted the rule.

BCA leadership, including BCA Chairman Will Brooke, BCA Tax and Fiscal Policy Committee Chairman Marty Abroms, BCA Judicial and Legal Reform Committee Chairman Debbie Long and BCA board member Jim Proctor, met with House Speaker Mike Hubbard, R-Auburn. Hubbard indicated the tort package will be brought to the House floor next week for final passage.

Williams Touts Jobs Creation and Retention Act Passed by Senate

A veteran Senate Democrat with decades of service was joined by a fresh-faced, political newcomer Republican at the weekly BCA Governmental Affairs Committee meeting on Tuesday, as the two discussed various issues being considered by the legislature's upper chamber.

Sen. Phil Williams, a first-term Republican representing Cherokee and Etowah Counties, said he considers the current legislature the most pro-business in the history of the state and cited an economic development incentive bill he is sponsoring as an example. [The Senate passed the measure, The Alabama Jobs Creation and Retention Act, late Wednesday.]

Williams, chief operating officer of a company that pairs businesses and industries with available federal incentives, tax credits and grant programs, said he was "shocked to see how little Alabama offers companies in terms of job creation incentives" when he entered the legislature.

SB 373 originated with an idea given to Williams by his local industrial development authority chairman. Under its provisions, new or existing businesses that meet certain payroll threshold markers may qualify for withholding tax abatements, which provide immediate capital for operations, expansion and other needs. Companies that do not meet the mandated markers would be subject to "clawbacks" that require repayment of the abatements, he added.

"This bill is very discretionary, so it's not a 'gimmee' that is handed out to businesses left and right," Williams said. "This bill has a protective layer of discretion that requires ADO and Revenue to do a written cost-benefit analysis and make a recommendation to the governor, who then provides his approval or disapproval to the Industrial Development Authority."

The legislation would benefit various disadvantaged areas of the state, according to Williams, and could prove vital to districts such as his, which is heavily dependent upon a local Goodyear manufacturing plant for jobs and opportunity.

"With 1,652 jobs, the Goodyear plant in my district is the largest private sector employer in the northeastern part of the state, and if you have read the news, you will know that Goodyear recently closed a similar plant in Tennessee," Williams said. "We are currently looking at ways for Goodyear to not only stay in our area, but to also grow and invest, and this bill provides those incentives."

He noted that his area recently lost the chance to be the home of the company that makes Hot Pockets because the state did not have the incentives that would be provided under SB 373.

Russellville Democrat Sen. Roger Bedford, first elected to the Senate in 1982, noted that the legislature, its procedures and the lawmaking process have changed dramatically since Republicans recently captured their first majority in both chambers in 136 years.

"It's different when you go from 22 (Senate Democrats) to 12, because everyone is a private in that army," Bedford said. "It's also interesting to watch a different approach and a different philosophy take shape."

Citing what he considered the lack of a "Republican farm team," Bedford said senators previously had to wait "six, eight, ten or 12 years" before being given committee chairmanship positions, but many freshman GOP lawmakers are finding themselves leading important legislative panels.

Bedford questioned whether the relative lack of legislative experience among Republicans led to temporary changes requiring State House visitors to sign a security sheet, receive a guest badge and make formal appointments to meet with senators and representatives.

"Now, we have bright, young, professional (freshmen lawmakers) come in, but they have no institutional knowledge of running a committee, and I think that's why we saw the leadership try to shut the public out," Bedford said. "During the special session (on ethics reform and accountability), members of the public came down to let these freshmen know they did not like what they were doing, but these guys were not used to the pressures you are put through down here."

He also lodged complaints about the Republican majority using cloture petitions and its super-majority to end Democrat-led filibusters and prolonged debate over measures before the body. Bedford said he and his fellow Democrats had been "cloutured more times in the past 40 days than we cloutured the Republicans in the previous eight years."

"I participated in sessions in the old Capitol where we would go 72 hours non-stop, and we would talk, read the bill, learn what was in it and reach a compromise," Bedford said. "But when you say you are going to cloture them in 20 minutes, there is no incentive to learn about the bill or an amendment and try to figure out if it is good or bad for your district."

[Note: Just a few hours following Bedford's remarks, Democrats engaged in a prolonged filibuster campaign that required Republicans to pass numerous cloture motions and forced a session that began on Tuesday afternoon to last until 6:30 a.m. on Wednesday morning before adjournment.]

Bedford, a previous chairman of the Senate Judiciary Committee, said he was glad to see a tort reform package pass through the chamber and liked the cooperative manner in which lawmakers addressed a venue determination clause involving wrongful death lawsuits. He does, however, believe it was mistake to statutorily change the interest on civil judgments from 12 percent to 7.5 percent, and said the higher rate, in his opinion, served as a deterrent for frivolous appeals in lawsuits.

Bedford said that rather than "balancing the budgets on the backs of teachers and state employees," the legislature should address closing "corporate loopholes or dealing with tax fairness."

He added his belief that those new to the work force will be less likely to accept public employee roles or teaching positions because the job security has lessened, and they will fear that benefits promised to them will not be made available when needed.

GOVERNMENTAL AFFAIRS TUESDAY MEETINGS

Speaker of the House Mike Hubbard

Senate President Pro Tem Del Marsh

Continuing a longstanding tradition, each Tuesday morning during the legislative session the BCA's Governmental Affairs Committee, above, was briefed by key legislators and state government officials on the latest issues of importance to business.

At left, Rep. Paul DeMarco, R-Homewood, and Sen. Cam Ward, R-Alabaster, brought the committee up to date on tort reform legislation.

Sen. Scott Beason

Sen. Roger Bedford

Sen. Gerald Dial

Rep. Blaine Galliher

Rep. Jay Love

State Finance Director David Perry

Sen. Trip Pittman

Rep. Oliver Robinson

Sen. Phil Williams

Gov. Robert Bentley welcomed BCA leadership to his office early in his term. From left, Second Vice Chair Carl Jamison, Chairman William Brooke, President and CEO William Canary, Gov. Bentley, Senior Vice President for Intergovernmental Affairs, Communications and Advocacy and Legal Advisor Anita Archie and 2010 Chairman Sandy Stimpson.

2010 GOVERNMENTAL AFFAIRS CONFERENCE

Political commentator Frank Luntz talked to then-gubernatorial nominee Robert Bentley as BCA's President and CEO William Canary and Sen. Arthur Orr looked on. Below, pollster Peter Hart and Luntz entertained the crowd at the 2010 BCA Governmental Affairs Conference at The Grand Hotel in Point Clear.

LEADERSHIP EXCHANGES

During 2010, BCA and the Chamber of Commerce Association of Alabama held a series of Leadership Exchanges across the state to bring together business and political leaders to talk about areas of common interest and brief them on BCA's goals and priorities. Above, Education and Workforce Preparedness Committee Chair Bob Powers spoke to a gathering in Eufaula about the importance of Pre-K education. At left, CCAA President Kirk Mancer addressed an Exchange group in Cullman.

Several hundred guests gathered at the Sheraton Hotel in Birmingham in September for the annual BCA Chairman's Dinner. Theme for the evening: "Politics Takes Center Stage."

Former U.S. Rep. J.C. Watts, R-OK, opened the evening's discussion.

Former U.S. Rep. J.C. Watts moderated a panel discussion with former Vermont governor and Democratic presidential contender Howard Dean and FOX News political analyst Dick Morris. At right, 2010 BCA Chairman Sandy Stimpson challenged the crowd to make a difference at the voting booth in November.

William J. Cabaniss of Birmingham, businessman and former U.S. Ambassador to the Czech Republic, received the 2010 Chairman's Award for Leadership and Distinguished Service from BCA Chairman Sandy Stimpson, who called Cabaniss a "statesman" and a "true gentleman."

Author and political commentator Fred Barnes was the guest speaker for the 2010 Annual Meeting of the BCA and Chamber of Commerce Association of Alabama at the Harbert Center in Birmingham.

Incoming BCA Chairman Will Brooke, right, presented 2010 Chairman Sandy Stimpson with a framed montage of photos and memorabilia from the Chairman's Dinner.

BCA First Vice Chairman Terry Kellogg, right, visited with Rep. Jim Patterson, R-Meridianville, at the 2011 Salute to State Leaders at the RSA Activity Center in Montgomery.

BCA President and CEO William Canary introduced Gov. Robert Bentley to BCA members Tom McCleod and Ron Perkins.

2011 ALABAMA MANUFACTURER OF THE YEAR AWARDS

U.S. Rep. Jo Bonner, R-Mobile, left, presented awards to the 2011 Alabama Manufacturers of the Year: A. Ray Shirley Jr., owner and founder of Applied Chemical Technology, Inc., Small Manufacturer of the Year; Y.D. Lim, president and CEO of Hyundai Motor Manufacturing Alabama, Large Manufacturer of the Year; and Randy Johns, training coordinator for Lafarge North America, Medium Manufacturer of the Year.

COMMITTEE DAYS

Jay Timmons, president of the National Association of Manufacturers, and Katie Strong Hays, executive director for congressional and public affairs at the U.S. Chamber of Commerce, were keynote speakers for 2010 Committee Days in Birmingham. Members of BCA's committees met together for two days to draft the *2011 BCA State Legislative Agenda*.

State Board of Education Endorses Students First Act

The State Board of Education on Thursday voted to endorse the Students First Act, a reform of Alabama's Tenure and Fair Dismissal Act. By a vote of 6-1, the board approved a resolution that read in part: "The State Board of Education seeks ways to always put students at the forefront of education, and continually seeks ways to improve education and promote student success in life and in the workplace. The Board lauds the professionalism and dedication of educators generally, but recognizes that every profession has its lowest performers; education administrators and local boards should never target an employee for personal or political reasons but should have the legal authority to reasonably discipline and terminate without prohibitive cost."

The legislation, SB 310 in the Senate, by Sen. Trip Pittman, R-Daphne, and HB 465 in the House, by Rep. Chad Fincher, R-Semmes, received a favorable report from the Education Policy Committee last week and could make it before the full Senate as early as next week.

Under current law, a teacher who is fired by a local school board is provided an arbitration hearing and remains on the payroll throughout the process. Under the Students First Act, teachers would have 30 days to notify the State Department of Education that they are seeking to appeal the dismissal to an administrative law judge chosen by the State Department of Education who would have the option of overturning or affirming the board's decision within 45 days. If the administrative law judge affirms the board's decision, the teacher would have the option of appealing to the circuit court. Under the Students First Act, the teacher's pay would cease upon notification of termination. Should the administrative law judge or an appeals court reinstate the teacher at a later date, back pay and benefits would be restored.

Board Members who voted in FAVOR of the resolution:

District 1 member Randy McKinney; District 2 member Betty Peters; District 3 member Stephanie Bell; District 4 member Dr. Yvette Richardson; District 6 member Dr. Charles Elliot; District 8 member Mary Scott Hunter.

Board Member who voted AGAINST the resolution:

District 5 member Ella Bell.

Gov. Robert Bentley and District 7 member Gary Warren were unable to attend the board meeting on Thursday due to the tornadoes that swept through Tuscaloosa and much of central and north Alabama on Wednesday.

BCA supports this legislation.

Senate Committee Version of Education Budget Closely Resembles House Version

The Senate Finance & Taxation-Education Committee members gave a favorable report to their version of the education budget for Fiscal Year 2012; it is similar to the version already passed by the House on several major items.

Both versions propose to expend about $5.588 billion from the Education Trust Fund. In K-12, both versions fund about 1,125 less state-funded teacher units statewide, while preserving approximately 2,000 essential support worker jobs and adding $25 million above the level recommended by Gov. Bentley for school transportation. According to State Superintendent of Education Joe Morton, the reduction in state-funded units should not actually cause any state-funded teachers to lose their jobs, because on average, some 1,500 teachers retire each year. Both versions are predicated on reduced contributions by the state for teachers' retirement and health insurance, larger contributions to be paid by education personnel for their share of retirement costs, and they fund the Children's Health Insurance Program (CHIP) next year by withdrawing the accumulated balance (over $30 million) in a fund that serves deaf and blind citizens.

However, the committee budget does differ from the version passed by the House on some smaller items. The committee reduced the appropriation to Auburn University's Agricultural Experiment Station by $1 million, reduced the appropriation to Auburn's Cooperative Extension System by $1.1 million and reduced the appropriation to the Alabama Innovations Fund by $4 million less than the $10 million recommended by the governor and passed by the House.

The committee budget increases the two-year college system by $2.8 million, funds two agricultural programs under the Alabama Commission on Higher Education by $300,000 each and adds $2.5 million to the Alabama Institute for the Deaf and Blind.

Governor's 'Full Employment Act' Moves Closer to Becoming Law

HB 230, by Rep. Blaine Galliher, R-Gadsden, received a favorable report from the Senate Job Creation and Economic Development Committee this week. The committee amended the bill to allow small banks to participate in receiving credits that are provided for creating jobs. The bill, dubbed the Full Employment Act, would provide to employers of 50 or fewer employees a one-time income tax credit, beginning in the current tax year, equal to $1,000 for each new job that is created that pays at least $10 per hour, after the employee has completed 12 consecutive months of employment. BCA supports this bill, which now goes to the full Senate for consideration.

Environmental Bills Update

HB 509, by Rep. Randy Wood, R-Anniston, was voted out of the House Commerce and Small Business Committee on Tuesday after it was approved without changes by the Environmental Subcommittee of the full Committee.

For several weeks, the sponsor and the law enforcement community have been in negotiations regarding the length of time vehicles would be held before being crushed and shredded, allowing local law enforcement to ensure the vehicle was not stolen. On Wednesday the parties agreed to language that will be offered in a floor amendment.

The bill was to be considered on Thursday, but the legislative workday was cut short for concerns over victims of Wednesday's tornadoes. The bill is expected to be taken up by the full House next Tuesday. Readers of Capital Briefing will recall that HB 509 is intended to correct a problem created last year when the Department of Revenue passed legislation that required "all" vehicles being sold for scrap or dismantling to have a title. Many older car owners no longer have the titles and will not go through the process to get a new title only to scrap-out a car that may not be worth more than a couple of hundred dollars.

BCA supports this legislation and on behalf of its members affected by last year's legislation, has worked to keep the bill moving forward.

Sen. Sessions Addresses Business Leaders Before Touring Storm Damage

U.S. Sen. Jeff Sessions (R-AL) was the guest speaker at a breakfast hosted by the Montgomery Area Chamber of Commerce on Thursday. The senator's remarks came just before he left to tour the state's storm damage.

Sessions singled out Hyundai for "winning award after award" and "continuing to produce investment in Alabama."

He also discussed his role as the ranking member of the Senate Budget Committee and the "unsustainable path" America is on, in regards to spending. Sessions called the budget submitted by the president "the most irresponsible budget in history."

Sessions closed his remarks by focusing on the strength of the Alabama delegation, calling the nine members the most "harmonious delegation in the country."

Attorney General to Prosecute Looters

In the wake of dozens of tornadoes that wreaked havoc throughout Alabama, Attorney General Luther Strange pledged that his office will be vigilant in protecting citizens from those who might exploit the tragedy for illegal profit. He also warned against looting and pledged that the Attorney General's Office will work with local law enforcement to make sure that anyone caught looting is prosecuted to the fullest extent of the law.

With a State of Emergency officially declared for every county of Alabama, the state's price gouging law now is in effect throughout the state. The Attorney General also reminds citizens to be careful of potential home repair fraud.

Strange urges consumers and officials to report any problems of alleged fraud or illegal price gouging to his Office of Consumer Protection by calling toll-free 1-800-392-5658 or though the Attorney General's main web page at www.ago.alabama.gov.

Illegal Immigration Bill in Line For Final Passage

HB 56, by Rep. Micky Hammon, R-Decatur, which seeks to curb illegal immigration in Alabama by requiring state and local government officials to enforce federal immigration laws and by cracking down on employers who hire illegal immigrants, unanimously passed the Senate Job Creation and Economic Development Committee. As previously reported, the legislation is modeled after the Arizona law and creates specific penalties for employers who "knowingly or intentionally" hire illegal immigrants. The bill could be up for debate on the Senate floor as early as Tuesday.

Taxpayer Bill of Rights Carried Over

HB 427, by Rep. Paul DeMarco, R-Homewood, was carried over by the Senate Judiciary Committee until next week because committee members had not had time to review the 100-plus page bill. The bill updates the Alabama Taxpayers' Bill of Rights act and creates an independent tax appeals tribunal, often referred to as the Alabama Tax Appeals Commission (ATAC). BCA supports this legislation.

Texting While Driving Could Soon be Illegal in Alabama

HB 102, by Rep. Jim McClendon, R-Springville, received a favorable report from the Senate Judiciary committee this week. If passed, persons found operating a motor vehicle on an Alabama public road, street or highway while using a wireless telecommunication device to write, send or read a text-based communication would be subject to a $25 fine upon a first violation, $50 fine upon a second violation and $75 fine upon a third violation.

The bill makes texting while driving a primary offense, and individuals would be charged with a two-point violation on their driving record if found to have violated the law. The bill now goes before the Senate.

BCA is monitoring this legislation to ensure that employers requiring the use of GPS devices for routine operations would not be subject to unfair penalties.

Washington Briefing
Administration Looking to Propose Corporate Tax Cut

CNBC's chief Washington correspondent John Harwood reported that the Administration is "talking about a top [corporate] rate as low as 26 percent. The current top rate is 35 percent. They're talking about fueling that decrease in the top rate by curbing or eliminating the deduction for domestic manufacturing and accelerated depreciation. And they may release their plan as early as May."

According to Harwood, economic advisors have "explored the willingness of business leaders to sacrifice loopholes in return for lowering the top corporate tax rate."

NLRB to Sue States that Banned 'Card Check' Unionization

In a letter sent last Friday, the National Labor Relations Board advised state officials that it will soon file federal lawsuits against Arizona and South Dakota to invalidate those states' constitutional amendments that prohibit employees from choosing to unionize through a procedure known as "card check."

The lawsuits will seek to assert that the Supremacy Clause of the U.S. Constitution preempts the state constitutional amendments. While four states — Arizona, South Dakota, South Carolina and Utah — have passed similar constitutional amendments, the NLRB is reserving "the right to initiate a suit against the other two states at the appropriate time."

Last year, some of the nation's largest unions — the AFL-CIO, SEIU and the Change to Win Coalition — pushed for Congress to approve "card check" legislation to change how unions are allowed to organize in the United States.

Under current law, employees are able to vote for or against unionization in a secret-ballot, federally supervised election. Under the card check bill, if more than 50 percent of workers at a facility sign a card, the government would have to certify the union, and a private ballot election would be prohibited — regardless of whether employees want a private ballot election.

Many expected the controversial card check legislation to pass Congress last year, and in response, several states passed constitutional amendments prohibiting card check.

BCA-supported HB 64, by Rep. Kurt Wallace, R-Maplesville, which would ensure, via constitutional amendment, that every individual in the state of Alabama is guaranteed the right to privately cast a ballot in all elections, including union elections, is moving now through the Alabama Legislature.

HB 64 passed in the House by a vote of 63-31. It received a favorable report by the Senate Constitution, Campaign Finance, Ethics and Elections Committee and is awaiting consideration by the full Senate.

As part of the *2011 BCA Federal Legislative Agenda*, the BCA opposes efforts to legislate, regulate or implement any provision of the card check legislation, and the BCA will monitor efforts of the NLRB with respect to unionization.

House Speaker Mike Hubbard, joined by bill sponsor Sen. Trip Pittman, BCA's William Canary and Anita Archie, and several representatives of the education community, spoke at a press conference on the Students First Act.

CHAPTER 12

May 6, 2011

SENATE PASSES 'STUDENTS FIRST ACT'

After hours of back and forth between different sides on Thursday and passage of several other bills throughout the day, the Senate late Thursday night passed the "Students First Act" of 2011 by a vote of 18-16.

Sponsored by Sen. Trip Pittman, R-Daphne, SB 310 is an overhaul of the Teacher Tenure Law and Fair Dismissal Act. The BCA worked closely with the Alabama Association of School Boards, School Superintendents of Alabama and the State Departments of Education and Postsecondary Education to prevent the bill from being gutted by the Alabama Education Association.

"BCA has long been championing a business/education alliance in Alabama, and the vote on the Students First Act is a significant first step toward better educating our students," said BCA President and CEO William J. Canary. "This not only protects our students, but it protects Alabama's best and brightest teachers as well."

The biggest change to the Senate-passed version since it was introduced in late March was an added provision that allows for teachers to be paid for 75 days upon termination. In the original bill, compensation was stopped immediately, and should a teacher win an appeal of his or her firing, back pay and benefits would be restored, which is still the case under the current legislation.

The appeals process for fired teachers also has been modified. Currently, teachers appeal to a federal arbitrator who often takes a year or longer to issue a ruling, all while the fired teacher is still paid. Under the legislation passed by the Senate Thursday, a teacher may appeal to the local board of education. Should the local board uphold the decision, the teacher may appeal to the executive director of the Alabama State Bar Association, who will then pick a hearing officer from a group of retired judges to hear the appeal.

As the clock ticked toward midnight, the issue that seemed to cause the biggest problem for opponents was a provision that took away an appeal for teachers who are laid off due to unavoidable reductions in the workforce or a shortage of revenues. Currently, a teacher who is laid off due to these factors can appeal to a hearing officer.

Before debate was cut off, Senate President Pro Tem Del Marsh, R-Anniston, told fellow senators that a refusal to invoke cloture was a "no" vote on the Students First Act. The Senate then followed with a 21-12 vote to end the debate and moved forward with a vote.

The bill now goes before the House of Representatives.

BCA supports this legislation.

18 senators who voted FOR the Students First Act were:

Sen. Gerald Allen, R-Tuscaloosa; Sen. Scott Beason, R-Gardendale; Sen. Slade Blackwell, R-Mountain Brook; Sen. Dick Brewbaker, R-Pike Road; Sen. Ben Brooks, R-Mobile; Sen. Paul Bussman, R-Cullman; Sen. Gerald Dial, R-Lineville; Sen. Rusty Glover, R-Semmes; Sen. Bill Holtzclaw, R-Madison; Sen. Del Marsh, R-Anniston; Sen. Shadrack McGill, R-Scottsboro; Sen. Arthur Orr, R-Decatur; Sen. Trip Pittman, R-Daphne; Sen. Paul Sanford, R-Huntsville; Sen. Clay Scofield, R-Guntersville; Sen. Bryan Taylor, R-Prattville; Sen. Jabo Waggoner, R-Vestavia Hills; and Sen. Phil Williams, R-Rainbow City.

16 senators who voted AGAINST the Students First Act were:

Sen. Cam Ward, R-Alabaster; Sen. Jimmy Holley, R-Elba; Sen. Greg Reed, R-Jasper; Sen. Tom Whatley, R-Auburn; Sen. Billy Beasley, D-Clayton; Sen. Linda Coleman, D-Birmingham; Sen. Priscilla Dunn, D-Bessemer; Sen. Jerry Fielding, D-Sylacauga; Sen. Vivian Figures, D-Mobile; Sen. Tammy Irons, D-Florence; Sen. Marc Keahey, D-Grove Hill; Sen. Quinton Ross, D-Montgomery; Sen. Hank Sanders, D-Selma; Sen. Bobby Singleton, D-Greensboro; Sen. Harri Anne Smith, I-Slocomb; and Sen. Rodger Smitherman, D-Birmingham.

House Passes Two Tax Bills That Bolster Upcoming Education Budget

As House and Senate conferees meet over the recess to work out their differences in the $5.588 billion FY 2012 education budget, two tax bills passed the House this week, providing an estimated $40 million to support the spending plan.

HB 434, by Rep. Jay Love, R-Montgomery, which passed the House by a vote of 93-4, would change the current apportionment method to double the weight of the sales factor for corporations subject to Alabama income tax that sell tangible property in multiple states. Currently, such companies apportion their income equally among three factors — sales, property and payroll. This change would reward companies that invest relatively more heavily in the state, in terms of company property and payrolls, compared to their sales in Alabama, by sourcing less income that is subject to Alabama's income tax. Alternatively, the change would source more company income to Alabama taxation when the company sells more in Alabama relative to its investments in property and payrolls in Alabama. Companies that sell tangible property exclusively in Alabama would not be affected.

Alabama currently stands as the only state in the Southeast that either does not double-weight the sales factor or employ a single sales factor, both of which benefit companies that make relatively greater investments in property and payrolls in their respective states.

HB 434 also provides that multi-state corporations that sell intangible property or services will be sourced to where the intangible property is used or where the service is delivered. This change would again reduce the amount of company income that is sourced to Alabama to be taxed when the company has relatively greater sales of intangible property or services to non-Alabama purchasers.

BCA is monitoring this legislation.

On a vote of 90-4, the Alabama House also passed HB 548, also by Rep. Love, which is supported by the BCA and the Business Association Tax Coalition (BATC) as the more preferable solution to the Department of Revenue's problems with the "gross income regulation." The bill resolves the issue in a fair manner based on sound tax policy, which should not hinder the affected companies that are struggling in this tepid recovery.

Members of the BATC are:

Alabama Association of Life Companies; Alabama Association of Realtors, Inc.; Alabama Bankers Association; Alabama Cable Telecommunications Association; Alabama Concrete Industries Association; Alabama Farmers Federation; Alabama Forestry Association; Alabama Hospital Association; Alabama Independent Insurance Agents, Inc.; Alabama Manufactured Housing Association; Alabama Nursing Home Association;

Alabama Poultry & Egg Association; Alabama Pulp and Paper Council; Alabama Retail Association; Alabama Road Builders Association; Alabama Roofing, Sheet Metal, Heating and Air Conditioning Contractors Association; Alabama Rural Electric Association; Alabama Society of CPAs; Alabama Trucking Association; American Council of Engineering Companies of Alabama; Associated Builders and Contractors of Alabama; Associated General Contractors of Alabama; Automobile Dealers Association of Alabama; Business Council of Alabama; Coalbed Methane Association of Alabama; Home Builders Association of Alabama; Manufacture Alabama; National Federation of Independent Business; and the Petroleum & Convenience Marketers of Alabama.

The department's problems stem from a conflict between a statute and a departmental regulation that define gross income for resident owners of "pass-through" entities that earn income in multiple states. The statute provides that the resident owner report his or her share of the entity's income worldwide, while the regulation provides that the resident owner report his or her share of income earned in Alabama. The regulation coupled with the application of 100 percent of the federal income tax deduction, as provided for by the Alabama Constitution, may greatly reduce or even eliminate the resident owner's Alabama income tax liability.

HB 548 provides clarity and consistency in specifying that the gross income of the resident owners will be their proportionate share of the income of the pass-through entity, regardless of where it is earned. The bill further provides the resident owner will receive an income tax credit equal to his or her proportionate share of income taxes paid on their behalf by the entity to other states or foreign countries.

Both bills now move on to the Senate for consideration.

BCA Members Step Up to Help with Tornado Recovery

Gov. Robert Bentley commended corporate citizens for helping answer the call to help Alabamians in need with donations to the Governor's Emergency Relief Fund. Business Council of Alabama members are among those who have stepped up to make donations, provide resources and offer help in a myriad of ways to their fellow citizens.

Hyundai Motor Manufacturing Alabama is the latest BCA member to contribute to the Fund, with a $1.5 million donation announced today. HMMA President and CEO Y.D. Lim indicated that providing "hope and comfort" was the goal of the gift.

"Our heartfelt sympathy goes out to everyone who lost loved ones in this terrible tragedy and to all of our fellow Alabamians who lost their homes and all of their possessions," said Mr. Lim. "We hope that our humble gift to the Governor's Emergency Relief Fund, which is given on behalf of all Hyundai Motor Company affiliates, will help bring necessary supplies and relief to our fellow citizens as quickly as possible, and that it will provide a measure of hope and comfort to those who are suffering at this time."

BCA member Mercedes-Benz U.S. International's Tuscaloosa plant and its parent company, Daimler AG, announced they were committing $1 million to charities in west and central Alabama. Specifically, they are donating $800,000 to the Tuscaloosa Disaster Relief Fund, $75,000 to the Salvation Army of Greater Birmingham Area, $75,000 to the Birmingham Area Red Cross and $50,000 to United Way of Central Alabama.

BCA member Blue Cross Blue Shield of Alabama has pledged $175,000 to the Governor's Emergency Relief Fund, and Walter Energy followed quickly with $250,000.

Other BCA corporate contributors pledging donations include: HealthSouth, $125,000; Great Southern Wood, $100,000; Norfolk Southern, $100,000 to the American Red Cross in Alabama, Mississippi and Tennessee, free rail transportation for movement of certain critical response supplies and zero-interest loans for employees who suffered property damage; AT&T, $75,000; Maynard, Cooper and Gale, $50,000; State Farm Insurance, $50,000; Farmers Insurance, $50,000, Navistar, $50,000; and Protective Life Insurance, $15,000.

"I am proud of our members who have generously given to help those in our state who need it most," said BCA President and CEO William Canary. "Their willingness to step up and show their support in tangible ways is an inspiration to all Alabamians."

Gov. Bentley also spoke highly of the corporate contributions. "The generosity of these companies should shine as a bright light to all of us, showing what giving hearts can achieve," he said. "These gifts will reach down to our communities and our neighbors and help them in this time of desperate need."

The purpose of the Governor's Emergency Relief Fund is to provide help to Alabamians who have exhausted all other avenues of disaster relief, such as FEMA, Red Cross, the Salvation Army and any other disaster relief programs. The Fund may receive donations from individuals, businesses and organizations.

"We appreciate our corporate citizens getting behind this effort," Gov. Bentley said. "With widespread devastation across the state, there will be plenty of opportunities for the Governor's Emergency Relief Fund to do good work. Whether you are a large corporation, a small business, or an individual, we all have a role to play in this recovery and renewal."

The Governor's Office of Faith-Based and Community Initiatives administers the Fund. The United Ways of Alabama serve as the fiscal agent. Donations to the Governor's Emergency Relief Fund are tax deductible and can be made by clicking www.servealabama.gov.

Dial Briefs BCA Committee on Process for Reapportionment

In his role as co-chairman of the Permanent Legislative Committee on Reapportionment, Sen. Gerald Dial, R-Lineville, on Tuesday briefed the BCA Governmental Affairs Committee about the process Alabama will utilize to redesign lines for congressional districts, state board of education districts and, ultimately, House and Senate districts.

Dial said lawmakers will immediately focus on revising districts for congressional and board of education seats while waiting to turn their attention toward legislative reapportionment next year. One reason for the schedule is that congressional candidates will have to qualify and campaign within new districts in 2012 while legislative candidates will not reappear on the ballot again until the 2014 election cycle.

In the very short term, the legislature will take a two-week working recess beginning May 9 and hold a series of five public hearings on redistricting in various venues across the state.

Dial said the committee will review census data along with testimony gathered during the public input period and develop a redistricting plan that legislators will consider immediately upon their return from the working recess.

"We are using the schedule for several reasons, but the most important is that it will save taxpayers' dollars by avoiding the need for a special session on redistricting," Dial said. "Given the financial situation of the state, we felt that calling a special session would be irresponsible."

Another reason for the schedule, according to Dial, is the need to leave ample time for U.S. Justice Department review and approval. Because Alabama is one of a handful of states that continue to fall under the pre-clearance requirements of the 1964 Voting Rights Act, any substantial change to that state's election process must undergo federal review.

A bill sponsored by Rep. Steve Clouse, R-Ozark, would move the 2012 primary elections from June to March and claims widespread support from both major political parties. The bill, which is designed to allow Alabama to play a larger role in the presidential nominee selection process, also moves congressional, judicial and other office primaries to the earlier date, so Dial said early Justice Department approval is even more essential.

"We have asked both the Democratic and Republican caucuses to nominate attorneys who will represent them and actually conduct the public hearings," Dial said. "We have also been advised that our position on redistricting should be 'we are going to be fair to everybody,' but anything we pass will likely wind up being challenged in court."

Dial said that upon lawmakers' return in two weeks, one redistricting plan will originate in the Senate and the other in the House, with both crossing chambers during the process.

"Ultimately, our goal is to see how this process works for congressional and BOE redistricting and to use it as a template when we tackle legislative redistricting next year," Dial added.

Immigration Bill One Step Away from Governor's Signature

A substitute version of HB 56, by Rep. Micky Hammon, R-Decatur, which seeks to curb illegal immigration in Alabama by requiring state and local government officials to enforce federal immigration laws and by cracking down on employers who hire illegal immigrants, passed the Alabama Senate on a party-line vote. The legislation creates specific penalties for employers who "knowingly or intentionally" hire illegal immigrants and closely resembles SB 256, by Sen. Scott Beason, R-Gardendale, that passed the full Senate last month.

The original HB 56 would have required every Alabama business to utilize the federal E-verify program by January 1, 2012 to ensure they are hiring legal workers and maintain a record of the verification for up to three years. The substitute bill does not mandate that an employer utilize the E-Verify program unless he or she wants to do business with the state. Instead, it allows for other forms of identification, such as a valid Alabama driver's license or any valid U.S. government-issued identification document to verify and document the legal status of workers.

Employers seeking state contracts, grants or incentives must submit a sworn affidavit attesting to the fact that they are not knowingly employing illegal immigrants, in addition to utilizing the E-Verify program. The substitute HB 56 includes a "whistle blower" provision that would award 50 percent of the damages collected by the courts to the person who reported the violation. Employers found by the courts to have knowingly hired an illegal immigrant would be subject to penalties; however, employers who can prove they utilize the E-Verify system to verify their workers would be immune from prosecution.

HB 56 now returns to the House where members will either agree to the changes and send the bill to the Governor, or non-concur and leave the fate of the legislation to a six-member conference committee.

BCA staff will continue to work with the bill's sponsors to ensure that employers are not unfairly burdened or penalized.

Senate Panel Approves Alabama Tax Appeals Commission/ Taxpayers' Bill of Rights II

HB 427, by Rep. Paul DeMarco, R-Homewood, was favorably reported from the Senate Judiciary Committee this week. The legislation has been listed on the *BCA Legislative Agenda* for several years and combines provisions for updating the original Alabama Taxpayers' Bill of Rights act and provisions to create an independent tax appeals tribunal, often referred to as the Alabama Tax Appeals Commission (ATAC).

The bill separates the tax appeals function from the Alabama Department of Revenue and is intended to give taxpayers more confidence that their tax appeals will be adjudicated in a fair and impartial manner by eliminating its connection to the department.

Based on the committee's discussion, however, some senators may want to make changes in the composition of the nominating committee and in the process used to appoint the chief judge.

Among the many provisions included in the legislation, the bill will: 1) allow taxpayers to appeal final tax assessments from self-administered cities and counties (and their private auditing firms), unless the governing body of the locality opts out; 2) extend the period that a taxpayer can appeal a preliminary or final assessment from 30 to 60 days; 3) conform to two sets of federal changes to the innocent spouse rule; 4) increase the penalties for negligence, fraud, frivolous returns and appeals to conform with federal law; and 5) correct the statute that imposes a minimum $50 penalty for late filing, even when the taxpayer owes no tax.

BCA supports this legislation.

Proposed Constitutional Amendment to Extend Forever Wild Passes Senate and Now Goes to the House

The Senate on Wednesday came to a halt as the chamber considered SB 369, by Sen. Scott Beason, R-Gardendale, which would have extended for 20 years the state's popular Forever Wild program.

Sen. Gerald Dial, R-Lineville, used procedural tactics to delay and stall a vote, and after several hours of debate on Wednesday, the Senate adjourned without taking a vote.

On Thursday, the Senate passed by a vote of 34-23 a revised version of the bill, a proposed amendment to the state constitution. Reauthorization of Forever Wild for an additional 20 years would be left to Alabama voters to decide on November 6, 2012. A three-fifths vote of the House is required for the amendment to appear on the ballot.

Forever Wild was established by constitutional amendment in 1992 with 83 percent voter support, the highest level of public support ever recorded for any state legislation establishing a government land acquisition program. This program receives payments into the Forever Wild Land Trust for acquisition of lands for public use.

Alabama's largest economic business is tourism. Hunting, fishing and wildlife viewing in Alabama has a $2.2 billion annual economic impact that benefits both local communities and the state. Forever Wild, since its inception, has preserved more than 200,000 acres of wilderness for hunting, fishing, bird-watching and other outdoor activities.

BCA supports the reauthorization of Forever Wild.

Job Creation Legislation Appears to Have Strong Support

The bills known as the Jobs Creation and Retention Act continued to move through the legislative process this week. If enacted, the bill would provide the state with an additional tool to attract, retain and expand industry and jobs in Alabama.

HB 478, by Rep. Barry Mask, R-Wetumpka, passed the House on a vote of 99-0, and its companion SB 373, by Sen. Phil Williams, R-Rainbow City, was favorably reported from the House Economic Development & Tourism Committee. The measure allows new and expanding industry and higher educational institutions to retain as much as 90 percent of state income tax withholdings from employees associated with the project that the company or university may use to pay the costs of constructing or equipping the new facility.

The legislation is similar to incentives offered by Kentucky, Georgia and Mississippi, and proponents contend it is needed to keep the state competitive with those states in attracting industry.

The heads of the Alabama Development Office and the Department of Revenue will negotiate the extent of the incentive to be offered on an individual project basis. Up to 90 percent of the employees' withheld taxes may be retained by the company for new and expansion projects, while up to 75 percent of the withheld taxes may be retained for projects deemed to retain jobs. The employees associated with the project will receive state income tax credits for the taxes withheld. Once the company recoups the costs of its capital investment, the employees' taxes will no longer be retained. Failure by a company to meet its agreed-upon jobs level or capital investment requirements could result in the state recapturing the withholding incentives or terminating the agreement.

BCA supports this legislation.

Senate Committee Approves Bill to Change Presidential Primary Date

The Senate Constitution and Elections Committee on Tuesday unanimously approved HB 425, by Rep. Steve Clouse, R-Ozark, that would change the presidential primary to the second Tuesday in March beginning in 2012, a move that would save the state nearly $4 million in fiscal year 2012.

The bill also deletes language in the statute that allows for the reimbursement of counties who recognize Mardi Gras as a holiday, should the primary election fall on Mardi Gras. This will save the state an additional $250,000.

Non-presidential primary elections will continue to be held on the first Tuesday in June, and Alabama now will have one less election in 2012 and every fourth year thereafter.

Currently, Alabama holds its presidential primary on the first Tuesday in February during presidential election years. During the 2006 legislative session, lawmakers passed a bill with the hope that Alabama would have more influence in the presidential nominating process. Legislatures from around the country had the same idea in 2006, and many states moved their primaries to the first Tuesday in February; Alabama, however, did not garner the influence it had hoped.

Rep. Clouse told committee members this week the original 2006 bill was passed in a bipartisan manner, and during these austere budget times, it was important to save the state the extra $4 million for fiscal year 2012. The House passed the bill on April 26, by a vote of 99-1. It now goes before the full Senate. If passed, the 2012 Republican and Democratic primaries would be held March 13, 2012.

Environmental Bills Update

HB 50, by Rep. Greg Canfield, R-Vestavia Hills, passed the Senate Thursday. Sen. Del Marsh, R-Anniston, sponsors the companion bill, SB 80. HB 50 amends the solid waste laws by removing an existing exemption from regulation fly ash waste, bottom ash waste, boiler slag waste and flue gas emissions control wastes from the burning of coal or other fossil fuels at electric generating plants. It also authorizes the Alabama Department of Environmental Management (ADEM) to regulate these wastes, once the federal EPA promulgates federal policy on management of such waste. BCA supports this legislation.

HB 106, by Rep. Steve Clouse, R-Ozark, passed the House Thursday and goes to the Senate. HB 106 amends state laws pertaining to civil penalties for violations of state environmental protection laws and orders, by removing minimum penalty amounts for certain violations and limiting the penalties for violations subject to monthly reporting based on average compliance, to not more frequently than once a month.

HB 406, by Rep. Alan Baker, R-Brewton, passed the Senate Thursday and goes to the Governor. HB 406 would set a two-year moratorium on the permitting of "new" commercial Subtitle D or Construction & Demolition waste landfills. During the two-year period, ADEM and the Alabama Department of Public Health will review their programs and propose legislation or update regulations as needed.

BCA President Touts Business-Education Alliance at Alabama Governor's STEM Summit

BCA President and CEO William Canary offered the keynote address at the Alabama Governor's Science, Technology, Engineering and Mathematics (STEM) Summit in Montgomery, which is hosted annually by the Alabama Math, Science, Technology and Engineering Coalition (AMSTEC). The Summit's goal is to bridge workforce needs, economic development and effective education.

In addressing the coalition of business and education leaders, Canary highlighted the importance of programs such as the Alabama Math, Science and Technology Initiative (AMSTI) to student achievement. "There are some in Alabama politics who wish to divide business and education by selling fear, but those of you gathered here today are advocates for hope. By supporting programs such as AMSTI, we are providing hope to our students and our future workforce."

Canary said that the STEM Summit is another great example of the success of a Business Education Alliance, and he thanked those BCA member companies such as Boise, The Boeing Co., Austal USA, Alabama Power and Michelin North America, among others, for their support of the STEM Summit and AMSTEC.

Following Canary's remarks, John Tully, on behalf of Michelin North America, received recognition for Michelin's longstanding support of AMSTEC.

Washington Briefing

Offshore Drilling Bill Passes House

The House on Thursday passed H.R. 1230, the Restarting American Offshore Leasing Now Act, sponsored by U.S. Rep. Doc Hastings (R-WA) by a vote of 266-149.

The bill would accelerate the offshore permitting process for the Gulf of Mexico and would require the Department of Interior to conduct four offshore oil and gas lease sales that were canceled or delayed since the moratorium: three in the Gulf of Mexico and one in the Mid-Atlantic region (Virginia).

Next week, the House is expected to consider H.R. 1229, Putting the Gulf of Mexico Back to Work Act, and H.R. 1231, Reversing President Obama's Offshore Moratorium Act.

BCA joined with more than 40 groups from across the country in calling for passage of these bills, which will expand American energy production, create jobs and lower prices.

NLRB Seeks to Determine Where Companies Can Locate

Alabama Attorney General Luther Strange, along with seven other state attorneys general, sent a letter calling on the National Labor Relations Board to withdraw its complaint made against Boeing last month.

On April 20, the NLRB filed a complaint against Boeing, alleging it violated federal labor law by opening an aircraft production facility in South Carolina, a right-to-work state. The NLRB claimed the jobs should have gone to Boeing's existing Washington state-based plant, which is unionized.

The letter of the attorneys general to the NLRB stated, "Our states are struggling to emerge from one of the worst economic collapses since the Depression. Your complaint further impairs an economic recovery. Intrusion by the federal bureaucracy on behalf of unions will not create a single new job or put one unemployed person back to work.... Your action seriously undermines our citizens' right to work as well as their ability to compete globally. Therefore, as Attorneys General, we will protect our citizens from union bullying and federal coercion. We thus call on you to cease this attack on our right to work, our states' economies, and our jobs."

If successful with the complaint, the NLRB effectively would set the precedent of prohibiting companies from expanding in right-to-work states.

Strange described the dispute as "an incredibly important issue for Alabama as a right-to-work state." He called the NLRB complaint "a direct threat to the kind of businesses climate Alabama needs to recruit industry and thrive."

On Tuesday, May 3, U.S. Sens. Lamar Alexander (R-TN), Lindsey Graham (R-SC) and Jim DeMint (R-SC) announced plans to introduce the Right to Work Protection Act, to prevent the NLRB from taking such action.

House Votes to Repeal Funding for Health Insurance Exchanges

The House on Tuesday voted 238-183 to pass H.R. 1213 which would repeal mandatory funding provided to states in the Patient Protection and Affordable Care Act for the creation and facilitation of state-based health insurance exchanges. However, H.R. 1213 would not prevent the federal government from running an exchange in a state that does not establish its own. The White House has threatened to veto the bill.

As part of the *2011 BCA Federal Agenda*, the BCA supports efforts to repeal the PPACA in its entirety.

Chapter 13
May 27, 2011
'Students First Act' Becomes Law

Gov. Robert Bentley has signed into law the "Students First Act," which overhauls the state's teacher tenure and fair dismissal law. The House of Representatives on Wednesday evening gave final approval to SB 310 by a vote of 56-43. No amendments were added.

"In a global economy, businesses understand the future is now," said BCA President and CEO William J. Canary. "Our students need the best teachers and the best education to compete in a worldwide market that demands a superior workforce. SB 310 is yet another step in the right direction in education reform to simply overcome the status quo."

The Students First Act was sponsored by Sen. Trip Pittman, R-Daphne, in the Senate, while its companion bill, HB 465, was sponsored in the House by Rep. Chad Fincher, R-Semmes, assisted by Rep. Steve McMillan, R-Bay Minette. Senators approved the bill in the upper chamber on May 5 by a vote of 18-16 before adjourning for two weeks.

Earlier this week, the House Ways and Means Education Committee held a public hearing on SB 310 before giving the legislation a favorable report. The packed committee room was filled with mostly proponents of the bill. BCA's Canary offered testimony in support of the bill, along with 13 other proponents who spoke. Opponents, composed of Alabama Education Association and American Federation of Teachers representatives, could only turn out four people to speak against the reform measure. The common theme from the AEA and AFT was "keep the status quo." This sentiment, repeated multiple times, clearly fell on deaf ears of the reform-minded education budget committee who voted 9-5 to send the bill to the full House.

Committee members voting FOR the Students First Act were:

Rep. Jay Love, R-Montgomery; Rep. Mary Sue McClurkin, R-Pelham; Rep. Terri Collins, R-Decatur; Rep. Jamie Ison, R-Mobile; Rep. Barry Mask, R-Wetumpka; Rep. Steve McMillan, R-Bay Minette; Rep. Bill Poole, R-Tuscaloosa; Rep. Mark Tuggle, R-Alexander City; and Rep. Phil Williams, R-Huntsville.

Committee members voting AGAINST the Students First Act were:

Rep. Jeremy Oden, R-Vinemont; Rep. Craig Ford, D-Gadsden; Rep. James Buskey, D-Mobile; Rep. Alan Harper, D-Aliceville; and Rep. Rod Scott, D-Fairfield.

Last Wednesday, the BCA, along with legislative leaders and education officials, called on the House to approve the legislation without any amendments to the bill. Even the smallest change to SB 310 would have meant that it would be returned to the Senate, where opposition had vowed to kill the reform. BCA, Alabama Association of School Boards, School Superintendents of Alabama, the Department of Education and the Department of Postsecondary Education worked as a team to ensure final passage.

Under the Students First Act, teacher tenure is protected and strengthened, but changes were made to the appeals process for fired teachers. A teacher may now appeal his or her firing to the local school board, removing the lengthy and expensive federal arbitration process that continued to pay ineffective teachers, often for years, and on at least one occasion while a former teacher was serving a prison sentence.

Should the local school board uphold the termination, the teacher may appeal to a hearing officer who is chosen from a group of retired judges, selected by the executive director of the Alabama State Bar. The process of

BCA President and CEO William Canary spoke at a public hearing on the Students First Act.

continuing to pay fired teachers while they drag out an appeal for a year or more will now be replaced by a 75-day severance pay.

"The Alabama House of Representatives has voted for excellence in our classrooms," said Robert Powers, chairman of BCA's Education and Workforce Preparedness Committee and president of The Eufaula Agency. "The days of mediocrity and the status quo in some of our classrooms are over."

The State Board of Education also endorsed the passage of SB 310 after they passed a resolution on April 28 by a vote of 6-1.

BCA is especially grateful to House Speaker Mike Hubbard and Senate President Pro Tem Del Marsh for their support in ensuring passage of the legislation.

Representatives voting FOR the Students First Act were:

Speaker Mike Hubbard, R-Auburn; Rep. Alan Baker, R-Brewton; Rep. Mike Ball, R-Madison; Rep. Jim Barton, R-Mobile; Rep. Richard Baughn, R-Lynn; Rep. Paul Beckman, R-Prattville; Rep. Alan Boothe, R-Troy; Rep. Duwayne Bridges, R-Valley; Rep. K.L. Brown, R-Anniston; Rep. Mac Buttram, R-Cullman; Rep. Greg Canfield, R-Vestavia Hills; Rep. Donnie Chesteen, R-Geneva; Rep. Steve Clouse, R-Ozark; Rep. Randy Davis, R-Daphne; Rep. Paul DeMarco, R-Homewood; Rep. Allen Farley, R-McCalla; Rep. Joe Faust, R-Fairhope; Rep. Chad Fincher, R-Semmes; Rep. Blaine Galliher, R-Gadsden; Rep. Victor Gaston, R-Mobile; Rep. Lynn Greer, R-Rogersville; Rep. Micky Hammon, R-Decatur; Rep. Ed Henry, R-Hartselle; Rep. Mike Hill, R-Columbiana; Rep. Jamie Ison, R-Mobile; Rep. Ken Johnson, R-Moulton; Rep. Ron Johnson, R-Sylacauga; Rep. Wayne Johnson, R-Huntsville; Rep. Mike Jones, R-Andalusia; Rep. Paul Lee, R-Dothan; Rep. Wes Long, R-Guntersville; Rep. Jay Love, R-Montgomery; Rep. Barry Mask, R-Wetumpka; Rep. Jim McClendon, R-Springville; Rep. Mary Sue McClurkin, R-Pelham; Rep. Mac McCutcheon, R-Capshaw; Rep. Steve McMillan, R-Bay Minette; Rep. John Merrill, R-Tuscaloosa; Rep. Barry Moore, R-Enterprise; Rep. Charles Newton, D-Greenville; Rep. Jim Patterson, R-Meridianville; Rep. Bill Poole, R-Tuscaloosa; Rep. Kerry Rich, R-Albertville; Rep. Bill Roberts, R-Jasper; Rep. Howard Sanderford, R-Huntsville; Rep. Harry Shiver, R-Bay Minette; Rep. Allen Treadaway, R-Morris; Rep. Mark Tuggle, R-Alexander City; Rep. Kurt Wallace, R-Maplesville; Rep. Dan Williams, R-Athens; Rep. Jack Williams, R-Birmingham; Rep. Phil Williams, R-Huntsville; Rep. Randy Wood, R-Anniston; and Rep. Greg Wren, R-Montgomery.

Representatives voting AGAINST the Students First Act were: Rep. Jeremy Oden, R-Vinemont; Rep. Elwyn Thomas, R-Oneonta; Rep. Todd Greeson, R-Ider; Rep. Steve Hurst, R-Talladega; Rep. Mike Millican, R-Hamilton; Rep. Arthur Payne, R-Trussville; Rep. George Bandy, D-Opelika; Rep. Elaine Beech, D-Chatom; Rep. Marcel Black, D-Tuscumbia; Rep. Daniel Boman, D-Sulligent; Rep. Barbara Boyd, D-Anniston; Rep. Napoleon Bracy, D-Mobile; Rep. Greg Burdine, D-Florence; Rep. James Buskey, D-Mobile; Rep. Merika Coleman, D-Midfield; Rep. David Colston, D-Hayneville; Rep. Chris England, D-Tuscaloosa; Rep. Craig Ford, D-Gadsden; Rep. Barry Forte, D-Eufaula; Rep. Juandalynn Givan, D-Birmingham; Rep. Dexter Grimsley, D-Newville; Rep. Laura Hall, D-Huntsville; Rep. Alan Harper, D-Aliceville; Rep. Alvin Holmes, D-Montgomery; Rep. Ralph Howard, D-Greensboro; Rep. Joe Hubbard, D-Montgomery; Rep. Thomas Jackson, D-Thomasville; Rep. Yvonne Kennedy, D-Mobile; Rep. John Knight, D-Montgomery; Rep. Richard Laird, D-Roanoke; Rep. Richard Lindsey, D-Centre; Rep. Artis McCampbell, D-Gallion; Rep. Thad McClammy, D-Montgomery; Rep. Darrio Melton, D-Selma; Rep. Joseph Mitchell, D-Mobile; Rep. Mary Moore, D-Birmingham; Rep. Jonny Mack Morrow, D-Red Bay; Rep. Demetrius Newton, D-Birmingham; Rep. John Robinson, D-Scottsboro; Rep. Oliver Robinson, D-Birmingham; Rep. John Rogers, D-Birmingham; Rep. Rod Scott, D-Fairfield; Rep. Patricia Todd, D-Birmingham; and Rep. Pebblin Warren, D-Shorter.

Representatives ABSENT or NOT VOTING: Rep. Terri Collins, R-Decatur; Rep. Becky Nordgren, R-Gadsden; Rep. Lesley Vance, R-Phenix City; Rep. April Weaver, R-Brierfield; Rep. Lawrence McAdory, D-Bessemer; and Rep. Owen Drake, R-Leeds.

House Sends Three Tort Reform Bills to Governor

On Thursday, the House passed SB 59, SB 207 and SB 212, which are a part of the tort reform package passed by the Senate last month.

SB 59, sponsored by Sen. Cam Ward, R-Alabaster, would decrease the statute of repose for commencing a civil action against an architect, engineer or builder from 13 years to seven years. The bill received final approval by a vote of 70-23.

SB 207, also sponsored by Sen. Ward, would provide that judgments, other than judgments based on a contract action, would bear a flat rate of 7 percent. The bill received final approval by a vote of 70-19.

SB 212, by Sen. Clay Scofield, R-Guntersville, would provide that a wrongful death action may only be filed in a county where the deceased could have filed a civil action, if living, and added that Rule 82 of the Rules of Civil Procedure would continue to apply to wrongful death actions. The bill received final approval by a vote of 71-22.

On Thursday, House Rules Committee Chairman Blaine Galliher, R-Gadsden, was notified that all objections had been removed from SB 187, which is also a part of the tort reform package.

SB 187, sponsored by Sen. Ben Brooks, R-Mobile, would require the federal expert witness rule, known as the "Daubert Standard," be applied in Alabama and be limited to scientific evidence. The U.S. Supreme Court mandated the Daubert standard in all federal courts in 1993; however, Alabama remains one of the final states that has not adopted the rule. SB 187 will be considered on the House floor next Tuesday as part of an economic development and legal reform special order calendar.

Tort reform has been a priority of the BCA's Legal and Judicial Reform Committee *Legislative Agenda* for the last several years.

Governor to Decide Fate of Budgets

The Alabama House and Senate gave their approval to compromise versions of a $5.588 billion education budget and a $1.767 billion general fund budget for Fiscal Year 2012. With both budgets predicated on several bills that have yet to pass the legislature, Gov. Robert Bentley is withholding any judgment on what specific actions he may take during the final four days of the current legislative session. It is clear, however, that of the two budgets that await his signature, the governor has serious concerns with the general fund spending plan.

The budget proposes to spend a total of $180 million more from the state general fund than in the current fiscal year, but $53.5 million less than the total recommended by the governor. The conference committee felt compelled to reduce the appropriations of the non-judicial agencies as originally passed by the House in an effort to increase the appropriation to the Department of Corrections by $25.8 million. Despite the additional funding for Corrections, the finance director expressed doubts that the agency will have sufficient funding next year because bills crafted to save money by revamping sentencing laws and controlling the costs of indigent defense remain doubtful for passage. Even the Medicaid Agency, whose funding the legislature usually protects at a premium, was reduced by the conference committee by more than $9.7 million, raising concerns that the Medicaid Agency also will be underfunded next fiscal year.

The House- and Senate-passed versions of the education budget had relatively minor differences before being assigned to conference. The education budget was reported from conference with funding increases of $1 million added to Auburn University's Agricultural Experiment Station, $1.1 million to Auburn's Cooperative Extension System and $1 million to the University of South Alabama's Cancer Center.

The conference committee retained the major change made by the two houses to the governor's budget, which involved increasing K-12 transportation funding by $25 million, adding $10 million to protect support worker positions and funding an estimated 1,125 less state-funded teachers. The state superintendent of education deems the reduction in teacher units acceptable, due to the nearly 1,500 teachers who retire statewide each year.

House Passes Redistricting Plan for State Board of Education

The House of Representatives on Thursday night approved a bill that would redraw the state's eight Board of Education districts. The plan was approved by a vote of 64-33. The biggest changes to the current districts are in south and west Alabama, changes that also have caused the most contention between senators and representatives. District Five is represented by Democrat Ella Bell and covers a portion of Montgomery and most of the Black Belt. District One is represented by Republican Randy McKinney who currently represents the two Gulf Coast counties and Escambia County.

Under the plan approved by the House, Ella Bell would lose a portion of Montgomery County and pick up a sizeable portion of Mobile County. Randy McKinney would lose his portion of Mobile County and pick up the four counties of Conecuh, Covington, Crenshaw and Butler. Legislators from the Mobile area have expressed concern about having a representative who lives in Montgomery but who represents portions of Mobile County.

Montgomery area legislators also are concerned about having three members represent them. Under the proposed plan, Stephanie Bell, Ella Bell and Betty Peters of Dothan would represent Montgomery County. Currently, only Stephanie Bell and Ella Bell represent Montgomery County.

School board districts in North Alabama would largely remain the same. A hot-button issue raised by Sen. Bill Holtzclaw, R-Madison, put Limestone and Madison counties into two different districts. Under a revised plan worked out in committee, a portion of Limestone County that covers the city of Athens and Athens State University was redrawn to be in District Eight, represented by Republican Mary Scott Hunter of Huntsville. The western portion of Limestone County is now slated to become part of District Seven.

On Thursday, the Senate became locked down in a filibuster by Democrats, and President Pro Tem Del Marsh, R-Anniston, agreed to carry over the redistricting bill. Senators will take up the measure when they return to Montgomery next week.

Business Death Penalty for Hiring Illegals Upheld by U.S. Supreme Court

On Thursday, the U.S. Supreme Court voted 5-3 to affirm the decision of the Ninth Circuit in the case of *Chamber of Commerce of United States of America v. Whiting* to allow for the punishment of employers who deliberately hire illegal immigrants. The U.S. Chamber of Commerce and various business and civil rights organizations (collectively the Chamber) challenged the validity of the Legal Arizona Workers Act that provides, "the licenses of state employers that knowingly or intentionally employ unauthorized aliens may be, and in certain circumstances must be, suspended or revoked." The law also requires the use of E-verify by all Arizona employers. The Chamber argued that, "the state law's license suspension and revocation provisions were both expressly and impliedly preempted by federal immigration law, and the mandatory use of E-Verify was impliedly preempted."

Chief Justice John Roberts, writing for the majority, concluded that the Arizona's licensing law is not expressly preempted, and that while federal law prohibits states from imposing "civil or criminal sanctions" on those who employ unauthorized aliens, it preserves state authority to impose sanctions "through licensing and similar laws." Chief Justice Roberts further wrote that, "license termination is not an available sanction for merely hiring unauthorized workers but is triggered only by far more egregious violations. Because the Arizona law covers only knowing or intentional violations, an employer acting in good faith need not fear the law sanctions (Emphasis added)."

The Court also upheld Arizona's use of E-Verify, asserting that employers enjoy safe harbor from liability when using E-Verify and that the law requires no more than that of an employer after hiring an employee. By not using E-Verify an "employer forfeits an otherwise available rebuttable presumption of compliance with the law."

Many states have enacted similar "business death penalty" legislation or are in the process of giving final approval to legislation, including Alabama. HB 56 by Rep. Micky Hammon, R-Decatur, creates specific penalties for employers who "knowingly or intentionally" hire illegal immigrants and is in the hands of a six-member conference committee composed of Hammon, Rep. Kerry Rich, R-Albertville; Rep. Charles Newton, D-Greenville; Sen. Scott Beason, R-Gardendale; Sen. Rusty Glover, R-Semmes; and Sen. Clay Scofield, R-Guntersville. BCA will continue to monitor the process of the legislation during the remainder of the session and work with the conferees to ensure that the voice of business is heard.

Governor Signs Law Guaranteeing Funding for Ethics Commission

Gov. Robert Bentley has signed a bill into law that guarantees future funding for the Alabama Ethics Commission. The law is aimed at protecting the commission from politicians who might want to stop an ethics investigation.

Ethics Commission Director James L. Sumner Jr. said the law would provide funding for the commission to operate at its current staffing level. With the new law, the agency's funding only can be reduced below the level mandated with a two-thirds vote of the Alabama House and Senate.

"Protecting its budget from political retaliation will help the Ethics Commission be the independent agency it needs to be to keep state and local governments accountable," bill sponsor Rep. Mike Jones, R-Andalusia, told the Associated Press.

Environmental Bills Update

SB 224, by Senate President Pro Tem Del Marsh, R-Anniston, passed the Senate Wednesday and was referred to the House Commerce & Small Business Committee.

Rep. Randy Wood, R-Anniston, sponsored the companion bill, HB 509, and will handle SB 224 as it moves through the House. SB 224 allows the owner of a motor vehicle who no longer possesses its title to transfer the vehicle to an automotive dismantler, parts recycler or a secondary metals recycler, if certain conditions are met. The conditions include requiring the owner to sign a statement attesting to the ownership, value and identifying characteristics of the motor vehicle. The BCA Environment & Energy Committee adopted this legislation as part of its *Legislative Agenda* during Committee Days. BCA supports this legislation.

On Wednesday, the House Economic Development and Tourism Committee gave a favorable report to SB 369, by Sen. Dick Brewbaker, R-Pike Road, that proposes an amendment to the Constitution of Alabama of 1901 to reauthorize the Forever Wild program for an additional 20 years. The amendment would be subject to a statewide vote November 6, 2012. A three-fifths vote of the House is required for the amendment to appear on the ballot.

BCA supports the reauthorization of Forever Wild.

Senate OKs Presidential Primary Date Change

By a vote of 21-11, the Senate on Thursday approved HB 425, by Rep. Steve Clouse, R-Ozark, that would change the presidential primary to the second Tuesday in March beginning in 2012, a move that would save the state nearly $4 million in fiscal year 2012. The bill also deletes language in the statute that allows for the reimbursement of counties that recognize Mardi Gras as a holiday, should the primary election fall on Mardi Gras. This will save the state an additional $250,000. Non-presidential primary elections will continue to be held on the first Tuesday in June, and Alabama will now have one less election in 2012 and every fourth year thereafter.

Currently, Alabama holds its presidential primary on the first Tuesday in February during presidential election years. During the 2006 legislative session, lawmakers passed a bill with the hope that Alabama would have more influence in the presidential nominating process. Legislatures from around the country had the same idea in 2006 and many states moved their primaries to the first Tuesday in February; therefore, Alabama did not garner the influence it had hoped.

Gov. Robert Bentley is expected to sign the bill.

In Other News

Verizon Donates $100,000 To Expand Technology Aimed at Rural Health Care Access

Business Council of Alabama member Verizon presented a $100,000 check last week to Sight Savers America, an Alabama-based non-profit, to expand the use of wireless technology for its award-winning KidCheck Program aimed at improving health care access for children in rural Alabama.

Gov. Robert Bentley, House Speaker Mike Hubbard, R-Auburn, and State School Superintendent Dr. Joe Morton were on hand for the announcement of the grant, along with BCA President and CEO William Canary and Senior Vice President for Intergovernmental Affairs, Advocacy and Communications and Legal Advisor Anita Archie.

Jeff Mango, president of the Georgia/Alabama Region of Verizon Wireless, said the grant has the potential to impact the lives of more than 16,000 Alabama students, particularly in rural areas of Alabama.

"We see the exciting potential of technology to help address disparities in the access to quality health care in rural areas," Mango said. "Verizon is proud to be able to help Sight Savers build on the initial success of Kid-Check. Supporting programs that use technology to improve health care access is among Verizon's top priorities."

Washington Briefing

State Senate Passes New Congressional Map

On Thursday, the Alabama Senate voted 19-11 to pass SB 484, a plan to redraw Alabama's seven congressional districts based on the 2010 census.

On Wednesday, the Senate Government Affairs Committee approved the plan offered by state Rep. Micky Hammon, R-Decatur, which the Joint Committee of Legislative Redistricting had green lighted last week.

Following nearly five hours of debate, state Sen. Scott Beason, R-Gardendale, presented a substitute bill similar to the one passed out of committee; however, under the Beason substitute all of Chilton County and much of western Coosa County would move from the 6th to the 3rd congressional district. Additionally, all of Pickens County would be added to the 7th District.

The plan now moves to the House.

House Committee OKs $1B Disaster Aid Package

The House Appropriations Committee gave final approval to the Department of Homeland Security's Appropriations bill on Tuesday.

An amendment, offered by U.S. Rep. Robert Aderholt (R-AL), chairman of the Homeland Security subcommittee, added $1 billion in disaster aid for those affected by the recent tornadoes and flooding of the Mississippi River. Under the amendment, the funding was offset with cuts to the Department of Energy Alternative Technology Vehicle loans.

The bill is expected to be approved by the full House and will then move to the Senate.

BCA Joins Multi-Industry Coalition Urging House To Keep Politics Out of Federal Contracting

The Business Council of Alabama joined a multi-industry coalition of 70 associations and chambers of commerce, led by the U.S. Chamber of Commerce, in writing a letter in support of the Cole amendment.

Rep. Tom Cole (R-OK) filed an amendment to the Department of Defense Reauthorization legislation (H.R. 1540) in response to the draft Executive Order under consideration by the Obama administration. The amendment would preclude the White House from requiring federal agencies to demand entities to disclose their political spending as a condition of being eligible for a federal contract.

The letter stated, "The Cole amendment would help ensure that political spending — or lack thereof — continues to play no role in federal contracting decisions. The amendment reaffirms the principle, currently embodied in federal procurement laws, that the Executive Branch has an obligation to procure goods and services based on the best value for the American taxpayers, and not on political considerations."

The draft Executive Order, which was leaked in April, has not been finalized, and is part of a broader effort to reduce the effect of the Supreme Court's 2010 *Citizens United v. FEC* decision that held that corporations, unions and nonprofits have the same free speech protections as individuals and can therefore spend money on elections.

The Cole amendment passed by a vote of 261-163.

Senate Rejects Two Budget Plans

The Senate on Wednesday rejected both the House Republican budget as well as the White House budget plan. The FY 2012 budget plan written by U.S. Rep. Paul Ryan (R-WI), chairman of the House Budget Committee, was voted down by a vote of 40-57. The plan, which would overhaul Medicare and Medicaid, has already passed the House.

While the vote on the Ryan budget was largely predicted, the Obama budget failed on a 97-0 vote, receiving no votes at all from either party.

No budget passed Congress last year, and after this week's votes, it is apparent there is still much work to be done if a budget is to be approved this year.

Next week, the House is scheduled to vote on a debt ceiling increase that is not expected to pass.

BCA Small Business Leaders Join U.S. Chamber in Rally for Small Business

Leaders of BCA's Small Business Committee participated in the U.S. Chamber of Commerce Small Business Summit this week in Washington D.C. Chairman Rick Roden, director of the Greater Jackson County Chamber of Commerce in Scottsboro, Co-Chairman Ron Perkins of Doozer Software in Birmingham and Mark Colson, BCA chief of staff met with small business owners, state and local chamber professionals and other key stakeholders from across the country.

The summit, which featured some of the nation's most prominent small business advocates, political leaders and thought provokers, emphasized "Putting America Back to Work," acknowledging that small businesses create the majority of jobs in America and if not hindered by government interference, will lead the economic recovery.

Perkins recently joined former BCA Chairman David Muhlendorf, CEO of Paper and Chemical Supply of Sheffield, as a member of the U.S. Chamber of Commerce's Council on Small Business. The council unites small business owners from across the nation to drive the U.S. Chamber's small business strategy and policy decisions.

The BCA continues to be a leading advocate for small business in both Alabama and Washington D.C. During the current Alabama legislative session, BCA was instrumental in passing a tax deduction for small businesses that provide health insurance to their employees. At the federal level, BCA successfully partnered with the U.S. Chamber for the repeal of the 1099 provision within the 2010 Patient Protection and Affordable Care Act. The BCA continues to recognize that small businesses provide the majority of Alabamians' jobs and that protecting entrepreneurial efforts sustains job growth in the short and long run.

Chapter 14

June 3, 2011

BCA-Backed Tort Reform Package Approved

The Alabama Legislature this week completed work on a five-bill tort reform package. For almost two decades, tort reform has been a priority of the BCA's Legal and Judicial Reform Committee, and the five bills now go to Gov. Robert Bentley for signature.

"For a state whose courts were once cited as 'judicial hellholes,' passage of these bills is a significant step towards restoring a measure of predictability and fairness to Alabama's civil justice system," said BCA President and CEO William Canary. "These bills were not allowed to see the light of day in past sessions, and we commend the legislature for working to ensure due process for each and every Alabama business."

BCA Board Chairman William W. Brooke agreed: "The BCA commends Speaker Mike Hubbard, R-Auburn, Senate President Pro Tem Del Marsh, R-Anniston, Sen. Ben Brooks, R-Mobile, Sen. Cam Ward, R-Alabaster, and Rep. Paul DeMarco, R-Homewood, for their leadership in making tort reform a priority for this legislature. The passage of this tort reform package sends a strong message that Alabama is open for business — open for new business and new jobs — and is no longer a haven for lawsuits."

The package:

- SB 59, sponsored by Sen. Cam Ward R-Alabaster, and Rep. Wes Long, R-Guntersville, would decrease the statute of repose for commencing a civil action against an architect, engineer or builder from 13 years to seven years. The bill received final approval by the House last week by a vote of 70-23.

- SB 207, sponsored by Sen. Ward, R-Alabaster, and Rep. Greg Canfield, R-Vestavia Hills, would provide that judgments, other than judgments based on a contract action, would bear a flat rate of 7 percent. The bill received final approval last week by a vote of 70-19.

- SB 212, by Sen. Clay Scofield, R-Guntersville, and Rep. Ron Johnson, R-Sylacauga, would provide that a wrongful death action may only be filed in a county where the deceased could have filed a civil action, if living, and added that Rule 82 of the Rules of Civil Procedure would continue to apply to wrongful death actions. The bill received final approval last week by a vote of 71-22.

- SB 187, sponsored by Sen. Ben Brooks, R-Mobile, and Rep. Steve McMillan, R-Bay Minette, would require the federal expert witness rule, known as the "Daubert Standard," be applied in Alabama and be limited to scientific evidence. The U.S. Supreme Court mandated the Daubert standard in all federal courts in 1993; until the bill's passage, Alabama was one of the final states that had not adopted the rule. SB 187 passed the House on Tuesday by a vote of 69-26; however, the House adopted an amendment, offered by Rep. Mike Jones, R-Andalusia, to exempt certain criminal and domestic abuse cases from the Daubert standard. The Senate concurred with the amendment on Wednesday.

- SB 184, by Sen. Brooks, R-Mobile, and Rep. Wes Long, R-Guntersville, would protect retailers, wholesalers and other distributors of products from being sued in product liability actions where the product comes in a "sealed container." The bill only protects retailers from the "innocent conduit" situations. SB 184 received final approval on Tuesday by a vote of 65-25.

Two Job Creation Bills Pass; Governor Expected to Sign Both

HB 230, by Rep. Blaine Galliher, R-Gadsden, known as the Full Employment Act, and SB 477, by Sen. Mark Keahey, D-Grove Hill, known as the Tariff Credit Act, passed the legislature on Thursday and have been forwarded to the governor for his signature. The bills represent two approaches to spur job creation in Alabama, on which many of the state's leaders had promised to focus at the beginning of the session.

HB 230 would provide to employers of 50 or fewer employees a one-time income tax credit, beginning in the current tax year, equal to $1,000 for each new job that is created that pays at least $10 per hour, after the employee has completed 12 consecutive months of employment.

SB 477 offers a tax credit during the period before the project becomes operational to foreign-based companies that are subject to tariffs imposed by the U.S. government. Eligible projects are for industrial, warehouse or research purposes with at least $100 million of capital investment that hire at least 100 new employees in Alabama. The taxpayer company (or if the credit is transferred to a transferee taxpayer) will receive a credit against state corporate income tax, individual income tax or financial institutions excise tax, as appropriate, to recoup the lesser of 25 percent or up to $20 million of the capital investment. The tariff credit is not affected or reduced if the company also qualifies for the existing capital credit. Failure to maintain target employment levels can result in claw backs by the state. No new tariff credits will be allowed after December 31, 2015, unless the credit is extended by a joint resolution of the legislature.

BCA supported these bills.

Fate of Budgets on Hold Until Final Legislative Day

With only one legislative day remaining in the current session, the state budgets remain in limbo awaiting the passage of bills that support both spending plans. A bill to require state employees and educators to pay a larger portion of their retirement costs, which supports both budgets, as well as a bill that supports the general fund budget that reforms the system for indigent defense, are both currently in conference committees.

Gov. Robert Bentley returned the General Fund Budget, SB 133, by Sen. Arthur Orr, R-Decatur, with an executive amendment that primarily added $3.3 million in funding from the General Fund to the state Medicaid Agency. The Senate adopted the executive amendment, but the House will take up the issue on the final day.

The governor has not submitted an executive amendment for the education budget, HB 123, by Rep. Jay Love, R-Montgomery, but is waiting to see if all supporting legislation passes before he signs the spending plan.

Environmental Bills Update

BCA-supported Salvage Vehicle Bill Goes to Governor for Signature; Good for Jobs, Good for Environment

The metal recycling industry is one step closer to being rid of unnecessary and burdensome regulations, thanks to House passage of SB 224, by Senate President Pro Tem Del Marsh, R-Anniston. A priority of the BCA Environment and Energy Committee, the bill is designed to increase the number of scrap vehicles and expedite the process for recycling them. Scrap vehicles that are not recycled may leak fluids into the environment or cause blight in communities.

The measure passed the House on Thursday night by a vote of 98-0, with an amendment that alleviated concerns of law enforcement. Rep. Randy Wood, R-Anniston, who sponsored the House companion bill, was out of town, so Rep. Mac McCutcheon, R-Capshaw, handled the bill on the House floor. Rep. McCutcheon's efforts to reach an agreement with law enforcement were critical to the bill's success. Rep. Allen Treadaway, R-Morris, who is a Birmingham police officer, worked with BCA members to draft an amendment that places a 48-hour hold time on cars more than 12 years old, are sold without a title, are bought by crushers and shredders, and are sold for scrap. SB 224 allows the owner of a motor vehicle who no longer possesses its title to transfer the vehicle to an automotive dismantler, parts recycler or a secondary metals recycler, if certain conditions are met. The conditions include requiring the owner to sign a statement attesting to the ownership, value and identifying characteristics of the vehicle. Several members of BCA and other interested parties worked with the Alabama Department of Revenue and other parties on the legislation. Sen. Marsh and Rep. Wood, who put much time and effort into passing the bill, are to be commended for keeping the bill moving and on special order calendars. BCA members affected by this bill were present at the State House to help educate members on the need for the legislation.

Other Environmental Bill News

HB 106, by Rep. Steve Clouse, R-Ozark, passed the Senate this week and went to the governor for his signature. HB 106 amends state laws pertaining to civil penalties for violations of state environmental protection laws and orders by removing the minimum penalty amounts ($100) for certain violations of laws and regulations enforced by the Alabama Department of Environmental Management. BCA supported this legislation.

HB 50, by Rep. Greg Canfield, R-Vestavia Hills, has been signed by the governor and is Act 2011-258. HB 50 amends the solid waste laws by removing an existing exemption from regulation on fly ash waste, bottom ash waste, boiler slag waste and flue gas emissions control wastes from the burning of coal or other fossil fuels at electric generating plants. It authorizes the Alabama Department of Environmental Management (ADEM) to regulate these wastes, once the federal EPA promulgates federal policy on the management of such waste. BCA supported this legislation.

The House has approved by a vote of 78-5 the reauthorization of Forever Wild, the state's program that for 20 years has purchased and preserved land for environmental and recreation purposes. The constitutional amendment must now be approved by voters in a November 6, 2012 referendum. BCA supports the reauthorization of Forever Wild.

Senate to Take Up School Board Redistricting Following Committee Approval of Amendment

The Senate Committee on Governmental Affairs on Tuesday considered HB 621, by Rep. Jim McClendon, R-Springville, which is the House-passed version of a redistricting plan for the State Board of Education. After Rep. McClendon's presentation, Sen. Dick Brewbaker, R-Pike Road, offered an amendment to change the apportionment of Montgomery County from three districts to two districts. McClendon promptly agreed with the Brewbaker amendment as did the committee by a 6-0-1 vote. Sen. Trip Pittman, R-Daphne, told McClendon that had he known he was so willing to take amendments, he would have offered one himself.

Senate President Pro Tem Del Marsh, R-Anniston, told committee members that he wanted them to give the bill a favorable report and settle their differences before he saw the bill on a Special Order Calendar. The committee agreed, and the bill with the Brewbaker amendment was given a favorable report by a 7-0 vote. The bill is expected to come before the full Senate on the final legislative day, June 9.

House Passes Bill Clarifying Ethics Act

The House voted 95-0 on Wednesday to approve SB 222, by Senate President Pro Tem Del Marsh, R-Anniston, and House Speaker Mike

Hubbard, R-Auburn. This bill amends the recently passed ethics act that prohibits a person from offering or giving anything to a public official, public employee or family member to influence official action. To clarify the act and make it effective and enforceable, SB 222 changes the term "corruptly" to "corruptly influencing," to alleviate any questions of vagueness and enforceability. This bill defines the term "corruptly" to mean "act voluntarily, deliberately and dishonestly to either accomplish an unlawful end or result or to use an unlawful method or means to accomplish an otherwise lawful end or result."

SB 222 now goes to the governor, who is expected to sign it into law. BCA supported this legislation.

Governor Signs Order Creating Health Insurance Exchange Study Commission

Gov. Robert Bentley on Thursday issued Executive Order Number 17 creating the Alabama Health Insurance Exchange Study Commission, which will make recommendations on how to move forward with the establishment of the Alabama Health Benefits Exchange.

The governor has charged the Commission with addressing the type of entity that should house the insurance exchange, the make-up of its governing board, an analysis of resources needed for operating and sustaining the Alabama Exchange, the specific functions of the Exchange, and the effects of the interactions between the Alabama Exchange and relevant insurance markets, existing health programs and agencies like Medicaid and Public Health. The business community will have two spots on the commission appointed by the Speaker of the House and the Senate President Pro Tem.

BCA Board Member Bubba Lee Appointed to ABC Board

BCA board member and former BCA Board Chairman Robert W. "Bubba" Lee, chief executive officer of Vulcan, Inc. in Foley, has been reappointed to the Alabama Beverage Control Board. Lee's term will expire April 12, 2016.

Lee was the first recipient of the inaugural Business Council of Alabama Chairman's Award for Leadership and Distinguished Service at the 2007 BCA Governmental Affairs Conference. Lee was chairman of the BCA

Board of Directors from 1995-96 and was chairman of the Board of Directors of ProgressPAC, BCA's political action committee, from 1992-94.

Legislature Approves Immigration Bill

After much debate and numerous revisions, the legislature has passed a conference committee version of a bill that would make it a crime to be in Alabama without a valid federal alien registration or other proof of legal presence in the United States. The Senate voted 25-7 and the House voted 67-29 to approve HB 56, by Rep. Micky Hammon, R-Decatur. The bill now goes to Gov. Robert Bentley, where it is anticipated that an executive amendment will be added to address the concerns of business.

Last week, the U.S. Supreme Court affirmed a lower court ruling that allows for the punishment of employers who deliberately hire illegal immigrants. The U.S. Chamber of Commerce and various business organizations had challenged the validity of the Legal Arizona Workers Act that allows revocation of the licenses of employers who knowingly employ unauthorized aliens.

Washington Briefing
New Congressional Redistricting Plan Clears Legislature

The legislature on Thursday gave final approval to SB 484, which redraws the state's seven congressional districts. The final plan differs from the plans that initially passed each chamber.

The House on Wednesday passed a plan by a vote of 65-37 that was identical to the plan approved by the Joint Committee on Legislative Redistricting, but it was different than the plan passed by the Senate last week.

The bills then went to a House-Senate conference committee to iron out the differences between the versions. The Senate late Thursday afternoon passed the new redistricting plan by a vote of 17-14, and the House followed by passing the plan by a vote of 57-45.

The new plan leaves Alabama's seven incumbents in their current districts. It splits the Shoals area and divides Montgomery County into three districts.

The plan now goes to Gov. Bentley for signature.

House Rejects Raising Nation's Debt Ceiling

The House on Tuesday rejected a proposal, H.R. 1954, to raise the nation's borrowing limit. In response to calls for a clean vote on the debt limit — meaning no other provisions were attached — House Republicans scheduled just such a vote, knowing it had virtually zero chance of passage without calling for budget cuts and fiscal responsibility.

The proposal, which would have raised the debt ceiling to $16.7 trillion, failed by a vote of 97-318.

Negotiations on raising the debt ceiling continued throughout the week. On Wednesday, the entire House Republican Conference met with the president at the White House, and the Democratic caucus followed on Thursday.

Chapter 15

June 10, 2011

Session's End: Finally,
a Level Playing Field for Business

The Business Council of Alabama on Thursday night praised the Alabama Legislature for one of the most productive legislative sessions in history and for making job creation a top priority. Pro-jobs legislation, which has been on BCA's agenda for nearly two decades, has been approved, and many of the items have already been signed into law by Gov. Robert Bentley.

"The new majority in the legislature proved early on in the session that they were no longer willing to accept the status quo of the last 40 years," said BCA President and CEO William J. Canary. "Speaker Mike Hubbard and Senate President Pro Tem Del Marsh led the charge to level the playing field for Alabama's business community in the legislature, and we commend them for tackling tough budget issues, emphasizing job creation and reforming education."

"This legislature has sent a clear message to businesses looking to expand that Alabama's international reputation as a place to do business is strengthened even more," said William W. Brooke, chairman of the BCA Board of Directors and managing partner of Venture Capital for the Harbert Management Corporation. "Creating jobs is vital to revitalizing our state's economy, and the legislature has met this challenge head on."

Small Business

One of BCA's top-tier small business agenda items that made its way through the legislature early this session was HB 61 sponsored by Rep. April Weaver, R-Brierfield, which provides small businesses a tax deduction in order to provide health insurance to their employees. This law allows qualifying employers and employees to deduct and additional 50 percent of the amount expended for health insurance premiums. Qualifying employers are those with less than 25 employees; qualifying employees are those whose annual wages do not exceed $50,000. The law now increases the 150 percent deduction, approved during the 2008 legislative session, to a deduction of 200 percent of qualifying premium payments. Gov. Robert Bentley signed this legislation into law on April 21.

Job Creation and Economic Development

BCA members proudly stood with Gov. Bentley on the steps of the State Capitol in late March as he announced his Full Employment Act. Sponsored by Rep. Blaine Galliher, R-Gadsden, and Sen. Arthur Orr, R-Decatur, HB 230 will provide businesses with 50 or fewer employees an income tax credit equal to $1,000 per new job paying more than $10 an hour. Once enacted, the tax credit will be available for the tax year during which the employee has completed 12 months of consecutive employment. The bill passed both houses unanimously and now awaits the governor's signature.

Education Reform

Two of BCA's education agenda items were also passed this session and have already been signed into law. SB 310 sponsored by Sen. Trip Pittman, R-Daphne, is a reform of the Teacher Tenure Law and Fair Dismissal Act. While preserving tenure, the Students First Act reforms the appeals process for fired teachers by eliminating the use of federal arbitrators. SB 310 also removes the appeals process for teachers who are laid off due to unavoidable reductions in the workforce or due to a shortage of revenues. In pursuit of a business/education alliance, the BCA worked closely with the Alabama Association of School Boards and the School Superintendents of Alabama to ensure passage of the Students First Act.

Rep. Greg Canfield, R-Vestavia Hills, was the sponsor of HB 57, another education agenda item supported by BCA. Known as the Responsible Budgeting and Spending Act, this legislation ends the practice of relying on revenue estimates that extend some 18 months in advance to determine the total amount of money available to appropriate from the Education Trust Fund. Beginning with the 2012 session, the legislature will begin to use a fiscally conservative formula to determine the total amount that can be appropriated in a given year. This amount will be based on the historical 15-year growth rate of recurring revenue. The goal is to prevent the governor from having to declare proration in the education budget. On March 11, Gov. Bentley signed the bill, the very first of his term as governor.

Environment

One of BCA's top environmental issues this session was reauthorization of the Forever Wild land preservation program, which is one of Alabama's biggest economic engines. Hunting, fishing and wildlife viewing in Alabama has a $2.2 billion annual economic impact that benefits both local communities and the state. The legislature this year approved a constitutional amendment to allow voters to decide whether or not to renew the program for an additional 20 years. Forever Wild was originally approved by voters in 1992 with 83 percent voter support. It will appear on the ballot on November 6, 2012.

Another important BCA Agenda item, SB 224, by Senate President Pro Tem Del Marsh, R-Anniston, was signed by the governor and is now Act 2011-633. This act provides for a procedure that allows the owner of a motor vehicle who no longer possesses its title to transfer the vehicle to an automotive dismantler, parts recycler or a secondary metals recycler, if certain conditions are met. This act will have a direct impact on job creation in the metal recycling industry, which has suffered over the past two years.

With the conclusion of the 2011 legislative session, creating jobs remains the key to economic recovery in Alabama where private sector unemployment still hovers above 9 percent. As the foremost voice for business in the state, BCA will continue working for legislation that will help business owners create jobs and improve the quality of life throughout Alabama.

Budgets Await Governor's Signature

The $5.588 billion education budget and the $1.767 billion general fund budget for Fiscal Year 2012 received the final votes needed to complete the legislative process on the final day of the legislative session. Several bills that support the two budgets also needed to pass on the final day of the legislative session, to avoid last-minute budget cuts.

Gov. Robert Bentley signed into law Thursday five tort reform bills that BCA has listed as a priority for nearly two decades. BCA President and CEO William Canary and Senior Vice President for Intergovernmental Affairs and Legal Advisor Anita Archie, along with bill sponsors from the House and Senate and representatives of other business associations, were on hand for the bill signing in the Old House Chamber at the State Capitol. Joining Gov. Bentley were, from left, Billy Norrell, Alabama Roadbuilders Association; Jim Pratt, Alabama State Bar Association; Tom Dart, Automobile Dealers Association of Alabama; Sen. Clay Scofield, R-Guntersville; Rep. Paul DeMarco, R-Homewood; Rosemary Elebash, NFIB; Skip Tucker, Alabama Voters Against Lawsuit Abuse; Rep. Wes Long, R-Guntersville; Sen. Cam Ward, R-Alabaster; Rep. Greg Canfield, R-Vestavia Hills; Allison Wingate, Alabama Retail Association; Sen. Ben Brooks, R-Mobile; William Canary, BCA; Anita Archie, BCA.

Gov. Bentley had returned the general fund budget, SB 133, by Sen. Arthur Orr, R-Decatur, with an executive amendment that primarily added $3.3 million for the state Medicaid Agency. Next year's general fund budget totals $180 million more than the current budget, is $53.5 million less than the total recommended by the governor, and does not include some $235 million in federal stimulus funds that underpinned the current general fund budget.

Anticipating that the legislature would fail to pass a bill raising the retirement contributions paid by educators and employees, Gov. Bentley returned the education budget with an executive amendment that would trim tens of millions from the spending plan. However, both houses agreed to the conference committee report on the retirement bill, so the governor's executive amendment was overridden on a "friendly" vote to non-concur.

The education budget calls for spending next fiscal year that will total $240.7 million more than the current year and $93 million more than the total recommended by the governor, but the budget also lacks some $462.5 million in federal stimulus funds that supplement the current year's spending plan.

Senate OKs BCA-Backed Amendment to Protect Right to Vote by Private Ballot

Ending a three-year effort to guarantee Alabamians' right to vote by private ballot, the Alabama Senate passed BCA-supported HB 64, by Rep. Kurt Wallace, R-Maplesville. Having not seen the light of day in the past two legislative sessions, HB 64 was approved in the Senate by a vote of 23-7 and now goes to Alabama voters for approval via constitutional amendment.

HB 64 would ensure that every individual in the state is guaranteed the right to cast a ballot privately in all elections, including union elections. BCA commends Rep. Wallace and Rep. Greg Canfield, R-Vestavia Hills, who sponsored similar legislation the past two years, for ushering HB 64 through the legislature.

Senators voting yes on HB 64 were:

Sen. Gerald Allen, R-Tuscaloosa; Sen. Scott Beason, R-Gardendale; Sen. Slade Blackwell, R-Mountain Brook; Sen. Dick Brewbaker, R-Pike Road; Sen. Ben Brooks, R-Mobile; Sen. Paul Bussman, R-Cullman; Sen. Priscilla Dunn, D-Bessemer; Sen. Gerald Dial, R-Lineville; Sen. Rusty Glover, R-Semmes; Sen. Jimmy Holley, R-Elba; Sen. Bill Holtzclaw, R-Madison; Sen. Del Marsh, R-Anniston; Sen. Shadrack McGill, R-Scottsboro; Sen. Arthur Orr, R-Decatur; Sen. Trip Pittman, R-Mobile; Sen. Greg Reed, R-Jasper, Sen. Paul Sanford, R-Huntsville; Sen. Clay Scofield, R-Guntersville; Sen. Bryan Taylor, R-Prattville; Sen. Jabo Waggoner, R-Vestavia Hills; Sen. Cam Ward R-Alabaster; Sen. Tom Whatley, R-Auburn; and Sen. Phil Williams, R-Rainbow City.

Voting no on HB 64 were:

Sen. Billy Beasley, D-Clayton; Sen. Roger Bedford, D-Russellville; Sen. Linda Coleman, D-Birmingham; Sen. Jerry Fielding, D-Sylacauga; Sen. Vivian Figures, D-Mobile; Sen. Tammy Irons, D-Florence; and Sen. Bobby Singleton, D-Greensboro.

Voting P (either not voting or not present) were:
Sen. Marc Keahey, D-Grove Hill; Sen. Quinton Ross, D-Montgomery; Sen. Hank Sanders, D-Selma; Sen. Harri Anne Smith, I-Slocomb; and Sen. Rodger Smitherman, D-Birmingham.

Legislature Approves Redistricting Plan for State Board of Education

In the final hour of the legislative session on Thursday, both houses approved a bill that redraws the lines for the State Board of Education's eight districts. After nearly four hours of the bill being read at length at the request of Sen. Rodger Smitherman, D-Birmingham, the legislation passed and was sent back to the House of Representatives so they could concur with minor changes made in the Senate.

The biggest changes to the current districts are in south and west Alabama, changes that also have caused the most contention between senators and representatives. District Five is represented by Democrat Ella Bell and covers a portion of Montgomery and most of the Black Belt. District One is represented by Republican Randy McKinney who currently represents the two Gulf Coast counties and Escambia County.

Under the plan approved by the House, Ella Bell will lose a portion of Montgomery County and pick up a sizeable portion of Mobile County. Randy McKinney will lose his portion of Mobile County and pick up the four counties of Conecuh, Covington, Crenshaw and Butler. Legislators from the Mobile area have expressed concern about having a representative who lives in Montgomery but who represents portions of Mobile County.

Environmental Bills Update

Several bills supported by BCA were passed during the session and have been signed by the governor:

HB 106, by Rep. Steve Clouse, R-Ozark, has been signed by the governor and is now Act 2011-612. This act amends state laws pertaining to civil penalties for violations of state environmental protection laws and orders, by removing the minimum penalty amounts ($100) for certain violations of laws and regulations enforced by the Alabama Department of Environmental Management.

HB 50, by Rep. Greg Canfield, R-Vestavia Hills, has been signed by the governor and is Act 2011-258. This act amends the solid waste laws by removing an existing exemption from regulation fly ash waste, bottom ash waste, boiler slag waste and flue gas emissions control wastes from the burning of coal or other fossil fuels at electric generating plants and authorizes the Alabama Department of Environmental Management (ADEM) to regulate these wastes, once the federal EPA promulgates federal policy on management of such waste.

HJR 197, by Rep. Paul DeMarco, R-Homewood, has been signed by the governor and is now Act 2011-131. The act urges the U.S. Congress to adopt legislation prohibiting the EPA from regulating greenhouse gas emissions without congressional approval. This was a model resolution by the American Legislative Exchange Council (ALEC) and is referred to as the "EPA Trainwreck Resolution" because of all the aggressive regulations that EPA is pushing to impose on business and industry.

HB 406, by Rep. Alan Baker, R-Brewton, has been signed by the governor and is now Act 2011-297. This act sets a two-year moratorium on the permitting of "new" commercial Subtitle D or Construction & Demolition waste landfills. During the two-year period, ADEM and the Alabama Department of Public Health will review their programs and propose legislation or update regulations as needed. BCA monitored this legislation.

Tough Immigration Bill Becomes Law

Gov. Robert Bentley signed into law Thursday what some are calling the toughest illegal immigration law in the country. HB 56 allows police to arrest persons suspected of being illegal immigrants if they are stopped for any reason and requires public schools to determine students' immigration status. Employers are also now required to use E-Verify to determine if their new workers are in the United States legally. Court challenges by the ACLU and the Southern Poverty Law Center are planned before the law takes effect September 1.

In Other News

Attorney General Joins Challenge to NLRB

Attorney General Luther Strange on Thursday joined in an amicus brief filed in opposition to the National Labor Relation Board's proposal to punish employers for creating new jobs in right-to-work states. The Alabama Attorney General and 15 others from both right-to-work and unionized states argue that the NLRB's unprecedented enforcement action would stifle job creation and economic opportunity.

On April 20, the NLRB's acting general counsel proposed an enforcement action against The Boeing Company for building a new final production line and creating 1,000 new jobs in South Carolina, a right-to-work state. The NLRB incorrectly claims that Boeing "retaliated" against its unionized employees in Washington state — which is not a right-to-work state — because the aircraft manufacturer exercised its business judgment to create new manufacturing capacity in South Carolina. Further, the NRLB is considering an enforcement action despite the fact that Boeing has created 2,000 new jobs in Washington, does not plan to eliminate any union jobs and only proposes to create new jobs in South Carolina.

Washington Briefing

Governor Signs Congressional Redistricting Plan

Gov. Robert Bentley on Wednesday signed the congressional redistricting plan approved by the legislature last week.

The plan redraws Alabama's seven congressional districts while leaving the state's seven incumbents in their current districts.

Senate Rejects Delaying Caps on Debit Card Swipe Fees

On Wednesday, the Senate voted to allow a controversial piece of last year's Wall Street reform law to move forward.

The vote on an amendment to delay the Federal Reserve from imposing new limits on the swipe fees retailers pay when customers use debit cards fell short of the 60 votes required for Senate approval; the vote was 54-45.

Last year, Sen. Richard Durbin (D-IL) added an amendment to the Dodd-Frank financial overhaul bill that capped swipe fees at 12 cents per transaction, down from the average of 44 cents. This rule takes effect July 21.

The amendment, introduced by Sen. Jon Tester (D-MT), would have delayed the Federal Reserve from imposing this new limit on swipe fees for another year and called for a study by the Federal Reserve and three other agencies to determine whether the fee limit is fair.

ACKNOWLEDGEMENTS

The Business Council of Alabama acknowledges the valuable contributions of the volunteer chairs and co-chairs of our BCA committees, several of whom made numerous trips to the Alabama State House during the 2011 session to testify before legislative committees on behalf of pro-business legislation.

GOVERNMENTAL AFFAIRS
Chair: Fred Blackwell,
Fred Blackwell & Associates
Co-Chair: Chester Vrocher, Boise

EDUCATION AND WORKFORCE PREPAREDNESS
Chair: Bob Powers,
The Eufaula Agency
Co-Chair: Ronnie Boles,
General & Automotive Machine Shop

ENVIRONMENT AND ENERGY
Chair: Tim McCartney,
McCartney Construction Co.
Co-Chair: David Roberson,
The Drummond Company

FEDERAL AFFAIRS
Chair: Suzanne Respess,
Children's Health Systems

HEALTH
Chair: Owen Bailey,
USA Children's and Women's Hospital

JUDICIAL AND LEGAL REFORM
Chair: Debbie Long,
Protective Life Corporation
Co-Chair: Greg Butrus,
Balch & Bingham LLP

SMALL BUSINESS
Chair: Rick Roden, Greater Jackson
County Chamber of Commerce
Co-Chair: Ron Perkins,
Doozer Software, Inc.

TAX AND FISCAL POLICY
Chair: Marty Abroms,
Abroms & Associates, P.C.
Co-Chairs: Ron Box,
Joe Money Machinery Company, Inc.,
and Jim O'Brien
Vulcan Materials Company

LABOR, WORKER AND UNEMPLOYMENT COMPENSATION & HUMAN RESOURCES
Chair: Freda Bacon,
Alabama Self-Insured Workers'
Compensation Fund
Co-Chair: Paige Goldman, Energen

APPENDIX

2011 LEGISLATIVE ACCOMPLISHMENTS

Students First Act
SB 310

This bill reforms the Teacher Tenure Law and Fair Dismissal Act. While preserving tenure, the Students First Act reforms the appeals process for fired teachers by eliminating the use of federal arbitrators. It also removes the appeals process for teachers who are laid off due to unavoidable reductions in the workforce or due to a shortage of revenues. In pursuit of a business/education alliance, the BCA worked closely with the Alabama Association of School Boards and the Superintendents Association of Alabama to ensure passage of the Students First Act.

✓ *May 26, 2011   Signed into law by the governor*

The Responsible Budgeting and Spending Act
HB 57

This bill ends the practice of relying on revenue estimates that extend some 18 months in advance to determine the total amount of money available to appropriate to the Education Trust Fund. Beginning with the 2012 session, the legislature will begin to use a fiscally conservative formula to determine the total amount that can be appropriated in a given year. This amount will be based on the historical 15-year growth rate of recurring revenue. The goal is to prevent the governor from having to declare proration in the education budget.

✓ *March 11, 2011   Signed into law by the governor*

Dropping Alabama's Deferred Retirement Option Program (DROP) SB 72

This bill, which eliminates new enrollments in Alabama's DROP program, is estimated to save the Education Trust Fund some $32.5 million and the General Fund $4 million in FY 2012, in addition to the savings realized from reducing the interest paid on the accounts of DROP completers.

✓ *March 24, 2011   Signed into law by the governor*

Environment and Energy

The Salvage Vehicle Bill
SB 224

This bill would remove unnecessary and burdensome regulations on the metal recycling inddustry by allowing the owner of a motor vehicle who no longer possesses its title to transfer the vehicle to an automotive dismantler, parts recycler or a secondary metals recycler, if certain conditions are met.

✓ *June 9, 2011 Signed into law by the governor*

Forever Wild
SB 369

This constitutional amendment would reauthorize, for an additional 20 years, Forever Wild, the state's program that for 20 years has purchased and preserved land for environmental and recreational purposes. The amendment must now be approved by voters in a November 6, 2012 referendum.

June 2, 2011 Passes legislature   *Next step: On November 6, 2012 ballot*

EPA Trainwreck Resolution
HJR 197

This Act urges the U.S. Congress to adopt legislation prohibiting the EPA from regulating greenhouse gas emissions without congressional approval.

✓ *April 14, 2011 Signed into law by the governor*

Health

Small Business Paperwork Mandate Elimination Act (1099 Repeal)
H.R. 4

This bill repeals the onerous paperwork burdens imposed on businesses by the expanded 1099 information reporting mandate contained in Section 9006 of the Patient Protection and Affordable Care Act. Without the repeal of this section, businesses would have been subjected to data collection and information filing on virtually all business-to-business transactions totaling $600 or more in a year.

✓ *April 14, 2011   Signed into law by the president*

Judicial and Legal Reform

Tort Reform
SB 59   SB 207   SB 212   SB 187   SB 184

SB 59 decreases the statue of repose for commencing a civil action against an architect, engineer or builder from 13 to seven years. SB 207 provides that judgments, other than judgments based on a contract action, would bear a flat rate of seven percent. SB 212 provides that a wrongful death action may only be filed in a county where the deceased could have filed a civil action, if living, and added that Rule 82 of the rules of Civil Procedure would continue to apply to wrongful death actions. SB 184 protects retailers, wholesalers and other distributors of products from being sued in product liability actions where the product comes in a "sealed container." The bill only protects retailers from the "innocent conduit" situations. SB 187 will require the federal expert witness rule, known as the "Daubert Standard," to be applied in Alabama and be limited to scientific evidence. The U.S. Supreme Court mandated the Daubert Standard in all federal courts in 1993; however, Alabama was one of the final states to adopt the rule.

✓ *June 9, 2011   Signed into law by the governor*

Small Business

Small Business Health Care Tax Deduction
HB 61

This bill allows employers and employees to deduct an additional 50 percent of the amount expended for health insurance premiums. Qualifying employers are those with less than 25 employees; qualifying employees are those whose annual wages do not exceed $50,000. The law now increases the 150 percent deduction, approved during the 2008 legislative session, to a deduction of 200 percent of qualifying premium payments.

✓ *April 21, 2011   Signed into law by the governor*

Labor and Employment

Full Employment Act
HB 230

This bill would provide to employers of 50 or fewer employees a one-time income tax credit, beginning in the current tax year, equal to $1,000 for each new job that is created that pays at least $10 per hour, after the employee has completed 12 consecutive months of employment.

✓ *June 9, 2011   Signed into law by the governor*

Tariff Credit Act
SB 477

This bill would allow the state to provide tariff tax credits to foreign-based companies that establish operations and create jobs in Alabama. Eligible projects are for industrial, warehouse or research purposes with at least $100 million of capital investment that hire at least 100 new employees in Alabama. No new tariff credits will be allowed after December 31, 2015, unless the credit is extended by a joint resolution of the legislature.

✓ *June 9, 2011   Signed into law by the governor*

Guaranteeing the Right to Cast a Private Ballot
HB 64

This constitutional amendment would guarantee Alabamians' right to vote by private ballot in all elections, including union elections.

June 9, 2011   Passes legislature   ***Next step: On November 6, 2012 ballot***

BCA's 2011 Federal Advocacy

At the Business Council of Alabama, it's our job to fight for business and industry. We know you feel at a competitive disadvantage when it comes to meeting the mounting bottom line costs that result from costly regulations, frivolous lawsuits, rising health care costs, unfair labor laws and more. Our members tell us every day.

While much of this book is dedicated to our work at the State House in Montgomery, BCA is the state's most powerful and effective advocate for business and industry in the halls of Congress. Some of BCA's federal advocacy for the first half of 2011 is listed below:

BCA Calls for Expanding Offshore Drilling and Expediting Permits in Gulf

In May, the Business Council of Alabama joined more than 40 groups from across the country in calling for passage of three bills (H.R. 1229, H.R. 1230 and H.R. 1231) designed to expand American energy production, create jobs and lower prices.

H.R. 1229, the Putting the Gulf of Mexico Back to Work Act, would expedite the approval process for drilling permits on the Outer Continental Shelf by requiring a maximum of 60 days response time to an application for a drilling permit. It stipulates that if no response were given within 60 days, that permit to drill would be deemed approved.

H.R. 1230, the Restarting American Offshore Leasing Now Act, would accelerate the offshore permitting process for the Gulf of Mexico and would require the Department of Interior to conduct four offshore oil and gas lease sales that were canceled or delayed since the moratorium: three in the Gulf of Mexico and one in the Mid-Atlantic region (Virginia).

H.R. 1231, Reversing President Obama's Offshore Moratorium Act, was written in response to the president taking new offshore drilling off the table following last year's Deepwater Horizon disaster. H.R. 1231 would require the Interior Department to lease areas on the Outer Continental Shelf for oil and gas development that are considered to have undiscovered, technically recoverable oil. It would also mandate that the Interior Department establish production targets.

All three measures have passed the House and are awaiting action in the Senate.

BCA, 87 Business Groups Write President

The Business Council of Alabama, along with 87 business groups and trade associations, signed a letter in May urging President Obama not to sign an executive order that would require disclosure of political contributions from companies bidding for federal contracts.

As stated in the letter:

"Rather than strengthening these existing safeguards, the draft executive order would politicize the procurement process. The proposed order will either encourage covered speakers to refrain from exercising their constitutional speech rights so as to avoid jeopardizing their competitiveness for federal contracts, or it will encourage speakers to alter their political messages in ways perceived to increase their chances of being awarded federal contracts. Either effect is a problem under the First Amendment …The Executive has a statutory obligation to procure goods and services based on the best value for the American taxpayer. It also has constitutional obligations to respect the legislative domain of Congress, to refrain from chilling protected political speech, and to avoid subjecting citizens to arbitrary laws. The draft executive order violates each of these duties and potentially turns the procurement process into a tool with which to reward political allies and punish political opponents. Accordingly, we urge you to abandon this dangerous and ill-advised proposal. American business people should not be forced to limit the exercise of their constitutional rights under a new and oppressive regulatory scheme."

BCA Joins Multi-Industry Coalition Urging House to Keep Politics out of Federal Contracting

The Business Council of Alabama joined a multi-industry coalition of 70 associations and chambers of commerce, led by the U.S. Chamber of Commerce, in writing a letter in June in support of the Cole amendment.

U.S. Rep. Tom Cole (R-OK) filed an amendment to the Department of Defense Reauthorization legislation (H.R. 1540) in response to the draft Executive Order under consideration by the Obama administration. The amendment would preclude the White House from requiring federal agencies to require entities to disclose their political spending as a condition of being eligible for a federal contract.

The letter stated "The Cole amendment would help ensure that political spending — or lack thereof — continues to play no role in federal contracting decisions. The amendment reaffirms the principle, currently embodied in federal procurement laws, that the Executive Branch has an obligation to procure goods and services based on the best value for the American taxpayers, and not on political considerations."

The draft Executive Order, which has not been finalized, is part of a broader effort to reduce the effect of the Supreme Court's 2010 *Citizens United v. FEC* decision that held that corporations, unions and nonprofits have the same free speech protections as individuals and can therefore spend money on elections.

BCA Small Business Leaders Join U.S. Chamber in Rally for Small Business

Leaders of BCA's Small Business Committee participated in the U.S. Chamber of Commerce 2011 Small Business Summit in Washington D.C. Chairman Rick Roden, director of the Greater Jackson County Chamber of Commerce in Scottsboro, and Co-Chairman Ron Perkins of Doozer Software in Birmingham met with small business owners, state and local chamber professionals and other key stakeholders from across the country.

The summit, which featured some of the nation's most prominent small business advocates, political leaders and thought provokers, emphasized "Putting America Back to Work," acknowledging that small businesses create the majority of jobs in America and if not hindered by government interference, will lead the economic recovery.

Perkins recently joined former BCA Chairman David Muhlendorf, CEO of Paper and Chemical Supply of Sheffield, as a member of the U.S. Chamber of Commerce's Council on Small Business. The council unites small business owners from across the nation to drive the U.S. Chamber's small business strategy and policy decisions.

BCA, 155 Organizations Write Congress Opposing Efforts by the White House to Force Businesses to Disclose Political Spending

In June, the BCA joined 155 organizations from across the country in writing each member of Congress supporting the "Keeping Politics Out of Federal Contracting Act of 2011" and urging members of Congress to become cosponsors to the legislation sponsored by Sen. Collins in the Senate and Rep. Issa in the House. The letter stated:

"'Keeping Politics Out of Federal Contracting Act of 2011,' offered in response to a draft Executive Order under consideration by the Obama Administration, would preclude the White House from forcing federal agencies to require entities to disclose their political spending — as well as that of their officers and directors — as a condition of participating in the federal procurement process.

"The legislation would help ensure that political spending — or the lack thereof —continues to play no role in federal contracting decisions. The legislation reaffirms the principle, currently embodied in federal procurement laws, that the

Executive Branch has an obligation to procure goods and services based on the best value for the American taxpayer and not on political considerations. It also reaffirms the principle that the Administration cannot enact through executive fiat legislation that which Congress has considered and explicitly rejected."

BCA, Southeast Organizations Write EPA to Oppose Utility MACT Rules

In June, the BCA joined a coalition of organizations located in the Southeast, a region whose economy depends heavily on the availability of affordable, reliable electricity, to write the administrator of the U.S. Environmental Protection Agency to express concern with the National Emissions Standards for Hazardous Air Pollutants From Coal- and Oil-Fired Electric Utility Steam Generating Units, otherwise known as "Utility MACT."

We believe these rules, if implemented within the stated timelines and with the stringency we believe is likely, will weaken industry in our region, cause job losses, and hurt power consumers.

As stated in the letter, "Our fear is that the Southeast will be particularly vulnerable to the consequences of Utility MACT rules. Our region remains the last bastion of heavy manufacturing, with hundreds of thousands of jobs and billions of dollars in economic impact that rely on the success of manufacturing. In this atmosphere, skilled labor has thrived and foreign manufacturing investment has flourished. Our region also relies more intently than others on coal-fired power generation. These two features are not coincidental; in fact, they are inextricably linked. The availability of abundant, reliable and inexpensive electricity from America's native coal resources has fueled this success."

The letter continued, "Put simply, we believe that the closure of significant numbers of coal-fired plants in the Southeast due to Utility MACT will mean economic setbacks for our region and strike a blow to manufacturing in one of the only regions in the United States where heavy industry is viable. We believe Utility MACT will mean the loss of high-paying, high-skill jobs and the advent of drastic price increases for consumers who cannot bear them in this economy."

BCA Urges Alabama Delegation to Restore Funding for State's Pediatric Training

The BCA asked each member of the Alabama delegation to restore the Children's Hospitals Graduate Medical Education FY 2012 funding after the president's budget proposal eliminated it altogether.

Alabama's pediatric physician work force continues to experience a significant shortage in general and subspecialty pediatrics. More than 50 percent of Alabama's pediatricians are 50-55 years old, and the Children's Hospitals Graduate Medical

Education program is the only pipeline to replace these physicians. If the funding level remains or is further reduced, Alabama will lose a minimum of 10 pediatric resident slots annually.

Alabama Children's Hospitals train more than 70 percent of our state's pediatricians, a key component of Alabama's primary care workforce and the state's health care infrastructure necessary for economic development. Restoring the Children's Hospitals Graduate Medical Education funding to the FY 2010 level is critical to ensuring future of Alabama's primary care workforce and future economic development.

BCA Joins NAM in Washington for Third Annual Manufacturing Summit

The Business Council of Alabama participated in the National Association of Manufacturers third annual Manufacturing Summit held in Washington D.C. in June. The summit emphasized "Manufacturing Means Jobs" and the pro-growth reforms needed to turn around our country's overall economic health.

The summit included a discussion with Senator John Thune (R-SD), chairman of the Senate Republican Policy Committee, to discuss his insights on the tax and regulatory issues Congress is facing and how these policies will impact manufacturers. He also spoke about energy supply and cautioned that current policies have our economy headed for a train wreck.

White House Chief of Staff William Daley discussed the Administration's efforts to get the economy back on track and the president's involvement in skilled workforce issues.

BCA is the exclusive affiliate for the NAM in Alabama.

BCA, Southern State Chambers of Commerce Challenge Wall Street Journal Editorial

In June, the *Wall Street Journal* ran an editorial regarding the National Labor Relations Board unfair labor charge against Boeing claiming, "When major firms move to the South, it's usually a harbinger of quality decline." The BCA joined state chambers of commerce from throughout the South in responding to this blatant attempt to discredit the quality, skilled work force of the Southern United States.

In a letter to the *Wall Street Journal*, the coalition emphasized, "Major corporations in general have continually chosen to locate facilities in the South due to the ability to compete in the global marketplace. In addition, over the last two decades, many businesses that have traditionally been located in heavily unionized states have moved their operations to the right-to-work South.... In today's litigious American climate, corporations must put a premium on producing a high quality product, and the South's work force has continuously delivered that product."

2011 STATE LEGISLATIVE AGENDA
Approved by the BCA Board of Directors on December 6, 2010

At the Business Council of Alabama, we realize that our members, who represent three-quarters of a million working Alabamians, trust us to do our very best to protect their business when it comes to politics and policy-setting in the state capital. On the following pages are BCA's legislative policies and priorities for 2011.

EDUCATION / WORKFORCE PREPAREDNESS

The Business Council of Alabama supports adopting policies and processes that ensure sound, sustainable funding for public education. BCA advocates that adequate and equitable funding for effective public education at all levels (pre-K through Ph.D., including AIDT, ATN & Career Tech) is essential if the system is to effectively prepare Alabama's children and young adults to meet the challenges of an increasingly complex economy and competitive workforce. Therefore, the BCA supports policies that promote access to quality education at all levels and strengthen public awareness and understanding that further educational investment is not only necessary, but also essential, in ensuring personal income growth and economic opportunity for all Alabamians. BCA contends that all education dollars go first to the classroom, including classroom educational support e.g., textbooks, library resources, educational supplies and technologies, and that all public education funds be appropriated to public educational entities with the exception of voluntary Pre-K programs.

In 2011, the BCA will actively work to:

- Adopt policies and processes that ensure sound, sustainable funding for public education.

- Enact legislation that reduces the growth in state-funded benefits for public educators and employees.

- Reform future teacher compensation to reflect their experience and performance in the classroom.

- Sustain funding, as appropriate, in the FY12 Education Budget for proven educational initiatives, such as the Alabama Reading Initiative, Alabama Math Science Technology Initiative, the Career/Technical Education Initiative, ACCESS and the Alabama Virtual Library, with a portion of the funding for each program allocated for periodic, independent evaluations according to national norms.

- Support a rational allocation of state funding resources among all segments of public education.
- Fundamentally reform teacher tenure and fair dismissal laws.
- Increase funding for pre-kindergarten educational programs administered by certifiably trained staff, and ensure that the programs demonstrate student academic preparedness for kindergarten through required appropriate accountability measures.
- Maintain funding for seamless training programs for existing industries and businesses to help employees advance on technical career paths; ensure adequate numbers of trainable workers are available to "back-fill" existing jobs as experienced employees are hired and promoted by new and emerging industries.
- Continue and maintain the regional and state workforce training development councils as the process for determining how to spend workforce training money.
- Continue consolidation of workforce development programs and activities, as necessary, into an efficient, focused and responsive system of workforce education and training, which utilizes all of the resources available under the Alabama Department of Postsecondary Education (including the AIDT and ATN) and emphasizes adult education programs.
- Enact legislation allowing for public charter schools in Alabama.

In 2011, the BCA will support efforts to:
- Increase the percentage of Alabama students who complete high school, and encourage students to take more challenging courses, so that more high school graduates will be prepared to be successful in higher education or in today's technical worksites. For those who do not complete high school, strengthen adult education programs to ensure more adults will earn a GED.
- Encourage public high schools and institutions of higher education to promote greater student understanding of personal financial management.
- Fund scholarships / salary supplements / incentives for teachers who agree to teach hard-to-staff subject areas or in underserved geographic areas.
- Ensure high caliber teacher training programs and administrative leader programs in colleges of education.
- Eliminate unfunded state mandates to local school boards.
- Ensure that the education and job training programs available to Alabama students culminate in nationally recognized credentials specifically relevant to job opportunities that are or will be available in the state.

Environment and Energy

The Business Council will work for sound environmental and energy legislation consistent with continued economic growth within the state. BCA has a long-standing policy that state environmental laws and regulations should be no more stringent than federal environmental laws and regulations, and the EPA and all 50 states should adopt and implement regulations in a manner such that no state's industry has an unfair advantage. In addition, the BCA supports adequate funding for The Alabama Department of Environmental Management (ADEM), so it may provide experienced personnel to carry out necessary services without wasteful overlap of programs.

In 2011, the BCA will actively work to:

- Establish incentives for alternative fuels, renewable energy production and use, and energy efficiency in conjunction with the BCA Tax and Fiscal Policy Committee and the Alabama Permanent Joint Legislative Committee on Energy.

- Retain primacy for federal programs by coordinating with state regulatory agencies.

In 2011, the BCA will support efforts to:

- Further strengthen penalties against those who sell stolen metal property.

- Support fair treatment of industry through joint legislative initiatives.

- Support legislation to keep Alabama metal recyclers competitive.

In 2011, the BCA will actively oppose:

- Implementing climate change policy or other regulations on the state level that would put Alabama at a business, manufacturing and/or economic development disadvantage.

- Enacting legislation and regulations that would have a detrimental effect on existing industry and that may have a negative effect on economic development.

HEALTH

The Business Council of Alabama strongly supports and will work to protect employer-sponsored health care coverage through private insurers and self-insured / ERISA plans. In that effort, BCA encourages innovative solutions that increase employers' choices in purchasing affordable, quality health care and prescription coverage while decreasing health care costs through free-market competition without government interference. To be successful, health care coverage, both in the public and private sectors, must encourage consumer involvement, promote wellness and prevention, and reward quality. The BCA opposes all health care and insurance-related mandates on employers and/or individuals because they increase costs without improving the quality of care, and the BCA opposes proposals for any type of single-payer system.

In 2011, the BCA will actively work to:

- Enact legislation to provide for tax relief for medical savings accounts.

- Increase the Small Business Health Care Tax Deduction from 150 percent to 200 percent in coordination with the BCA Small Business and Tax & Fiscal Policy committees.

- Ensure that any implementation of the Patient Protection and Affordable Care Act is as cost effective as possible to Alabama businesses.

In 2011, the BCA will actively support efforts to:

- Explore options for the Alabama Medicaid program to prevent the costs of uncompensated care from shifting to employer-sponsored health care plans.

- Maintain the current composition of the Certificate of Need Board or efforts to increase payer and consumer business representation on the CON Board.

- Increase representation of payers of health care services to state health and medical boards.

- Continue to expand efforts to provide consumers (patients) with medical providers' quality performance data that is transparent and verifiable for the purpose of assessing and improving health care merit, accessibility and affordability.

- Identify and promote measurable programs and policies, such as electronic medical records, electronic prescribing, wellness programs, e.g. the Alabama KidCheck Program and the Patient Centered Medical Home, which will result in long-term containment of health care costs.

- Develop innovative solutions for prescription drug coverage at a reasonable cost while opposing mandated prescription drug pricing.

In 2011, the BCA will actively oppose:
- Mandating employer-provided health care benefits or any legislation, resolution or regulation that would increase health plan costs.
- Enacting or expanding licensure laws where there is no evidence-based impact on quality of care or outcomes.

JUDICIAL AND LEGAL REFORM

The Business Council of Alabama supports transparency in all aspects of the judiciary and the judicial system and advocates for the current open and democratic election process for Alabama's judges. Specifically, the BCA opposes any proposal to adopt an appointment process for selecting Alabama judges, proposal for nonpartisan elections for judges, or any other proposal that decreases the transparency of the selection process. Partisan elections provide the voting public with a source of distinguishable information regarding judicial candidates.

The Business Council of Alabama supports participation and transparency in all aspects of the governmental process and accordingly, strongly supports ethics reform that affords all persons the opportunity to participate fully and equally in the political process and all voters the opportunity to ascertain easily and in a timely manner what persons or entities may be supporting or opposing governmental candidates or lobbying governmental officers. Specifically, the BCA supports the right to exercise free speech in all aspects of the political process and the timely and easily accessible reporting of all political contributions, financial commitments or expenditures.

In 2011, the BCA will actively work to:
- Promote transparency in all aspects of government.
- Tie post-judgment interest to the federal index.
- Reform non-economic damages.
- Establish limits on product liability awards.
- Enact a Statute of Repose for product liability claims.
- Eliminate the presentation of unqualified "junk science" evidence to a jury by requiring that the Daubert standard be applied in all state legal proceedings. Applying the Daubert standard to testimony will ensure that scientific evidence presented by an expert witness is both relevant and reliable when presented to a jury.

- Maintain the doctrine of contributory negligence.
- Establish appropriate venue for cases brought in Alabama state courts.
- Establish a privilege for accountant work papers.
- Support proposals affecting frivolous lawsuit outcomes and uphold the current loser pay provision in Rule 11 of Alabama Civil Procedures, which holds litigators accountable for filing frivolous claims.

In 2011, the BCA will actively oppose:

- Restricting or eliminating contractual arbitration agreements.
- Narrowing or the abolishing the statute of limitations from toxic substance torts or wantonness claims.
- Infringing on employers' right to provide a safe workplace for employees by restricting firearm possession on company property when appropriate and/or creating any new causes of action against employers because of such policies.

In 2011, the BCA will also support efforts to oppose:

- Allowing private attorneys to sue on behalf of the state of Alabama under the False Claims Act, regardless of the attorney general's position.
- Allowing officials not directly responsible to the voters to be the ultimate decision-makers with respect to prosecution of crimes and claims brought by the state of Alabama.

SMALL BUSINESS

The Business Council of Alabama recognizes that small businesses provide the majority of Alabamians' jobs and that protecting entrepreneurial efforts sustains job growth. BCA supports protecting economic development funds currently allocated for small business development programs and encourages recognition of, and support for, entrepreneurial enterprises as essential to the state's economic development program. The BCA will not support unjustified reallocation of existing economic development funds already committed for specific projects.

In 2011, the BCA will actively work to:

- Enact legislation that defines "Small Business" as a business entity, including any affiliates that meet any of the following: (1) is independently owned and operated and employs less than 100 full-time employees, or (2) has gross annual sales of less than $6 million.

- Increase the Small Business Health Care Tax Deduction from 150 percent to 200 percent.

- Evaluate and examine, in conjunction with the BCA's Health Care Committee, initiatives that aim to address the bottom-line challenge of rising health care costs.

- Form coalitions with associations and other groups to bring more awareness and focus on resolving the challenges that threaten the economic viability of small businesses.

- Enact legislation that requires a small business regulatory flexibility analysis and a small business economic impact statement when a state agency proposes a new rule or rule change. This legislation should mirror federal provisions and require a five-year review of all state agency rules and their effect on small business.

- Encourage state agencies to use their best efforts to contract with Alabama small businesses.

In 2011, the BCA will monitor:

- Small business government contracts to ensure that small business government contracts go to small businesses instead of subsidiaries of large companies.

Tax and Fiscal Policy

In keeping with long-term Business Council of Alabama policy, should any tax or tax reform initiatives be proposed, BCA will not consider supporting such legislation unless it is applied fairly without levying a disproportionate burden on any individual segment of Alabama's economy. Any tax reform proposal must be tied to governmental accountability and the elimination of wasteful spending.

In 2011, the BCA will actively work to:

- Create the Alabama Tax Appeals Commission (ATAC) as an independent state tax agency, headed by a judge selected in a non-partisan manner who has specific training in state and local taxation. The legislation would also abolish the Administrative Law Division of the Alabama Department of Revenue.

- Enact the Alabama Taxpayers' Bill of Rights II, an updated and expansion of the original landmark legislation enacted in 1992, which extends the appeal deadlines for taxpayers.

- Increase the Small Business Health Care Tax Deduction from 150 percent to 200 percent in coordination with the BCA Small Business and Health committees.

- Establish a privilege for accountant work papers.

In 2011, the BCA will support efforts to:

- Resolve the Revenue Department's problems and litigation over its "gross income regulation" that affects partnerships, S-corps, LLCs and other "pass-through" entities, which earn income both in and outside of Alabama. The legislation would: (1) prospectively recognize the non-Alabama income; and (2) provide a pass-through tax credit for income/franchise taxes paid to other states and foreign countries by the entity, on behalf of its resident owners.

- Streamline and simplify our sales/use tax system so that in-state and out-of-state retailers are on a level playing field.

- Enact a constitutional amendment authorizing a road and bridge construction program to be funded by the Alabama Trust Fund with 100 percent of the appropriations distributed by the Alabama Department of Transportation for state highways, roads and bridges and other transportation purposes. No part of any appropriation may be allotted if such allotment would cause the balance in the Alabama Trust Fund to fall below $2 billion.

In 2011, the BCA will oppose:

- Establishing unitary combined reporting in Alabama.

In 2011, the BCA will monitor efforts to:

- Regulate and set minimum standards for individual tax preparers.

LABOR AND EMPLOYMENT

The Business Council of Alabama strongly supports Alabama's right-to-work status for its benefits to economic growth, industrial recruitment and job creation. To this end, BCA works to protect Alabama's competitive edge nationally and internationally by fighting efforts to create a state minimum wage above the national minimum wage and opposing attempts to negatively influence the current balance between business and labor as it relates to unionization and contract negotiations. Employer-subsidized lockouts, whereby locked-out employees are eligible for unemployment compensation, prolong labor disputes and have a chilling effect on industrial recruitment.

In 2011, the BCA will actively work to:

- Allow for meaningful drug and alcohol testing in workers' compensation claims.

- Reduce oral and written reporting times in an effort to decrease fraud in unemployment and workers' compensation claims.

- Maintain an employer's right to choose the treating physician and second opinion physician in workers' compensation claims.

- Find solutions to medical cost issues, including consideration of changes to the Workers' Compensation medical fee schedule and evaluation of the need for an outpatient surgery fee schedule.

- Ensure that immigration laws impacting Alabama businesses do not impose additional burdens on, or penalize, Alabama employers.

- Support a constitutional amendment establishing the right to cast a secret ballot in all elections in Alabama.

In 2011, the BCA will actively oppose:

- Expanding state unemployment compensation benefits that incur increased taxes on Alabama business.

- Legislation that attempts to limit employers' freedoms to implement "employment at will" policies.

2011 FEDERAL LEGISLATIVE AGENDA
112TH CONGRESS - 1ST SESSION
Adopted by the BCA Board of Directors on March 22, 2011

ECONOMIC DEVELOPMENT

The BCA will support efforts to:

- Secure federal contracts and support and enhance federal programs leveraging Alabama's military, defense and aerospace, biotech and medical research, and research and development opportunities.

- Advocate changes and improvements to Sarbanes-Oxley to reduce the negative impact to business created by the existing statute by providing further clarification to the existing law in order to eliminate several unintended consequences; to reduce the disproportionate costs of compliance; and to ensure the U.S. markets are not at a competitive disadvantage to foreign markets.

- Support the development of a heavy-lift launch vehicle to keep our nation the world leader in the human exploration of space.

- Preserve, promote and protect the integrity and viability of the federal government's small business programs in order to ensure that work awarded under such programs is performed to the maximum extent possible by authentic small businesses that legitimately comply with applicable size standards established by the Small Business Administration.

EDUCATION/WORKFORCE DEVELOPMENT

The BCA will support efforts to:

- Federally fund the needed resources to expand the Alabama Reading Initiative beyond grades K-3.

- Work with the Department of Defense to rebuild the "compact" between the military and employers so that companies, especially small and midsize companies, continue to hire members of the National Guard and Reserve in this era of increased call-ups for citizen-soldiers.

- Reform immigration policy to strengthen our national security, including increasing protection of our borders, while providing a supplemental workforce for American businesses and industry. Simplify and expand the caps in the

H2B program to make it an effective tool in offsetting the growing workforce shortages in various sectors of the U.S. economy, and in particular Alabama's economy, wherein there are no qualified Americans willing and able to take positions, and ensure that the temporary worker must intend to return to their homeland once their visa is expired.

- Reauthorize the Job Training Improvement Act of 2005 with guidelines that allow more flexible funding and responsiveness to critical training needs.
- Support programs that will enlarge the pool of skilled workers for the manufacturing sector.

The BCA will monitor efforts to:

- Reauthorize the No Child Left Behind Act (also known as the Elementary and Secondary Education Act) in order to strengthen and improve its provisions and funding, while respecting the fundamental features of this historic law that are designed to raise student achievement and close achievement gaps.

ENVIRONMENT AND ENERGY

The BCA will support efforts to:

- Amend the Federal Water Pollution Control Act (commonly known as the Clean Water Act) to provide that civil penalties assessed and collected by the United States in connection with the Deepwater Horizon oil spill will by equally disbursed to the five affected Gulf Coast states for the purpose of economic, environmental, ecological and public health recovery and restoration.
- Ensure that Alabama has adequate water to meet the state's needs for municipal and industrial water supply, navigation, energy production, economic development, irrigation and recreational uses.
- Delay implementation of EPA's greenhouse gas regulations under the Clean Air Act.
- Increase royalties for offshore drilling for Gulf Coast states.
- Base environmental legislation and regulation on sound scientific study and provide safeguards to the environment without hindering economic development or imposing undue regulations on the business community.
- Reduce America's dependence on foreign energy sources and increasing reliance on domestic energy sources; promote energy conservation; encourage research and investment in and enact incentives in developing clean energy sources, clean coal, nuclear power and advanced gas technology.

- Invest federally in carbon capture and sequestration technology and efforts such as the Asia-Pacific Partnership on Clean Development and Climate to reduce greenhouse gas emissions.

- Ensure that any clean energy mandate includes hydroelectricity, natural gas, nuclear and coal with carbon capture and sequestration along with all other clean energy technologies so that the most affordable clean energy solutions can be deployed in Alabama.

- Encourage sustainable business practices such as life cycle costing in public sector procurement for water projects.

The BCA will oppose efforts to:

- Impose regulations or fiscal policy that threaten the drilling and completion of domestic oil and gas wells.

- Impose mandates related to the production of alternative fuels and alternative and renewable energy.

- Establish caps or taxes on carbon emissions, which would put Alabama businesses in a competitive disadvantage with other nations.

- Expand the jurisdiction of the Clean Water Act to allow federal agencies to regulate ditches, culverts and pipes, desert washes, sheet flow, erosional features, and farmland and treatment ponds as "waters of the United States," subjecting such waters to all of the requirements of the CWA (as proposed by EPA in recent draft guidelines presently under review by the Administration).

- Reduce or withdraw the state's delegated authority to administer the federal Clean Water Act in Alabama.

FINANCIAL SERVICES

The BCA will support efforts to:

- Represent the interests of its bank and financial services members by working closely with the Senate Banking Committee and the House Financial Services Committee to ensure that the regulations under the newly enacted Dodd-Frank Wall Street Reform and Consumer Protection Act are implemented in a reasonable and proper manner to ensure the stability of the financial services industry and the availability of credit to consumers.

The BCA will monitor efforts to:

- Support uniform national standards in the regulation of financial services and products in the areas of information security and consumer privacy.

- Enact legislation to increase customer access to services from banks and trust companies on an interstate basis, while strengthening the traditional dual banking system.

HEALTH CARE

The BCA will support efforts to:

- Repeal the Patient Protection and Affordable Care Act in its entirety.

- Maintain equitable funding and formulas for the Medicare and Medicaid programs (wage index language, federal funds designated to states, sustainable growth rate, etc).

- Fund graduate medical education (adult and pediatric) and medical research.

- Ensure all employers, regardless of size, have vehicles (tax incentives, etc) to provide affordable health care coverage for their workforce.

The BCA will oppose efforts to:

- Change, through legislation or regulation, the federal funding formula that would negatively impact the state-federal Medicaid and Medicare programs and providers.

- Create new mandated benefits.

- Weaken workers' compensation requirements.

- Increase the cost of health care or liability to the employer or weaken the Employee Retirement Income Security Act (ERISA).

- Implement a national single payer health care plan.

The BCA will monitor efforts to:

- Contain health care costs through medical malpractice reforms and technology, quality and safety initiatives.

LABOR RELATIONS

The BCA will support efforts to:
- Protect right-to-work statutes.

The BCA will monitor:
- Efforts of the National Labor Relations Board with respect to unionization.

The BCA will oppose efforts to:
- Legislate, regulate or implement any provision of the Employee Free Choice Act (as enrolled in the 111th Congress as S. 560 and H.R. 1409).

LEGAL REFORM

The BCA will support efforts to:
- Reform asbestos litigation to ensure fair treatment of victims and end the pervasive, growing problem posed by a $250 billion present and future liability for manufacturers.
- Enact civil justice reform, including reform of the collateral source rule; punitive damage awards; damages from non-economic loss; comprehensive product liability; and medical liability as well as abolition of the rule of joint and several liability and adoption of a rule of pure and several proportionate liability.

The BCA will oppose efforts to:
- Erode the Federal Arbitration Act.

The BCA will monitor efforts to:
- Protect the right to free speech in the judicial process.

OSHA

The BCA will support efforts to:
- Implement more scientific research and emphasis on current best practices before new ergonomics regulations are issued.
- Adopt new occupational safety and health standards and regulations through the current statutory and regulatory framework that both Congress and the Executive branch have established, thereby preserving for all stakeholders a voice in the process of developing new standards and regulations.

- Review current occupational safety and health standards and regulations so that they are working as intended. Prior to any new rulemaking, OSHA should practice due diligence in reviewing whether existing standards and regulations address emerging safety and health issues. OSHA should work to limit the regulatory burden on employers whenever possible.

- Allow employers to stay abatement requirements, pending the full completion of a challenge to the citation through the Occupational Safety and Health Review Commission, should they choose to do so.

REGULATORY REFORM

The BCA will support efforts to:

- Provide regulatory relief by advocating the review and repeal of outdated, unnecessary regulations.

- Require proposed regulation additions and changes are based on sound science and subject to impartial scientific peer review, risk assessment and cost/benefit analysis, which places the least burden on sustainable economic development.

TAX

The BCA will support efforts to:

- Permanently repeal both the Estate Tax and the Alternative Minimum Tax (AMT).

- Create tax credits and incentives for small businesses and individuals who purchase or provide health care coverage, including prescription drugs, for their employees and themselves.

- Enact the Business Activity Tax Simplification Act (BATSA) to clarify the requirement of physical presence as the nexus standard governing the assessment of corporate income taxes and comparable taxes.

- Make research and development tax credits permanent.

- Implement accelerated depreciation for capital investment.

- Streamline and simplify our sales/use tax system so that in-state and out-of-state retailers are on a level playing field.

- Support efforts to repeal the 1099 provision passed under the Patient Protection and Affordable Care Act.

The BCA will oppose efforts to:

- Impose retroactive tax increases on American businesses through modifications of tax rules applicable to closed or existing multi-year transactions.

- Change congressional tax policy where "revenue offsets" are used to underwrite the projected cost of tax cuts, and those offsets result in undue tax increases or undue new taxes on businesses.

- Alter the tax consequences of existing corporate compensation plans, including but not limited to: taxing non-qualified deferred compensation plans and limiting deductions for compensation to business executives.

- Repeal the inventory method known as Last-In, First-Out (LIFO), which many manufacturers and retailers have employed for decades.

TRADE

The BCA will support efforts to:

- Enact fair trade initiatives that will enhance Alabama's growth and export capability in the globally competitive marketplace.

TRANSPORTATION AND INFRASTRUCTURE

The BCA will support efforts to:

- Enact a need-based, multi-year federal transportation program as soon as possible.

- Continue to expand, update and strengthen Alabama's multi-modal transportation infrastructure.

- Ensure that the reauthorization of the federal transportation program does not change the current balance of funding for roads and bridges versus other modes of transportation.

- If necessary, transfer money to the Highway Trust Fund from the general fund to maintain Highway Trust Fund solvency while Congress completes work on a multi-year highway bill.

- Invest in the nation's water infrastructure through increased funding for the Clean Water and Drinking Water State Revolving Funds and the removal of limits on private activity bond financing for water and wastewater projects.

The BCA will monitor efforts to:

- Address future Inland Waterways Trust Fund shortfalls.

ALABAMA BUSINESS: IT'S TIME TO PUT THE PRIVATE SECTOR AND TAXPAYER FIRST!
By William W. Brooke

Change has finally come to Alabama. As Governor Bentley and the Alabama Legislature begin their terms of office, we at the Business Council of Alabama stand ready to help meet the governor's goal to create jobs. We are committed to doing everything we can to stimulate positive growth in the private sector, so that our state reaches full employment, existing businesses can expand and new industries continue to locate here.

Governor Bentley's goal could not be more timely. The November elections signaled a new day in our state's history, as the forces that have long prevented real progress and reform were turned back at the ballot box, and a pro-business majority was elected in both houses of the legislature.

It has been said that elections have consequences, and general election voters certainly proved that saying to be true. Tired of the Montgomery mindset that set the expansion of government, and its rules and regulations as the top priority, the citizens of Alabama chose to firmly place the needs of taxpayers, small businesses and private industry atop the State House agenda.

As the state's leading advocate for business, the BCA is uniquely positioned to help Alabama's new leadership meet the challenges that lie ahead. Our group represents some 750,000 working Alabamians through its member companies, and more than 80 percent of our members are small businesses. In addition, our formal relationship with the Chamber of Commerce Association of Alabama, whose members include 124 local chambers of commerce, representing more than 60,000 local business owners, allows us to speak for more than one million working Alabamians.

As BCA President and CEO William Canary has stated, "Our mission is simple: We fight every day for businessmen and women to be able to sign the front of a paycheck, so that others can sign the back."

The 2011 Regular Session of the Alabama Legislature must have a primary focus on job creation and place an emphasis on important economic development initiatives such as fostering innovative technologies, offering access to workforce training and expanding tourism. We also must leverage our higher education system as an economic development mechanism, while establishing innovative new incentives that grow existing industry and business, demanding the highest return on investment.

Jobs are indeed vital to revitalizing our state's economy, but without a first-class education system, the schoolchildren of today will not be able to function in the workforce of tomorrow. It is our obligation to provide that opportunity to them; anything less is unacceptable.

The BCA has long been an advocate for the professional teacher and has a record of support for quality classroom initiatives for our children. At the top of our legislative priorities we have pledged to enact policies that promote sustainable funding for public education and ensure that Alabama's limited education dollars are spent in the classroom on such proven educational programs as distance learning, the Alabama Reading Initiative, and especially, a first-rate voluntary pre-kindergarten program.

William W. Brooke

Studies have shown that every $1 spent on high-quality early childhood programs returns $7 to $9 in future savings. Disadvantaged children with quality early learning opportunities have fewer remedial education needs in later years and are more likely to graduate from high school, earn more money and contribute more tax dollars, enjoying a higher quality of life as they become more productive members of the business community.

The days when political forces in Alabama worked to pit business and education against each other are over. The business community is the number one consumer of the product called education, and the time has come for the creation of a true Business/Education Alliance in Alabama.

Similar organizations have been operating successfully in other states and cities, with measureable results and reforms. The BCA is ready to marshal the strength of our member businesses and unite with like-minded educators to begin this historic initiative.

It is time to fundamentally change how Montgomery operates and leave our children and grandchildren a more prosperous future, along with a more accountable and efficient state government. The business community of Alabama is committed and ready to do its part.

It's time for us all to come off the sidelines and lead. Let's get to work!

This article was published in several of the state's daily newspapers.
William W. Brooke, managing partner of Venture Capital, Harbert Management Corporation, Birmingham, is chairman of the Business Council of Alabama.

WHAT A DIFFERENCE 6 PERCENT MAKES...
By William J. Canary

There is no doubt that creating jobs generates revenue for Alabama's Education Trust Fund, a fact that Governor Robert Bentley and the new legislative leadership obviously understand.

It's hard to believe that just four short years ago, Alabama's unemployment rate rested at 3.3 percent, roughly, and the state spent $6.7 billion on education. Most sectors of our economy were booming, and the devastating effects of the Great Recession had not yet taken their toll on Alabama families and businesses.

We know all too well what happened next. As the economy spiraled out of control, hundreds of thousands of Alabama families were affected, and businesses were forced to make incredibly difficult decisions. Private sector cuts were inevitable — first to health and retirement benefits and then salaries. Finally, when all of the fat had been cut, and furloughs and four-day work weeks still left revenue too short, business owners had no choice but to let people go, and some were even forced to shutter their doors for good.

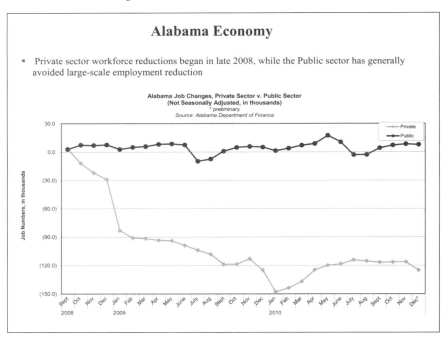

Alabama Economy

- Private sector workforce reductions began in late 2008, while the Public sector has generally avoided large-scale employment reduction

Alabama Job Changes, Private Sector v. Public Sector
(Not Seasonally Adjusted, in thousands)
* preliminary
Source: Alabama Department of Finance

In 2010, unemployment peaked at just more than 11 percent, leaving almost a quarter-million Alabamians out of work and $1 billion less flowing into state education coffers. Today, we have nearly 200,000 Alabamians looking for jobs, a 9.2 percent unemployment rate and a proposed education budget totaling $5.5 billion for fiscal year 2012. But, now there is no one-time stimulus money coming from Washington and no rainy day account to bail out the state.

The education budget recently passed by the Alabama House of Representatives demanded very tough decisions. Teachers and education personnel have been asked to contribute more to their retirement, the average classroom size is increased by a half-

William J. Canary

a-student and most of the teachers who retire in the next year will not be replaced. Most importantly though, the budget does not require a single state-funded teacher to be laid off; teachers will not be forced to join the 200,000 unemployed citizens in Alabama because of the education budget.

At the same time, this budget protects critical programs such as Alabama Math, Science and Technology Initiative, the Alabama Reading Initiative, the ACCESS Distance Learning Program and funding for Pre-Kindergarten education, all of which have helped move Alabama from 40th place to 25th in national education rankings.

House Speaker Mike Hubbard and Senate President Pro Tem Del Marsh recognize that growing our state budgets requires a growing economy, and they already have taken action to help businesses create jobs. The legislature increased the tax deduction for small businesses that provide health insurance, which the governor signed into law last week. Similarly, Gov. Bentley is championing tax incentives for creating jobs in new and existing industries through the Full Employment Act (HB 230 and SB 173) and Jobs Creation and Retention Act (HB 478 and SB 373).

While viewing job creation as a solution — a means to an end — is common sense, various labor unions and a handful of politicians believe fixing the state's budget problems is as simple as raising taxes. Instead of supporting legislation that will help grow our economy, they demonize the business community and preach about "sharing the sacrifice," yet they refuse to acknowledge the sacrifices being made. Business owners who stopped taking a salary and laid off good employees because there was not enough work as well as those struggling to weather a devastated Gulf Coast tourism industry certainly can explain the meaning of "sacrifice" to these union leaders.

Politics of division seems to be a sport in Alabama, but our students are the ones who suffer when these tactics are used to divide business and education. Today's students are tomorrow's workforce, which is why we continue to advocate for a Business Education Alliance to unite the business and education communities for a simple purpose: putting our students first. We will never be able to fully compete for the jobs of the future unless we prepare our students now.

Six percentage points separate the unemployment rate of today with that of 2007. More than $1 billion separates the respective education budgets during this time. Rather than burden our state's job creators with new, punitive taxes, we should provide them with incentives needed to employ Alabamians in tough economic times. Both our students and our future depend on it.

William J. Canary is president and CEO of the Business Council of Alabama, Alabama's leading business and industry organization, which represents, through its members companies, nearly three-quarters of a million working Alabamians. This article was published in several of the state's daily newspapers and in Business Alabama *magazine.*

ALABAMA'S NEW PRODUCTIVE, RESPONSIVE LEGISLATURE

By Rep. Mike Hubbard,
Speaker of the Alabama House of Representatives

Unfortunately, people in Alabama haven't been accustomed to seeing much productivity and responsiveness from the legislature. In the 2010 election cycle, we vowed to change that.

Alabama voters, fed up after decades of broken promises and political paralysis in Montgomery, elected a new class of leadership to the House and Senate last November. Today, I'm proud to report that we've lived up to our promise to enact conservative, good-government reforms that move Alabama forward.

When the final gavel of the 2011 Regular Session sounded and the legislature adjourned, it ended the most productive legislative session in decades, if not ever. Lawmakers worked together to complete an ambitious agenda focused on boosting the Alabama economy by jumpstarting job growth and enacting long-needed government reforms.

We passed balanced, responsible budgets that avoid teacher layoffs and pay cuts, while looking out for taxpayers' interests. We revamped the budgeting process to ensure future budgets won't force our schools to deal with proration. We saved taxpayers the expense of having to call a special session of the legislature by moving forward with congressional and State School Board redistricting plans.

We also passed every single bill proposed in the Republican Handshake with Alabama, a series of reforms GOP candidates vowed to pass during the 2010 election cycle. The Handshake agenda addressed everything from ending corruption in Montgomery to combating illegal immigration to taking control of long-abused state finances.

But of all the Handshake's many promises, none was more important than creating jobs and opportunity through economic development. With so many Alabamians still

Speaker Mike Hubbard

without work, it's up to state leaders to innovate and keep finding ways to jumpstart private sector jobs in Alabama. We have to continually re-examine our laws and policies to ensure we are giving new and existing businesses an opportunity to succeed.

That's why I formed the Speaker's Commission on Job Creation, a select group of business and community leaders tasked with gathering ideas that could help improve the state's business climate and boost job growth. We went around the state and did something almost unheard of in government — we listened. We listened to small business owners and large business owners about what kinds of struggles they face in trying to grow their businesses. We listened to those who know best how government could do a better job removing obstacles to private sector success.

One of the innovative ideas recommended by the Commission directly resulted in the "Made in Alabama" Job Incentives Act.

A centerpiece of the legislature's accomplishments this session, this new law embraces the outside-the-box thinking we must utilize to compete with other states for new jobs and opportunities. Alabama can now offer state tax incentives to international companies interested in locating here to directly offset federal trade tariffs they may be subject to. Alabama is the first state in the nation to offer such incentives, giving us a unique competitive advantage for recruiting jobs.

It also embodies forward-thinking, responsive government. Lawmakers asked for ideas, found a good one, and soon more Alabamians will have jobs because of it.

In fact, we've already heard from several companies interested in locating facilities in Alabama potentially creating thousands of new jobs as a direct result of this new law.

The legislature also took steps to end the widespread government corruption that has plagued our state for decades. Tough laws requiring officials and candidates to disclose government contracts and potential conflicts, a new measure of transparency in our campaign finance system and a strong statute shielding the Alabama Ethics Commission from retaliation by elected officials they investigate are just a few of the protections we put in place.

Because illegal immigrants drain tax dollars without contributing to the system, steal scarce jobs from those who need them and, by their very presence, break our laws, we passed the nation's toughest illegal immigration law. Now, Alabama will never become a sanctuary state for those who enter into this country illegally.

Other long-needed reforms, including photo voter identification to prevent mischief at the ballot box, new protections for our innocent unborn and a streamlined process to dismiss teachers who break the law and abuse our classrooms were also passed and must not be overlooked.

None of this could have been accomplished without the leadership of Senate President Pro Tem Del Marsh, R-Anniston, and his fellow Republican senators, each of whom worked seamlessly with their counterparts in the House.

I'm proud that Republicans can say we kept our promise to enact these landmark reforms. But it wasn't about politics. It was about ushering in a new era of responsive government in Alabama that seeks to build trust with the people.

The 2011 regular session was, without question, the most successful in modern history. If just a few of these measures had passed this year, it would have been a tremendous accomplishment. Enacting all of these reforms in the very first year of the quadrennium was a triumph of historic proportions for the people of Alabama.

And we're just getting started.

Rep. Mike Hubbard, R-Auburn, is the speaker of the Alabama House of Representatives.

The following article was originally published in the March 2011 issue of
The Alabama Lawyer magazine.

The 2010 Changes To Alabama's Ethics Law
Edward A. "Ted" Hosp
Maynard, Cooper & Gale, PC

In early December 2010, the Alabama Legislature was called into special session by outgoing Governor Bob Riley. The stated purpose of the session and the legislation introduced during that session was to increase accountability and transparency in government at the State, County and local levels. More specifically, one of the primary focuses of the session was to limit the perceived influence that lobbyists and those who hire lobbyists have on the political process. Thus, two of these bills, Senate Bill 14 ("SB14"), by Senator Bryan Taylor, and House Bill 11 ("HB11"), by Representative Paul DeMarco, made extensive changes to the definitions of lobbying, lobbyists, and the items and hospitality that lobbyists and principals – those who hire lobbyists – can provide to public officials and public employees.[1] In fact, these bills so transformed the law that at the first mandated ethics training session in Montgomery on January 24, 2011, Ethics Commission Executive Director Jim Sumner declared that "life, as we have known it in the past, no longer exists."

To say that there is significant confusion and disagreement over what the new laws actually did would be an understatement. *See* COMMISSION SAYS NEW ETHICS LAWS CONFUSING, *Montgomery Advertiser*, 2/3/2011. The changes are still being analyzed, and many of the new provisions will require interpretation through Advisory Opinions issued by the Ethics Commission before their full impact is understood.[2] Additionally, the Legislature may address some of the issues that have arisen

---

1 The Code contains separate definitions for "public officials" and "public employees." The definition of public official is very broad, and includes any person elected or appointed to a government position at the State, County, or municipal level. Public officials therefore include many individuals who serve in an unpaid capacity, whether as a member of local city councils or as a member of local government boards or commissions. Additionally, the definition of "family member" for public officials is significantly more broad than the definition of family member for public employees. Thus, restrictions as to what can be provided to family members are different for these two categories. With that exception, the restrictions on what can be provided to public officials and public employees discussed herein are the same and therefore this paper will use the term public official.

2 SB14, which dealt extensively with what can and cannot be provided to public officials and public employees and became Act 2010-264, has an effective date of March 15, 2011. Thus, those changes to the law do not take effect until that date. HB11, which expanded the definition of lobbying and became Act 2010-262, had an effective date of January 1, 2011. Therefore the additions to the definition of lobbyist became effective on that date.

through technical amendments when the 2011 Regular Session begins on March 1, although early indications are that they are reluctant to do so.

This article analyzes SB14 and HB11 in an attempt to provide as clear a picture as possible of the new restrictions on public officials, lobbyists, and those who employ lobbyists – as well as to whom those restrictions apply.

I. WHAT IS LOBBYING?

Under prior law, and pursuant to language re-passed in SB14, the definition of "lobbying" includes any attempt to influence legislation, including the veto or amendment of legislation.[3] The definition of lobbying also includes any attempt to influence the adoption and modification of regulations instituted by any regulatory body. Therefore, if the purpose of contact with the government is to influence the content of legislation or regulation, an attorney would likely fall under the definition of a lobbyist.

Consistent with prior interpretation of the law, and based on the language in the definition of lobbying as well as the "attorney exception" to the definition of "lobbyist" (see 36-25-1(20)(b)(2)), it does not appear that lobbying includes attempting to influence the application of regulations to a particular situation – for example, an attempt to obtain a license or to convince a government entity that a party is not in violation of an existing rule or regulation. Additionally, "professional services" involving drafting legislation or regulations, or assisting clients in interpreting the impact of particular measures does not render a person a lobbyist. Ala. Code § 36-25-1(20(b)(2).

The purpose of HB11, however, was to add a new code section that expanded the definition of lobbying to include any attempt to influence the award of any contract or grant by any department of the executive, legislative or judicial branch of state government. Ala. Code § 36-25-1.5. While this is a significant change to the law, note that HB11 applies only to those seeking contracts and grants with the state. Therefore, those seeking contracts and grants with county or city governments, or their departments and agencies, would not fall under the definition of "lobbying" and should not be considered "lobbyists."

As discussed more fully below, there appears to be a conflict between the new definition of lobbying contained in HB11, and one of the exceptions to the definition of "lobbyist" contained in the existing code and re-enacted as part of SB14. Thus, there exists some confusion as to the circumstances under which a person

---

3 According to the definition of "legislative body," this includes measures considered by the state legislature, county commissions, city councils or commissions, town councils, and municipal councils or commissions, and committees of those bodies. See Ala. Code § 36-25-1(18).

seeking to obtain a contract for goods and services with the executive or legislative branches of state government will be considered a lobbyist.[4]

II. WHO IS A LOBBYIST?

A. Generally

Under SB14, a lobbyist "includes any of the following:"

1. A person who receives compensation to lobby. That is, anyone paid to influence legislation, regulations or the award of contracts of grants by the state;

2. A person who lobbies as a "regular or usual part of employment;"

3. A consultant to any government entity who is employed to influence legislation or regulations regardless of the funds from which that person is paid;

4. Any employee or consultant of a lobbyist who regularly communicates with members of a legislative body.

   Ala. Code § 36-25-1(20)(a).

   As noted above, the definition of lobbyist in Ala. Code § 36-25-1(20) as re-enacted by SB14 begins with the phrase "[t]he term lobbyist <u>includes</u> any of the following." Therefore, the examples given and listed above may not be exclusive. This creates the possibility that the Ethics Commission could interpret other activities by an individual as rendering that person a lobbyist.

   What is perhaps more instructive than the definition of who is a lobbyist is that the code also specifies who is <u>not</u> a lobbyist. A lobbyist does not include:

1. Elected officials acting on matters which involve that person's official duties;

2. A person or attorney drafting bills or advising clients or rendering opinions regarding the construction or effect of pending legislation, executive action, or rules or regulations;

3. Reporters and members of the press;

4. Citizens who do not expend funds to lobby or who merely give public testimony on a particular issue;

5. A person who appears before a legislative body, a regulatory body, or an executive agency to either sell or purchase goods or services;

---

4 Lobbyists are required to pay a fee and register with the State Ethics Commission, and must undergo mandatory ethics training. Additionally, under the new law, lobbyists may be under significant additional restrictions with regard to what they can and cannot do in their interactions with public officials and employees. Therefore, the determination of whether a person crosses the threshold and becomes a lobbyist is a significant one.

6. A person whose primary duties or responsibilities do not include lobbying, but who may organize social events for members of a legislative body so long as that person has only irregular contact with members of the legislative body;

7. Persons who are members of associations who retain lobbyists but who do not personally lobby;

8. State government agency heads or their designees who provide information or communicate with other entities regarding policy and the positions affecting that agency.

Ala. Code § 36-25-1(20)(b).

B. Are Sales People Now "Lobbyists"?

Although the exception to the definition of lobbyist set forth in § 36-25-1(20)(b)(5) for those appearing before a legislative or executive body to sell or purchase goods or services appears to be broad, as noted above, it is also in conflict with the Legislature's attempt in HB11 to include as lobbyists individuals "seeking to influence the award" of contracts and grants with the state. A question therefore arose as to whether or not a salesperson who attempts to makes sales to a State government entity fell under the new definition of a lobbyist. This issue was a contentious one during the session, and there were numerous attempts to include language in the final bill that would clarify that salespeople were not intended to be included in the definition of lobbyist. Those efforts were ultimately unsuccessful, however, on February 2, 2011, the Ethics Commission issued Advisory Opinion 2011-02, clarifying this issue. According to that opinion, individuals and entities who engage in sales activities with the State government as part of their normal job activities are not considered by the Commission to be lobbying. Similarly, the opinion states that individuals and entities who respond to requests for proposals are not lobbyists. In contrast, those hired purely for the purpose of influencing a decision of the State government with respect to a contract or grant, or those hired to "open doors" for a business are considered lobbyists, however, and must register. Ethics AO 2011-02.

III. WHO IS A PRINCIPAL?

A principal is any person – including any business – that employs a lobbyist. The revised definition of principal removes the statement previously contained in Code that a principal could simultaneously serve as his or her own lobbyist, and added the statement that "a principal is not a lobbyist, but is not allowed to give a thing of value." Clearly in some instances, particularly with regard to associations, a principal _may_ also be a lobbyist. The current thinking of the Ethics Commission staff appears to be that the language stating that a principal was not a lobbyist was added to the code only to indicate that a principal was not _automatically_ also lobbyist.

IV. WHAT CAN A LOBBYIST OR PRINCIPAL DO (OR NOT DO)?

As discussed in detail below, when the new law was first passed, there existed some confusion regarding the impact of changes to code § 36-25-7. The language in new section 7 provides that no one – not a lobbyist, a principal or a citizen – is permitted to provide anything to a public official if the giving of that thing is to influence official action. If not given to influence official action, there appears to be no limitation on what an individual or entity who is not a lobbyist or principal may provide to a public official. This is not the case for lobbyists and principals, as a new code section 36-25-5.5 places specific restrictions on those individuals and entities. New Code § 36-25-5.5(a) states that no lobbyist, or subordinate of a lobbyist or principal shall offer or provide a thing of value to a public employee or public official or family member of [those individuals].

Ala. Code § 36-25-5.5(a). This new code section similarly prohibits public employees or public officials and their family members from soliciting or receiving a thing of value from a lobbyist, subordinate of a lobbyist or principal. In what appears to be a minor drafting error, the plain language of this provision does not include a prohibition that relates to principals – only to subordinates of principals. However, it is clear that the Legislature intended this prohibition to apply to principals as well as lobbyists. As noted above, contained in the definition of "principal" is the statement that "a principal . . . is not allowed to give a thing of value." As a result, it should be assumed that principals, like lobbyists, are prohibited from providing to public officials and public employees any "thing of value."

Under § 36-25-5.5, neither a lobbyist nor a principal can provide to a public official or the official's family members a "thing of value." As noted above, it appears that anyone not considered a lobbyist or a principal may be permitted to give to a public official anything – including a thing of value, so long as the thing provided is not for the purpose of influencing official action, as prohibited by § 36-25-7. Again, the intersection between section 5.5 and the language of § 36-25-7, and how the Ethics Commission has dealt with this issue thus far, is dealt with below.

VI. WHAT IS (AND IS NOT) A THING OF VALUE?

If it is assumed that no conflict exists between section 5.5 and section 7, and that lobbyists and principals are permitted to give to public officials things that are not "thing[s] of value," then it is important to have a clear understanding of exactly what that term does and does not mean. "Thing of value" is defined very broadly, and includes essentially anything and everything that has any value. Thus, as in the past, the numerous exceptions to the definition are more relevant and helpful.

General Exclusions from "Thing of Value:"

The following items are specifically excluded from the definition of a "thing of value," and therefore appear to have been intended by the Legislature to be allowed to be provided to public officials and public employees so long as they are not given for the purpose of influencing official action:

1. Campaign contributions or contributions to an inaugural or transition committee;

2. Anything given by a family member "under circumstances which make it clear that the gift is [the thing given] is motivated by a family relationship;"

3. Anything given by a friend under circumstances which make it clear that the gift is given due to the friendship;

4. Items of little intrinsic value such as plaques or certificates, or items and services of de minimus value;

5. Anything that is available to the general public such as loans, discounts, and "opportunities and benefits, and rewards and prizes given in contests or events including random drawings;"

6. Benefits earned by a public official or employee through a non-government employer where it is clear that those benefits are provided for reasons unrelated to the person's public service.

Ala. Code § 36-25-1(33)(b)(1-7, 10)

B. Group Meetings, Receptions and Conferences

There are several exceptions to the definition of "thing of value" that deal with group meetings, receptions and conferences. Under those exceptions, a "thing of value" does not include:

1. Reimbursement for transportation and lodging for public officials or public employees attending an education function or a widely attended event when the person providing the reimbursement is a primary sponsor. This exclusion only applies if the public official is a meaningful participant in the event, or if the public official's attendance is "appropriate to the performance of his or her official duties or representative function;"

2. Reimbursement for travel and expenses in connection with participation in an economic development function;

3. Hospitality, meals and other food or beverages provided as an integral part of an educational function, economic development function, a work session,[5] or a widely attended event.

---

5   There is no definition for "work session" in the legislation.

Ala. Code § 36-25-1(33)(12-14).

1. Educational Function

An educational function must be organized around a formal program or agenda concerning matters within the scope of the participant's official duties for other matters of public policy, economic trade or development, ethics, government services or programs, or government operations.

The definition states that "taking into account the totality of the program or agenda [it] could not reasonably be perceived as a subterfuge for a purely social, recreational, or entertainment function." Ala. Code §36-25-1(12). If the function is primarily attended by individuals from Alabama, it must take place in Alabama. If it is predominately attended by individuals from other states, it must still take place in the continental United States. Ala. Code § 36-25-1(12).

Transportation and lodging may be provided for an educational function, but only by a primary sponsor of the event, and only if the public official is a "meaningful participant" in the event. Ala. Code § 36-25-1(33)(12). There is no definition of a "primary sponsor," however, the legislation's use of the more broad term "a principal sponsor" rather than the restrictive term "the primary sponsor" indicates that an event may have more than one primary sponsor.

Additionally, according to the exceptions to the definition of a thing of value, hospitality may be provided at an educational function, but the language states that the hospitality must be "an integral part" of the event. Ala. Code § 36-25-1(33)(14).

2. Economic Development Function

An economic development function is one reasonably "and directly related to the advancement of a specific, good faith economic development or trade promotion project or objective." Ala. Code § 36-25-1(11). In order to qualify as an "economic development function," therefore, the event must concern an actual project or proposal, and cannot be a function relating to economic development in general.

Travel and lodging of a public official or employee may be paid to "facilitate a public official's or public employee's participation in an economic development function." Ala. Code § 36-25-1(33)(13). As in the case of an educational function, hospitality may be provided as part of an economic development function if the hospitality is an integral part of the function. Ala. Code § 36-25-1(33)(14).

3. Widely Attended Event

A widely attended event is "any gathering, dinner or reception at which it is reasonably expected that more than 12 individuals will attend." According to this definition, the participants must have "mutual interests," but the attendees must include "individuals with a diversity of views or interests." Ala. Code § 36-25-1(35). If the event is one organized around a formal agenda, and the public official or employee is a meaningful participant, transportation and lodging may be provided by a primary sponsor of the event. Ala. Code § 36-25-1(33)(12). Hospitality may be provided if it is an integral part of the event. Ala. Code § 36-25-1(33)(14).

In general, the exception for widely attended events appears to be broader than the exceptions for educational functions and economic development functions. As a result, it appears that so long as more than twelve (12) people are expected to attend, most events that would qualify as educational functions or economic development functions would also qualify as a "widely attended event."

4. General Rules for Group Events and Functions

There is no limitation on the amount that can be spent on travel, hospitality or entertainment for a public official or public employee if the event qualifies under one of the group event exceptions. However, travel and lodging can <u>only</u> be provided by a primary sponsor of the event. It also can only be provided if the event is one organized around a formal agenda or program, <u>and</u> if the official is a meaningful participant, meaning that he or she performs a role such as speaker or panel participant – or if the event concerns his or her role as a public official.

Hospitality, including food and beverages, can only be provided at a group event if it is an "integral part" of the function. Unfortunately, there is no definition of "integral part" of a function, although the dictionary definition of the word is "essential to completeness." At this time, it is not clear when the provision of hospitality will be considered "an integral part" of an event, or how that term will be interpreted.

Unlike a previous code section that restricted the provision of hospitality in certain circumstances to three consecutive days, there is no time limitation in the newly passed law.

C. Meals and Beverages Provided by Lobbyists and Principals

Also excepted from the definition from a thing of value are meals or beverages provided by a lobbyist to a public official not exceeding $25 per meal, with an aggregate limit of $150 per year. Principals are permitted to spend $50 per meal on a public official, with a limit of $250 per year. It is important to remember, though, that if the provision of hospitality falls within a group event exception such as an educational function or a widely attended event, it is not a thing of value, and therefore does not fall within the $25 or $50 limitation, nor does it count towards the $150 or $250 aggregated amount permitted for the calendar year.

Reporting Hospitality Provided to Public Officials

Under prior law, the definition of "thing of value" indicated that when more than $250 in hospitality was spent on a public official or public employee during a single calendar day, the entire amount spent was required to be reported by the provider to the Ethics Commission.

Although SB14 eliminated this reporting requirement within the definition section, lobbyists and principals still must file quarterly reports pursuant to Ala. Code § 36-25-19(a). Those reports require an itemization of the items outside the definition of "thing of value" provided to a public official in excess of $250 in a twenty-four (24) hour period.

GIVING SOMETHING TO INFLUENCE OFFICIAL ACTION

Without question, the most confusion and disagreement regarding the new provisions of the Ethics Act have centered on the changes made to § 36-25-7. Previously, this code section prohibited the giving and receiving of a thing of value for the purpose of influencing official action. Although the language used in this section did not on its face appear to require an explicit quid pro quo agreement (*i.e.*, it used the phrase "influencing official action" as opposed to "in exchange for an official act"), it was generally viewed as an anti-bribery statute that required some sort of quid pro quo. In any event, though, because section 7 only prohibited the giving of a "thing of value", individuals and businesses knew that they were safe so long as the thing given – hospitality or whatever – fell within one of the many exceptions to the definition of a "thing of value."

Although there are still numerous exceptions to the definition of "thing of value," SB14 modified § 36-25-7 to remove the requirement that the thing given to influence official action be a "thing of value." Thus, under the new section 7, if anyone offers to a public official anything, "whether or not the thing . . . is a thing of value," in order to influence official action, that person has violated the law. Ala. Code § 36-5-7(a-c). On February 2, 2011, the Ethics Commission issued Advisory Opinion 2011-01 to the Association of County Commissioners of Alabama, and examined several of the exceptions to the definition of "thing of value." The opinion is helpful in understanding what is permitted with regard to group functions and meals provided by lobbyists or principals. It is particularly useful, however, in that it clearly interpreted what was allowed to be given through the lens of § 36-25-7.

According to AO 2011-01, businesses and individuals including lobbyists and principals may sponsor group events and meals pursuant to the exceptions set forth in the code, and public officials may attend such events and activities. However, implicitly acknowledging the language of section 7, the Commission pointed out that the individuals and businesses providing the meals at these events may not use the event "as an opportunity to lobby the public official/employee, or use it for a sales opportunity." Ethics AO 2011-02 at 9.[6] Stated elsewhere in the Opinion, the Commission found that meals could be provided as long as "the meal is not used as an opportunity to influence official action on the part of the county official/employee."

The change in the language of section 7 appears to create a potential problem for many entities interacting with government officials, but especially for lobbyists, whose primary purpose is to influence official action. If a lobbyist takes a public official to dinner to discuss a policy or legislation, that meal may be interpreted as having been provided "for the purpose of influencing official action." If so, it does not matter that the meal or event may fit within one of the exceptions contained in the definitions because under § 36-25-7 if a thing given or received is for the purpose of influencing official action it is prohibited under all circumstances.

Therefore, based on the language now found in § 36-25-7, and on the interpretation of that language given by the Ethics Commission in Advisory Opinion 2011-01, it is risky for any entity – whether a lobbyist, principal or citizen – to provide anything at all to a pubic official if the giving of that thing is in any way connected with the discussion of, or attempt to influence any policy, legislation or regulation.

CONCLUSION

There is no question that the changes enacted by the Alabama Legislature to Alabama's Ethics Act in December 2010 were substantial. As a result, many if not most of the rules and procedures that entities interacting with public officials and public employees had in place are no longer valid. Under the new ethics laws, anyone considering providing a meal, a gift, a sponsorship for an event—anything at which public officials or public employees will be present—must give serious thought beforehand as to how and whether to proceed. Whether or not the provision of that item is allowed will depend on numerous factors including the character of the provider (lobbyist or principal), the purpose of the expenditure, the content of the event, and the possible subjects that may be discussed. Because violations of the Ethics Act are class B felonies, it is recommended that parties contemplating such activities exercise caution, and consult either the Ethics Commission staff or an attorney before proceeding.

---

6 Advisory Opinion 2011-01 also recognizes that prior to the 2010 changes, the language in § 36-25-7 had been interpreted to require a quid pro quo. As stated in the Opinion, "[s]ince 1995, when the previous Ethics law went into effect, all the activities set out in this opinion were permissible under the above-listed exceptions, unless they were offered in exchange for official action on the part of the public official or the public employee." Ethics AO 2011-01 at 7.

NETWORKING, EDUCATION ON ISSUES ARE
KEY DRAWS FOR BCA EVENTS

The Business Council of Alabama organizes several events, conferences, seminars and special programs every year to keep its members on the cutting edge of issues and events of importance to Alabama business and industry.

The premier fundraising event for ProgressPAC, the BCA's political action committee, is the Chairman's Dinner, which has featured guest appearances by former Secretary of State Condoleezza Rice, President and Mrs. George H. W. Bush, political commentators Sean Hannity and James Carville, and TV personality Bill O'Reilly.

In September 2010, politics took center stage as hundreds of business and elected leaders gathered to hear from a trio of nationally known speakers: former U.S. Rep. J.C. Watts, R-OK, former Vermont Governor and Democratic presidential candidate Howard Dean and Fox News political analyst and former Democratic strategist Dick Morris. Watts moderated a spirited discussion amongst the three on the economy, health care and foreign policy issues.

"The quality of men and women leading this organization is of such a high caliber that they deserve and expect to hear from accomplished leaders who are held in high regard," BCA president and CEO William J. Canary said. "It's always an honor to bring such esteemed individuals to Alabama so they can see for themselves the quality of the people and the leaders of our great state."

In the fall, BCA and the Chamber of Commerce Association of Alabama partnered for the third year to host a series of Leadership Exchanges, regional dinner meetings designed to bring together business and policy leaders for the exchange of ideas on issues of importance to business and industry and Alabama's long-term economic growth. Each of the gatherings — held in Calera, Eufaula, Foley, Cullman and Wetumpka — were targeted, invitation-only events for community, business and governmental leaders from each region. Attendees each received a copy of the BCA book, *What if No One Were Watching: 2010*, and were briefed on BCA's commitment to Alabama's pre-kindergarten programs.

In November, volunteer leaders representing all aspects of Alabama's business community joined to craft the *2011 BCA Legislative Agenda*. The two-day working session in Birmingham brought together volunteers from each of BCA's committees who worked together to draft goals, policies and actions on areas from small business to tax matters. The work sessions were highlighted for the first time with visits from two nationally known guest speakers, Jay Timmons, then executive vice president of the National Association of Manufacturers, and Katie Strong Hays, executive director of Congressional and Public Affairs for the U.S. Chamber of Commerce.

In December 2010, the BCA teamed with the Chamber of Commerce Association of Alabama for a joint annual meeting at the Harbert Center in Birmingham. The combined groups, known as The Partnership, hosted author and commentator Fred Barnes, Fox News commentator and editor of *The Weekly Standard.*

During the business portion of the Annual Meeting, the CCAA and BCA elected their respective boards of directors and officers for 2010.

In the past, the BCA Annual Meeting has attracted such diverse speakers as U.S. Chamber of Commerce President and CEO Tom Donohue; Doro Bush Koch, sister of former President George W. Bush and daughter of former President George H. W. Bush; and author and former U.S. Ambassador to the United Nations Sichan Siv.

In the spring of 2011, BCA again joined with the Alabama Technology Network to present the annual Alabama Manufacturer of the Year Awards, an annual recognition of Alabama manufacturing enterprises that exhibit excellence in leadership, performance, profitability and workforce relations. Congressman Jo Bonner, R-Mobile, gave the keynote address and presented awards to all the winners.

The 2011 Alabama Manufacturers of the Year were Hyundai Motor Manufacturing Alabama, LLC, Montgomery (large manufacturer); Lafarge North America, Calera (medium manufacturer); and Applied Chemical Technology, Florence (small manufacturer).

"This year marks the 12th consecutive year the BCA has partnered with ATN to recognize manufacturing excellence in Alabama," said BCA President and CEO William J. Canary. "This year's award winners reflect the skill, performance, agility, innovation and commitment to product excellence that sets Alabama manufacturers apart, and the BCA is proud to join ATN in bringing the accomplishments of these hard-working, high-performing companies to light."

The Governor Bob Riley Building a Better Alabama Award was presented to Jay Timmons, president and CEO of the National Association of Manufacturers. The award, presented in 2010 to former Gov. Bob Riley and named in his honor, is designed to recognize individuals who work tirelessly to promote manufacturing and economic development in Alabama.

THE PARTNERSHIP: BCA, CCAA WORKING TOGETHER ON BEHALF OF BUSINESS

In 1937, as Alabama teetered on the brink of recovery from the Great Depression, representatives of the chambers of commerce from the leading cities of Alabama — Huntsville, Mobile, Dothan, Tuscaloosa, Anniston, Alexander City, Selma and Dothan, along with utility and media representatives — met in Mobile to found what was originally known as The Alabama Association of Commercial Organizations. The intent of this group, as originally stated, was to "foster the commercial, industrial, and recreational welfare of the state…"

This group of like-minded business and civic leaders maintained a loose association through the years, and in 1997, adopted the name Chamber of Commerce Association of Alabama (CCAA). In 1999, the volunteer leadership of CCAA saw the need to take CCAA from a volunteer-led organization to a professionally staffed group that would allow it to become more involved in events that would shape the future of Alabama's business community. Ralph Stacy, former executive director of the Greenville Area Chamber of Commerce and past Chairman of CCAA, was named the CCAA's first president and CEO and set about the task of bringing more than 120 local chambers across the state together to help form a true grassroots business network.

In 2003, William J. Canary accepted the post of president and CEO of the Business Council of Alabama (BCA). Since its formation in 1985 by the merger of the Alabama Chamber of Commerce and the Associated Industries of Alabama, BCA had always maintained contact with CCAA and supported the efforts of local chambers. Canary saw the great potential that the more than 60,000 members of local chambers offered to the efforts of BCA in the halls of government and set in motion a plan to formalize the relationship of the two organizations. In October 2003, an historic agreement was signed linking the two through The Partnership.

In the seven years following formation of The Partnership, both groups have been able to find common ground on business issues that affect the men and women who make up Alabama's business community. In addition to bringing local business leaders of all types together in the Leadership Exchange format, The Partnership maintains contact during the legislative session through a series of conference calls with key BCA staff, elected leaders and others involved in the political process to keep local chambers and their leadership up to date on business issues. Through the *Capital Briefing* publication, members of The Partnership receive a weekly update on keep local chambers and their leadership up to date on business issues. Through the *Capital Briefing* publication, members of The Partnership receive a weekly update on the goings-on in Montgomery and Washington in a format that allows quick distribution to their local members if so desired. The Partnership also coordinated trips to the State House for several chambers who wanted to visit with their local legislators.

The mission of CCAA is "to build a better Alabama…through strong Chambers of Commerce." The Partnership, anchored by BCA's unwavering support, helps bring that mission to reality. That same spirit set forth in 1937 is still alive and well today in the form of The Partnership.

BCA Establishes
Manufacturing Advocacy Council
Regional Leaders to Ensure Continued Competitiveness of Alabama Manufacturers

The Business Council of Alabama, Alabama's exclusive affiliate for the National Association of Manufacturers with more than 1,300 manufacturing members, proudly announces the launch of the *Manufacturing Advocacy Council.*

This select group of BCA members will bring together their experience, skill and innate understanding of the manufacturing process to promote and enhance a positive business climate for Alabama manufacturers.

The BCA's *Manufacturing Advocacy Council* is comprised of a cross-section of Alabama's manufacturing community, manufacturers who are members of BCA, BCA's board of directors and BCA's regional advisory committees. The council is aligned with the state's workforce development regions of the Governor's Office of Workforce Development with at least one manufacturer from each region serving the council.

The *Manufacturing Advocacy Council* will serve as a national model for the NAM and will reinforce the strong, exclusive partnership of BCA with the NAM to strengthen our message of supporting manufacturing and the need to compete in the global marketplace.

One of the first initiatives of the council will be working with the NAM's Manufacturing Institute to build in Alabama a coalition of business, education, workforce and economic development leaders to develop a nationally credentialed high-quality manufacturing workforce.

BCA is proud to be at the forefront of this groundbreaking new effort. We continue to advocate for a Business Education Alliance, an alliance that will unite the business and education communities for the simple purpose of putting our students first, and this new partnership with the Manufacturing Institute through the *Manufacturing Advocacy Council* is another component of that alliance.

"Manufacturers are a critical segment of our economy, and the *Manufacturing Advocacy Council* is yet another way the BCA is working to support the companies that are making jobs and world-class products here in Alabama," said BCA President and CEO William Canary.

The BCA and the members of the *Manufacturing Advocacy Council* will be front and center, working to advance policies that will be good for jobs and the economy.

BCA Officers and Board of Directors

The Business Council of Alabama is grateful to the volunteer leaders who give of their time and talents with the understanding that businesspeople in our state must unite in support of policies that enhance the free enterprise system in Alabama.

2011 BCA Officers

Chairman, William Brooke, Venture Capital - Harbert Management Corp., Birmingham

First Vice Chairman, Terry Kellogg, Blue Cross and Blue Shield of Alabama , Birmingham

Second Vice Chairman, Carl Jamison, JamisonMoneyFarmer PC, Tuscaloosa

Immediate Past Chairman, Sandy Stimpson, Scotch & Gulf Lumber LLC, Mobile

Legal Counsel, Fournier J. Gale III, Regions Financial Corporation, Birmingham

Treasurer, Charles Nailen, Jr., BBG Specialty Foods, Inc./Taco Bell, Dothan

2011 BCA Board of Directors

Martin Abroms, Abroms & Associates, Florence; Dick Anderson, Huron Valley Steel Corporation, Anniston; Cathy Anderson-Giles, Equity Holding Company, Mobile; Freda Bacon, Alabama Self-Insured Worker's Comp. Fund, Birmingham; Owen Bailey, USA Children's and Women's Hospital, Mobile; Eason Balch, Jr., Balch & Bingham LLP, Birmingham; Bill Barranco, Wilson, Price, Barranco, Blankenship & Billingsley P.C., Montgomery; Fred Blackwell, Fred Blackwell & Associates, Smiths Station; Ronnie Boles, General & Automotive Machine Shop, Huntsville; Jim Bolte, Toyota Motor Manufacturing of Alabama, Huntsville; Ron Box, Joe Money Machinery Company, Birmingham; David Boyd, Balch & Bingham LLP, Birmingham; Gregory Brown, B. R. Williams Trucking, Oxford; Terrence Brown, HealthSouth Corporation, Birmingham; Bill Brunson, The National Security Group, Elba; John Buchanan, Regions Financial Corporation, Birmingham; William Bullock, Jr., W. J. Bullock Inc., Fairfield; Joseph Busta, Jr., University of South Alabama, Mobile; Robert Campbell, Bradley Arant Boult Cummings LLP, Birmingham; Karen Carter, State Farm Agency, Montgomery; Steve Cawood, Goodwyn Mills & Cawood, Montgomery; Shane Clanton, BBVA Compass, Birmingham;

Paul Cocker, GKN Westland Aerospace, Tallassee; Ab Conner, Conner Brothers Construction Company, Auburn; Philip Dotts, Public FA, Huntsville; William Dow, Warren Averett Kimbrough & Marino LLC, Birmingham; Garry Neil Drummond, Drummond Company, Birmingham; Frank Filgo, Alabama Trucking Association, Montgomery; Jim Fincher, 3M, Decatur; George Flowers, GDF Inc., Dothan; Susan Foy, Russell Medical Center, Alexander City; Randall George, Montgomery Area Chamber of Commerce, Montgomery; Carol Gordy, Natural Decorations, Brewton; Winthrop Hallett, III, Mobile Area Chamber of Commerce, Mobile; Jack Hawkins, Troy University, Troy; Denson Henry, Henry Brick Company, Selma; Brian Hilson, Birmingham Business Alliance, Birmingham; Sheila Hodges, Meyer Real Estate, Gulf Shores; LaShaunda Holly, Jackson Area Chamber of Commerce, Jackson; Steve Holt, Shoals Chamber of Commerce, Florence; Mark Hope, Wells Fargo Bank, Montgomery; Horace Horn, Jr., PowerSouth Energy, Montgomery; Erik Johnsen, International Shipholding Corporation, Mobile; Eddy Kilman, J. Smith Lanier, Opelika; Bryan Kindred, DCH Health System, Tuscaloosa; Patricia King, Sunny King Automotive Group, Anniston; Keith King, Volkert Inc., Mobile; Robert Lee, Vulcan Inc., Foley; Greg Leikvold, BF Goodrich Tire Manufacturing, Tuscaloosa; Linda Lewis, Chamber of Commerce of Walker County, Jasper; Chris Lewis, L & S Enterprises, Birmingham; Debbie Long, Protective Life Corporation, Birmingham; Ralph Malone, Pinnacle Gage and Tool, Huntsville; Kirk Mancer, Cullman Area Chamber of Commerce, Cullman;

Doug Mannion, Rheem Water Heating, Montgomery; Douglas Markham, Books-A-Million, Birmingham; Cameron Martindale, Montgomery Area Chamber of Commerce, Montgomery; Fred McCallum, Jr., AT&T Alabama, Birmingham; Tim McCartney, McCartney Construction, Gadsden; Mary Sue McClurkin, McClurkin Enterprises, Pelham; Charles McCrary, Alabama Power Company, Birmingham; James McManus, II, Energen Corporation, Birmingham; Ben McNeill, United Food and Fuel/CITGO, Montgomery; Jeff Miller, Research Solvents & Chemicals, Pelham; Donald Morgan, Morgan Properties, Cullman; Harris Morrissette, China Doll Rice and Beans, Inc. / Dixie Lily Foods, Saraland; Bill Morton, Robins & Morton, Birmingham; David Muhlendorf, Paper & Chemical Supply, Sheffield; John Northcutt, Robertson Banking Company, Demopolis; Caroline Novak, A- Plus Education Foundation, Montgomery; Tim Parker, Parker Towing Company, Tuscaloosa; Ray Perez, Honda Manufacturing of Alabama, Lincoln; Ron Perkins, Doozer Software, Birmingham; Greg Powell, FI-Plan Partners, Birmingham; Robert Powers, Eufaula Agency, Eufaula; James Proctor, II, McWane, Birmingham;

Joseph Rella, Austal USA, Mobile; Suzanne Respess, Children's Health System, Birmingham; Van Richey, American Cast Iron Pipe Co., Birmingham; Rick Roden, Greater Jackson County Chamber of Commerce, Scottsboro; Steve Roy, AAA Cooper Transportation, Dothan; Markus Schaefer, Mercedes-Benz U. S. International, Tuscaloosa; John Seymour, Decatur-Morgan County Chamber of Commerce, Decatur; Lolly Steiner, Auburn Chamber of Commerce, Auburn; Stephen Still, Maynard, Cooper & Gale P.C., Birmingham; Charlie Story, Public Affairs Consulting, Daphne; John Russell Thomas, Aliant Bank, Alexander City; Michael Thompson, Thompson Caterpillar, Birmingham; Ken Tucker, The Boeing Company, Huntsville; Frances Turner, Turner Motor Company, Selma; Russell Tyner, Baptist Health, Montgomery; Chester Vrocher, Boise, Jackson; David Ward, Hager Companies, Montgomery; Donna Watts, South Baldwin Chamber of Commerce, Foley; Cameron West, Huntingdon College, Montgomery; Margie Wilcox, Mobile Bay Transportation Co., Mobile; Cheryl Smiley Williams, The Coleman Group DBA: Spherion Staffing Services, Mobile; Donta' Wilson, BB&T, Birmingham; Jan Wood, Wetumpka Area Chamber of Commerce, Wetumpka; and Alan Worrell, Sterling Bank, Montgomery.

INDEX

In Memoriam

L. Ralph Stacy
1957-2010

*Senior vice president for Strategic Communications
at the Business Council of Alabama,
executive director of The Partnership
and our friend and colleague.*